Hearts and Minds Matter

CREATING LEARNING ENVIRONMENTS WHERE ALL STUDENTS BELONG

Jackie Eldridge
and
Denise McLafferty

 FriesenPress

Suite 300 - 990 Fort St
Victoria, BC, V8V 3K2
Canada

www.friesenpress.com

ISBN
978-1-5255-8241-7 (Hardcover)
978-1-5255-8242-4 (Paperback)
978-1-5255-8243-1s (eBook)

1. EDUCATION, TEACHER TRAINING & CERTIFICATION

Distributed to the trade by The Ingram Book Company

HEARTS AND MINDS
M A T T E R

DEDICATIONS

From Jackie with love and respect!

I want to thank my children Bryce, Matthew and Brittany who have always been guiding lights for me. They bring me such joy and I am so proud of the caring and loving human beings they have become. Watching them grow, I saw the seeds of emotional intelligence and resilience growing from their earliest years. I also want to thank my daughter-in-law Carrie for her love and encouragement. All four of these amazing people truly demonstrate the very essence of what it means to live with heart and mind!

I must also thank Melanie Scott who stood by me during this process and gave me the guidance I needed to dream big and stay the course. Your friendship and coaching skills were just what I needed.

I must give special mention to Beth Parker who co-developed the emotional intelligence cards with me and whose editorial skills were invaluable. It's been an adventure and I have loved every minute.

I am also indebted to Elizabeth Kerr for her constant friendship, guidance, and creative talent. Re-connecting with you after many years helped bring me to this very place.

I cannot go without thanking the rest of my soul sisters at Verity for their unending encouragement, advice, editing, help and fun.

Dr. Barrie Bennett, you are such an influence in my teaching and writing and I feel like you started me on this journey all those years ago. Thank you for introducing me to the concepts in this book and for the guidance you gave to me when we co-taught and beyond. Everything I knew about teaching and learning changed for me when I met you!

Finally, Denise McLafferty, my colleague, co-creator, co-author, business partner and my friend. You are a gift and I am so happy I met you and that we stayed connected as we shared a common vision and belief in the power of inclusion and belonging. It's been quite the journey and there has been so much learning along the way. Thank you, girlfriend! It's not over yet!

From Denise

As my life journey has taken many curves, even some "dead-ends", (that luckily, I have been able to recover from), I have always had my incredible sisters there for me. A bottomless well of support, encouragement, and love. Jean, Anne, and Helen, I hope you know how much I love you and appreciate all the help and guidance you have given me forever. I am so blessed to have such amazing "anchors" in my life.

To my daughter Devon, I love you desperately and I am so proud of the resilient, creative, spontaneous, compassionate, and inspiring young woman you are. You have been a consistent cheerleader for me as I have taken on this "post-retirement" journey. Thank you for being there! I hope you realize how much I appreciate your encouragement and how much I love you. I look forward to all our future "safaris" together!

I too must thank Barrie Bennett. I often tell people (and I have also told Barrie this), that he was the person who kept me in education. When I was feeling disillusioned and unsure about my future, I luckily attended one of Barrie's "Instructional Intelligence Institutes". That learning experience was so inspiring. His enthusiasm, innovative teaching strategies and perspectives on students and their learning, totally re-energized me, gave me new motivation, and helped me realize that I could make a difference. Thank you for that Barrie! Luckily for me, we got the chance to work together many times since then. I am so fortunate to have you as a colleague and mentor. Barrie, you are a truly exceptional person, and I am in awe of the work you do and the incredible impact you have made on teachers and classrooms worldwide.

And to Jackie, my incredible co-trainer, co-author, and co-owner, you are the Energizer bunny - you just keep on "going and going". In addition to dragging me out of retirement into this consulting world, you have continued to push me beyond my comfort zone, resulting in me stretching myself in new and exciting ways. Without this support and encouragement, I would not be where I am today. You are an extraordinary lady! Thank you for coming into my life. Our journey together has been long, and I am confident that we have many more adventures ahead of us. All my love!

TABLE OF CONTENTS

FORWARD

Having worked in many school districts in several countries over the last 48 years, I've noticed that all district vision statements argue the value of citizenship and the development of the social-emotional side of learning. Why?

Interpersonal relationships, a component of emotional intelligence, is one of the most powerful predictors of success in school and throughout one's life. Learning to effectively work in groups (cooperative learning) has one of the highest effect sizes on student academic learning and achievement. That said, when group work is not enacted effectively, it is one of the least effective approaches to student learning. The challenge then, to us as educators, is to learn to structure groups to effectively impact both social-emotional and academic learning so that children grow up to be resilient adults.

Additionally, we know that creating classroom environments that foster a sense of belonging in a safe place in order to survive, thrive and become resilient, is critical to ensure that all students achieve their true potential. When teachers explicitly use the tools necessary to build inclusive classrooms, they are creating learning spaces where all students develop socially, emotionally, morally, and academically.

Two issues must be considered. First (and for good reason) the attention in most districts in most countries is on literacy and numeracy. Clearly, those two areas of inquiry are likewise key to being successful in life. Yet, interestingly, when we look at job ads in countries like Ireland, Australia, Canada, and the United States, the most common variable that organizations are seeking is employees who are skilled interpersonally...who can work as part of a team...who can work with all stakeholders...that have highly developed communication and problem solving skills. They don't ask for employees who can only work on their own and who can only work with their best friends.

The second issue relates to figuring out how to build that social-emotional side of learning into a classroom, school, and district culture to respect district vision statements and to increase academic achievement in all subject areas. This text, by Jackie Eldridge and Denise McLafferty, is designed to assist and guide educators to refine and extend that social-emotional side of learning.

This text is an excellent example of merging theory and practice. Michael Fullan, one of the top educators in the world, posits that there is nothing so practical as good theory and nothing so theoretical as good practice. These authors respect those dimensions. They provide a delightful balance of theory and practice; the practice and theory play off each other. A rich variety of practical ideas and processes are provided to build that 'interpersonal intelligence' into the teaching and learning process. Importantly, they also look at current brain research to add to the relevancy of their work.

The authors respectfully merge the voices of key educators in the social-emotional side of learning; people such as Jeanne Gibbs and her Tribes program, and the work of David and Roger Johnson, who have won international awards for their research in cooperative learning.

Having worked with both authors over the last twenty-five years, both at the University of Toronto and in a large-scale systemic change project with York Region District School Board, I know how passionately they work to support teacher, principal, and student learning. They model mindfulness and a deep respect for the interesting complexity of the teaching and learning process.

I know you will enjoy your journey with these two educators.

Dr. Barrie Bennett
Professor Emeritus
Ontario Institute for Studies in Education
University of Toronto

Jackie Eldridge and Denise McLafferty

INTRODUCTION

A deep sense of love and belonging is an irreducible need of all people. We are biologically, cognitively, physically, and spiritually wired to love, to be loved, and to belong. When those needs are not met, we don't function as we were meant to. We break. We fall apart. We numb. We ache. We hurt others. We get sick.

~ Brene Brown

This quote makes it clear that feelings of exclusion can cause great harm to those who do not feel like they belong. Children are especially vulnerable in this area because they do not always have the skills to successfully integrate with others. Many have not yet developed the emotional intelligence to understand how to become included or how to include others. Instead, they find themselves on the outside of classrooms, which, in turn, creates all kinds of challenges for students and teachers alike.

As Brené Brown writes, "When [our] needs are not met, we don't function as we were meant to".

Renowned addiction specialist, Gabor Mate's research is also extremely clear. Early traumatic events like being excluded lead to any number of addictions (alcoholism, drug dependency, gambling, etc.). Emerging neuroscientific evidence suggests that physical pain (e.g., scraping your knee) and social/emotional pain (e.g., from exclusion) are felt in the same way because of the manner in which the brain processes the experience. Exclusion hurts emotionally and physically. In *Hearts and Minds Matter, Creating Learning Environments Where All Students Belong*, along with our signature professional development program also known as Hearts and Minds Matter, we encourage the many positive attributes of inclusion because we understand that human potential is boundless, given the right learning environments. To inspire this potential, human beings need to feel a sense of belonging in a safe place. Only then, can they survive, thrive, and become resilient adults. People can and will make a difference in a world given the right circumstances.

Grounded in research on 1) human needs and wants, 2) culturally relevant and responsive pedagogy, 3) brain-compatible learning, 4) emotional intelligence (EQ), 5) resilience, 6) trauma-informed practice, 7) effective group work, and 8) mindfulness, *Hearts and Minds Matter* provides educators with the tools necessary to understand the power of belonging in safe, inclusive classrooms where students achieve their potential without fear.

Jackie Eldridge and Denise McLafferty

In 1943, Abraham Maslow proposed his famous hierarchy of needs, which demonstrates the levels that individuals must go through in order to self-actualize. At the lowest level, are the physiological needs of food, water, and shelter. When these needs are not met, the higher levels cannot be achieved. Educators understand these concepts. There has been a great deal of research that demonstrates that children cannot learn when they are hungry or living in poverty where basic needs may not be available to them. Schools try to help as best as they can.

Safety and belonging are the second level of Maslow's hierarchy and the one that supports all of the other levels. It is critical that educators understand the importance of this stage because many children in today's schools do not feel safe or enjoy a feeling of belonging. There are many reasons why this might be the case: a classroom bully, a teacher who consistently yells, unattainable standards, instruction that doesn't meet the students' needs, chaotic classrooms, etc. It is not hard to imagine how students in these circumstances are being held back from developing their self-esteem and self-actualization. Now, imagine a school where every child feels safe and included in the classroom. Their potential would dramatically increase and they could achieve even greater things!

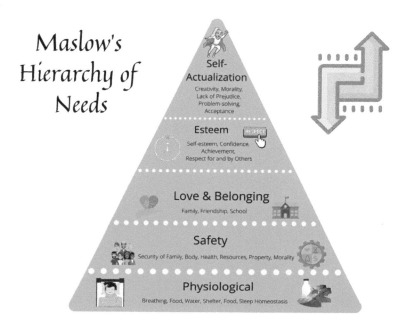

We believe that understanding Maslow's hierarchy gives educators an edge when working with students. The need for safety and belonging in particular is one of the major factors in helping children develop their emotional intelligence and their resilience.

Currently, there is a great deal of research that indicates emotional intelligence is more important than IQ as a predictor of success in life. Children who develop solid emotional intelligence skills are more likely to succeed because they are able to understand themselves and others. When teachers understand the importance of nurturing emotional intelligence in children, they see all kinds of benefits. More emotional connectedness with and among students leads to more opportunities for growth, cooperative learning, increased empathy among classmates, and fewer incidents of misbehaviour. Students feel welcomed by all, and they feel safe to learn and make mistakes without fear of reprisal. When misbehaviour is reduced, academic achievement improves. Teachers are able to teach more content because they are not spending exorbitant amounts of time managing their classes. When academic achievement increases, so does self-esteem and a sense of a bright future. Such benefits only serve to increase a child's opportunity to become resilient.

Hearts and Minds Matter understands how important the impact of emotional intelligence is for all who are involved in the education of students. This is why emotional intelligence is one of the key components in our work. The current research in education fully supports the need for teaching and modelling emotional intelligence. Degrees of the topic have always been part of the curricular landscape in schools. There is, however, a critical need to put it all together and understand that emotional intelligence is a defined set of skills that leads to children becoming resilient in their lives. Without an emphasis on this important content, true connection does not occur.

At this time in history, we are seeing more disconnection than connection. People (including our students) are rushed, stressed, and exhausted, leaving little time to connect with others. They are locked into personal devices, often to the exclusion of everyone and everything around them. At the same time, the daily news is filled with stories of hatred, abuse and tragic events that paint a strong picture of a disconnected world. As a result of all these influences, deep relationships do not develop, there is an increase in conflict, and people feel more and more isolated from others.

We are also seeing an increase in mental health challenges that could otherwise be avoided if people knew how to develop a sense of belonging or how to access and join the community when they are feeling excluded. In order to do so, people must have emotional intelligence skills, and these skills can be taught, but they must first be modelled. Parents and teachers are the most logical ones to meet these needs as they are typically the "first responders" for children. When the role models have the skills, and they practise them regularly, children are more inclined to pick them up at an early age. It is also true that when educators and parents teach emotional intelligence and provide feedback to children, the skills taught become integrated much more deeply than if people simply expect children to pick them up through osmosis. This kind of teaching is actually a thoughtful and intentional undertaking.

It is also necessary that the teaching of these skills, just like academic skills, be done in an emotionally safe environment that is judgement-free, where mistakes are welcomed, and risks are encouraged to be taken. Our brains require this safety in order to receive information and allow it to move through all of the neural pathways to the cerebral cortex—the centre for long-term memory and thinking. When classrooms are not safe and students feel threatened, the information goes directly to the amygdala, the centre for fight, flight, or freeze. It is important to note that once this pathway is engaged, people shut down, stop thinking clearly, and are unable to learn to their maximum potential. If schools and/or classrooms are not safe, students may stay locked into fight, flight, or freeze. Going back to Brown's original quote, we can see the harm that can be done.

We all have stories of teachers who were amazing and supportive. These teachers inspired us to be better people and our memories of them stay with us. We also have stories of teachers who were bullies or cruel, or simply lacked empathy. Such teachers humiliated students and ostracized them because they were somehow different than their vision of the perfect student. The images of these teachers are forever etched in our minds!

It is sad that children must endure such stress in places that are meant to nurture them and help them grow. It is also very stressful for those students who do not have the skills or understanding to realize that it's the behaviour of others that is impacting what is happening in the class, not them; or that the lack of compassion on the part of the teacher, is not their fault. For some, it can be devastating!

The research on the brain is clear and compelling, yet schools and classrooms continue to be unsafe for some. Imagine a world where every teacher understood the power of the safe place, the potential for all students to develop resilience, and the great contributions that can be made to children's

Jackie Eldridge and Denise McLafferty

development and skills. Imagine a world where teachers understood that trauma exists even in the youngest of children, and if children could be taught from a trauma-informed approach, we would not be adding to the already challenging life these children are experiencing.

Trauma-informed practices are finding their way into the education vernacular and influencing the ways teachers teach and schools are run. According to The Trauma and Learning Policy Initiatives:

> Once schools understand the educational impacts of trauma, they can become safe, supportive environments where students: make the positive connections with adults and peers they might otherwise push away; calm their emotions so they can focus and behave appropriately; and feel confident enough to advance their learning—in other words, schools can make trauma sensitivity a regular part of how the school is run.

While understanding the critical importance of the brain research and the creation of emotional safety, we must also realize how these learnings extend into teaching and learning. Teachers who bring brain-compatible learning to their teaching are opening a world of opportunity to their students. This research enlightens us about time-on-task, memory, the integration of new content, and the vast array of strategies that are available and their use in different teachable moments. Essentially, understanding the brain helps us understand teaching and learning.

Resilience develops when people feel they belong, when they have the skills necessary to get along with others and to bounce back in the face of adversity. It is nurtured when people learn to become autonomous, socially competent, and strong problem-solvers. It also develops when people learn to see past their challenges to a world with a bright future; a place where they can find a sense of purpose. While there are many factors associated with resilience, autonomy, social competence, problem solving and a sense of a bright future are among the most important. When children are taught in safe learning environments, where emotional intelligence is a focus and teachers are using effective instruction, they gain access to skills that help them develop resilience. Such resilience makes it possible to meet all of life's challenges in ways that serve to make them healthy and happy human beings.

Through *Hearts and Minds Matter,* we want teachers to fully understand and appreciate these qualities, and to see how they can, in fact, choose to help their students develop these skills simply by teaching content in ways that allow children to learn and practise the skills. It is not about adding anything else to a teacher's already busy workload; it is simply a new way of approaching the art and science of teaching. We must learn that children need to be taught using approaches that nurture both their hearts and their minds.

In this book, we outline ways to reach *all* children. We teach from the heart instead of being solely focused on achievement and standardization. Academic success is important, but it cannot be accomplished without attending to the social-emotional needs of each child and what they bring to the learning environment. Early social emotional skills are related to how socially, emotionally, academically, and professionally skilled we are later in life. For example, having higher social-emotional skills in kindergarten is related to important outcomes at age 25 (Jones, Greenberg, & Crowley, 2015). These outcomes include educational success, career success, and other key life outcomes. (Psychology Today, January 2017).

Throughout this book, we provide relevant and current research, as well as real-life examples of the ways in which this kind of teaching benefits all students and sets them up for life beyond the classroom. These skills are ones that we all need in order to be emotionally intelligent and resilient. They are life skills as well as learning tools.

Having been teachers ourselves, we are fully aware of the demands placed on teachers these days. We are very cognizant of the stress that teachers feel when they are asked to teach new and unfamiliar content. As such, we do not want to overwhelm; instead, we are demonstrating attitudes and skills that facilitate learning in ways that reflect good teaching and solid management strategies.

It is not about adding-on; it is about embedding effective instruction into the daily routine, while providing children with the tools and opportunities to develop their emotional intelligence and resilience. It is about using strategies that are grounded in Maslow's hierarchy of needs, emotional intelligence, and brain research. We provide the reader with a range of instructional strategies, tactics, skills, and resources that are developed by people in the field familiar with classroom life, its demands and all of its rewards. We also have included some personal stories to inspire and motivate teachers to be the best they can be.

When teachers have the proper tools and the freedom to create, they inspire students to stretch themselves and maximize their potential!

> *One looks back with appreciation to the brilliant teachers,*
> *but with gratitude to those who touched our human feelings. The curriculum*
> *has so much necessary raw material, but warmth is the vital element*
> *for the growing plant and for the soul of the child.*
> *~ Carl Jung*

Jackie Eldridge and Denise McLafferty

CHAPTER ONE

Human Needs and Inclusion

What Does the Research Say?

Over many years, educational research has focused on the needs of children and the importance of designing teaching/learning environments to support them. In all of this research, there is one ingredient that most researchers agree upon—classrooms must be inclusive.

In this chapter, we explore:

✓ *The research on human needs*

✓ *Maslow's hierarchy of needs and how to utilize this hierarchy in teaching and learning*

✓ *Risk factors for attaining each level of need*

✓ *Connections to behaviour management theorists, William Glasser and Rudolph Dreikurs*

✓ *The ways this research plays out in classrooms*

In his 1943 paper, "A Theory of Human Motivation" and in his subsequent book, *Motivation and Personality*, published in 1954, Abraham Maslow developed his famous hierarchy of needs, which suggests that people must have their basic physiological needs met before moving on to the other, more advanced needs of security and safety, love, belonging and acceptance, self-esteem and self-actualization. Researchers continue to explore his work and add that people self-actualize irrespective of where they find themselves on the hierarchy. Current research also explains that people can move in and out of each level depending on life's experiences. Regardless, current education and business theorists alike still embrace Maslow's work and acknowledge it as a powerful motivator for human beings.

The key to Maslow's work, especially in education, is his **humanist** approach to human growth and development, instead of focusing on deficiency. As a humanist, he believed that everyone wants to self-actualize so they can reach their full potential. They simply need the right circumstances to help them along the way. We all want to belong and feel loved, and we can all benefit from increased self-esteem so that we can reach for the stars. Understanding Maslow's work is a crucial piece in the educational puzzle.

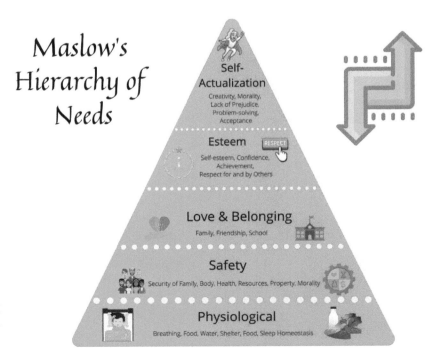

Jackie Eldridge and Denise McLafferty

Knowing the interconnectedness of our needs and the realities of school life is especially valuable, given the amount of time children spend in classrooms. When they are welcomed and have a positive school experience, they shine, and they will carry their school stories with them into adulthood. Conversely, when school is not a safe place, they can easily fall through the cracks or fall behind, making their educational experience challenging, as they labour to get through it all. Those who struggle are the adults who hated school and could not wait for it to end.

These narratives are not new ones. Many adults can recall accounts where each day was difficult because their needs were not met. That is a sad statement considering we spend at least fourteen years of our life in school. Faculties of education are filled with neophyte teachers who talk about being inspired to become teachers because they had such wonderful experiences. There are also those who choose to become teachers in order to make changes to a system in which they struggled so significantly. The latter clearly had teachers who did not understand the needs of children.

Maslow's hierarchy of needs has five levels. It is important to understand how these needs fit into the school landscape and are connected to each other.

Level One: Physiological Needs

Our basic physical needs are located at the bottom of the pyramid: the need for food, water, sleep, and warmth. If these needs are not met, it can be difficult to move ahead in our lives. At this level, we are in survival mode, and the challenge of day-to-day living is focussed on having these basic needs met. Educators understand this crucial part of human development. They are constantly checking to see if their students are fed, had enough sleep, are wearing appropriate clothing, so that they are ready for the school day. Schools make a difference in the lives of children who are struggling in these areas. It is the reason why many schools provide breakfast, lunch or snack programs, and teachers keep mittens and hats on hand, or sponsor clothing drives to ensure they have what they need in harsh weather conditions. Once these essential needs have been met, people can move to the next level of needs: safety and security.

Level Two: Security and Safety Needs

Maslow's second level in the hierarchy starts to become more complex. We all need to feel safe and secure. We want to know what is happening so that we have some measure of control and order in our lives. When people do not feel safe, a variety of behaviours can be manifested. When these behaviours appear, teachers are faced with challenging classroom management issues. When classrooms are not safe places because chaos exists or the teacher is unpredictable, children try to claim control of their lives through whatever means they can. For instance, without safety and security, children may act out or withdraw. Acting out is only one of the potential outcomes. Children often underperform or are unmotivated to work because they feel unsure and/or unsafe. As a result, their focus will be less likely on academic achievement or pleasing the teacher, and simply on survival. It is not that these children are not intelligent, but rather, they simply cannot focus their attention on school and survival at the same time. Some of the basic security and safety needs include:

- ♥ Freedom from emotional and physical harm
- ♥ Safety against accidents and injury
- ♥ Safety of routine

Teachers can work towards building a safe learning environment so that students know what is expected from them and their classmates. Routine and predictability are also important so that children feel secure in knowing what is coming.

Level Three: Love, Belonging and Acceptance Needs

Maslow's third level in the hierarchy includes love, belonging and acceptance. At this level, the need for emotionally safe relationships drive human behaviour in various positive ways. Potential in human beings is enhanced when they contribute more fully to their own growth and development and to the relationships they build within their own environments. Some areas of this need include:

- ♥ Family
- ♥ Friendships
- ♥ Romantic attachments
- ♥ Social groups
- ♥ Community groups
- ♥ Religious and/or spiritual affiliations

We all want to belong. We all want to feel loved and accepted by other people. When we feel excluded, we feel threatened, which can manifest itself in inappropriate behaviour. As is the case with the previous level, when this need is not met in children, the child will act out.

In classrooms where teachers have not built inclusion, students may behave inappropriately in order to feel included and part of the classroom community. Attention-seeking behaviour is a way to be recognized. Negative attention, for some students, is better than no attention, and for these students is as powerful as positive attention. Even the most well-behaved child acts out if they feel they do not belong. It is one of the reasons people join gangs—it is a place where they feel welcomed and connected. In chapter three, we address the connections between the last two levels of Maslow and the recent research on the brain. It is clear from this work that children thrive within safe and inclusive settings, while at risk when the environment is threatening. A sense of belonging and the resulting benefits from feeling like a valued member of the classroom community, provide all students with a solid foundation for learning.

Addiction research also supports the importance of love and belonging. Many people who take this path express that they always felt excluded. Addiction became their friend when no one else seemed to care. More and more, we hear about younger and younger children becoming addicted to an extensive range of escapes (e.g., drugs, alcohol, social media, shopping, video games, gambling, etc.) Drugs and alcohol are at the top of the list. Addictions among young people have reached crisis proportions: 2.8 million Canadians are addicted to drugs and/or alcohol and almost 21 million Americans have at least one addiction, yet only ten percent of them receive treatment in either country.

Risk factors for substance abuse problems in youth include:

- ♥ Alcohol or other drug problems among family members
- ♥ Poor school performance
- ♥ Poverty, family conflicts, chaos, or stress
- ♥ Friends who drink or use drugs
- ♥ Social isolation or exclusion because of factors such as race, ethnicity, gender, or sexual orientation
- ♥ Emotional, physical, or sexual abuse
- ♥ Discrimination or oppression.

The protective factors for substance abuse problems include:

- ♥ Positive adult role model
- ♥ Good parental or another caregiver supervision
- ♥ Strong attachments to family, school, and community
- ♥ Having goals and dreams
- ♥ Being involved in meaningful, well-supervised activities (e.g., sports, volunteer work).

These risk and protective factors are closely aligned with the research on resilience, addressed in chapter five. When we understand these factors, we can develop connections with students so they can develop the skills needed to avoid these paths.

Level Four: Self-Esteem Needs

Meeting the need for appreciation and respect leads to improved self-esteem. When the needs at the bottom three levels have been satisfied, children really start to flourish. Their self-esteem now allows them to take risks, try new things, and feel good about who they are. Learning potential is dramatically increased. On the other hand, low self-esteem is the source of many problems in our lives. It prevents us from moving forward and shuts us down from any form of self-actualization. While developing our own esteem may seem like an individual practice, one actually develops self-esteem in relationship to acceptance from others. There is an innate challenge when looking for acceptance from others: our potential acceptors often have self-esteem issues themselves. When this is the case, those whose esteem is under-developed are eager to put others down in order to boost themselves up.

It is also apparent in today's society that people use put-downs as a common way of interacting with each other. Social media, television and radio are all inundated with criticisms, putdowns, bullying, and the like. Schools are rife with put-downs. One only has to listen to children and teens putting themselves and others down to understand how challenging the level of self-esteem can be to attain. Some middle and secondary school teachers have suggested they believe this kind of communication is simply the way that people of that age communicate. At Hearts and Minds Matter, we say, no—there is no child development expert who has found this to be true. It has simply become an acceptable way of treating each other, and this will never change if we do not discourage this kind of behaviour or hold people accountable for treating others in such disrespectful ways.

Some characteristics of low self-esteem:

- ♥ Continual negative thoughts and feelings
- ♥ Fear of making mistakes and risk-taking
- ♥ Constant dissatisfaction and frustration
- ♥ A tendency to be suspicious and defensive of many things
- ♥ Lack of boundaries and assertiveness
- ♥ Fear of abandonment
- ♥ Fear of being hurt
- ♥ Constant avoidance
- ♥ Fear of change

Identifying children with low-self-esteem is often easy because they typically see the world around them as negative. They tend to see themselves as victims, feeling like people are out to get them. They are reluctant to express and assert themselves, and they often miss out on experiences and opportunities. They also feel powerless to change things. These behaviours only serve to lower their self-esteem even further. Children who exhibit these traits find school challenging, and they will likely withdraw or act out.

When teachers understand the ramifications of low self-esteem, they are able to work hard to assist students in this area. They understand the connections to student achievement and classroom management. We all want to accomplish our goals and have our efforts recognized. When teachers consciously contribute to building self-esteem, they are providing a platform for children to feel included and safe, supported, appreciated, and respected. In this kind of classroom, students also have a sense of self-worth that allows them to fail because they have the confidence to take risks, get back up and try again. When children feel valued, they are motivated to participate and contribute to their classroom community, and they feel confident in their abilities. Those who lack self-esteem and the respect of others, feel inferior and will try everything they can to be recognized. Their choices to do so may not always be the best.

According to Maslow's definition of self-actualization: It may be loosely described as the full use and exploitation of talents, potential, capabilities, etc. Such people seem to be fulfilling themselves and maximizing what they are capable of doing. Those who have a need to self-actualize are interested in self-awareness, self-growth and being the best they can be. As they self-actualize, they are inspired, creative and striving to reach their full potential. Additionally, William Glasser introduced the *Choice Theory of Behavior Management* in 1996. His theory is based  on the core idea that the most important need people have is for love and belonging. In order for anyone to be able to satisfy any of their needs, they must have a certain closeness or a feeling of connectedness with people they care about. This correlation between Glasser and Maslow shows again the importance of creating safe classrooms with supportive and nurturing teachers.

Like Maslow, Glasser identified several human needs that must be satisfied by individuals:

- ♥ Survive
- ♥ Belong
- ♥ Gain power
- ♥ Be free
- ♥ Have fun

Glasser suggested that we feel frustrated when a need is not met and satisfied when it is. He outlines the following ways to fulfill these needs:

- ♥ Having our basic needs met
- ♥ Loving, sharing, and cooperating with others
- ♥ Achieving, accomplishing, being recognized and respected
- ♥ Making choices in our lives
- ♥ Laughing and playing

There are obvious and important connections between the theories presented by Maslow and Glasser. Their work factors greatly into the understanding of how we must design and manage our classrooms. Psychiatrist and educator, Rudolph Dreikurs, also explored these same ideas. He outlines a myriad of ways that children behave in order to have their needs met, along with positive teacher responses. When teachers take the time to investigate the reasons children are behaving the way they do, they are better equipped to deal with misbehaviour, and be proactive in working towards change. Without this kind of understanding, the inclination is to simply tell the child to stop. In this case, there is no empathy, feedback, or next steps.

Dreikurs identified four main goals for misbehaviour in children:

GOALS	CHILD'S NEEDS	CHILD'S BEHAVIOUR	POSITIVE TEACHER RESPONSE
ATTENTION	Contact/Belonging—physical or emotional contact	Calling out, breaking the rules, inappropriate behaviour	Don't sweat the small stuff, catch them doing something good and praise, positive flooding
POWER (REBELLION)	Ability to influence their environment; have a measure of control	Talking back, aggression, passive-aggression	Remove yourself from the conflict, give the child a chance to cool off, take some deep breaths yourself, give students choice and voice
REVENGE	Protection from physical or emotional harm, wants to preserve self-esteem, has felt threatened	Sabotage lessons and activities, getting back through false reports to administration, social-media bullying	Refuse to be hurt, withdraw from conflict, open and authentic dialogue, show love and concern
INADEQUACY (AVOIDANCE)	Self-esteem, permission to take risks	Helplessness, refusal to even try, excuses, school absence	Patience, encouragement, chunking of assignments, provide baby steps, positive flooding

Other current classroom management researchers such as Bennett and Smilanovich are clear that student needs must be met in order for classrooms to run smoothly. Dr. Barrie Bennett also suggests that inclusion is key. He advocates for the conscious building of cooperation in classrooms since learning is socially constructed and students benefit from a blend of independent and cooperative learning structures. In chapter seven, we include Dr. Bennett as a guest author on cooperative learning. Dr. Bennett describes the need for teachers to understand cooperative strategies, tactics and skills because these are paramount to meeting student's needs, and to creating effective classroom design and instruction.

Classroom management is perhaps one of the biggest challenges that teachers face. It can be difficult to meet the needs of so many individuals at one time. If a teacher has good strategies for managing the class, then the year runs smoothly and all curriculum areas are covered. However, if teachers do not understand their students' needs and there is no solid management plan in place, the year can be long and arduous. This classroom might be chaotic which exacerbates the problem because the students are searching for ways to get their needs met. This will be stressful for both students and the teacher. A vicious cycle soon begins. In order to avoid this disastrous situation, teachers must be able to create an environment where the physiological, social, and psychological needs of all students are considered. It is a conscious decision.

Jackie Eldridge and Denise McLafferty

What Does it Look Like in the Classroom?

Physiological Needs

Note: Refer to the Classroom Resources section where noted.

- ♥ *Ensure that Student's Physiological Needs are Being Met*: Allow for snacks and water throughout the day; speak to parents if you have concerns; speak to the administration if parents can't provide for their child's needs; encourage parents to take their child to a doctor for regular check-ups; provide a quiet corner where students can rest if needed; and ensure a strong physical and health education program so students get exercise and learn to manage their own physiological needs.

- ♥ *Build a Safe Learning Environment*: Establish routines and alliances or agreements from the first day of school and post them for all to see; get to know your students and their specific needs and interests by using interest inventories (see Classroom Resources); spend the first few weeks focusing on inclusion-building as opposed to rushing into curriculum; provide multiple opportunities for the students to get to know each other and to work with as many different students as possible (see Classroom Resources); observe the ways students interact and work with each other so you know who works well together and who doesn't; model appropriate behaviour yourself and talk through your own problem solving and decision-making; provide many opportunities for reflection and classroom dialogue (see Classroom Resources); give the students voice in your classroom; allow the right to pass if students are not feeling safe, comfortable or prepared; and encourage risk-taking; downplay and welcome mistakes.

- ♥ *Understand Behaviours and Ensure Effective Classroom Management*: Discuss needs with students; ensure you are meeting their needs; be firm, fair and consistent with routines and alliances/agreements and consequences; hold students accountable; involve parents when necessary; talk to students regularly; give them a voice in decision-making; give students responsibilities; believe in yourself in terms of dealing with misbehaviour; understand that students want and need boundaries; seek to understand the child; don't make assumptions; be informed about trauma-informed practices (See Chapter Six); be prepared ahead of time and make a plan—understanding all that goes into your daily routine (transitions, picking up resources, what happens when work is finished early, what are your potential consequences, etc.); think about employing restorative justice and/or healing circles; include student voice in decision-making and problem solving; empower students; ensure that you understand the connections between effective instruction and classroom management (e.g., make your lessons interesting, engaging, culturally responsive and relevant, meaningful, include fun in your day, use authentic assessment practices, differentiate instruction where possible); build in mindfulness practice to help students learn to self-regulate and calm themselves down (See Chapter Eight); ask for help when needed; involve parents, in short… **BUILD INCLUSION!**

Security and Safety Needs

All of the strategies included under the *Physiological Needs* would also be relevant in this section.

♥ *Create Predictable and Consistent Routines*: All of us need predictability in our lives; this is especially critical for children. In the classroom, ensure there is information throughout the room that clearly indicates what is going to happen on a day-to-day basis. This should include classroom norms/alliance; daily schedule; tasks of the day; student jobs; learning centre expectations; and include a notice board located beside the daily schedule labelled '*changes for today*'. By notifying the students of any modifications to the normal schedule, this too builds safety, and when they enter the classroom daily, that will be the first area they check. By including this wide-range of visual "scaffolding" for students, we create security and safety – there will not be any surprises. For some students, change will not be an issue, but we have to consider the needs of every student in the classroom (e.g., special needs) and therefore, we need to overprepare to maximize success for everyone. The more predictable, the better!

♥ *Ensure Consistency of Expectations*: When we create classroom routines and expectations, it is one thing to work with our students to establish these, but another to implement consistently every day; that's the real work! When students know that "what we say, is what we mean", they feel secure and safe knowing what will happen and that it applies to everyone. All members of that classroom community have to commit to following the norms/expectations and as the classroom teacher, you are the "head role model". Students are watching your behaviour all the time, so remember, "What you do speaks so loudly, they cannot hear what you say"!

Love, Belonging and Acceptance Needs

♥ *Provide Belonging and Love*: Ensure that each student is recognized and valued by you and the others involved in the classroom (other students, classroom assistants, etc.). Continue to build inclusion throughout the year. Encourage mutual respect, appreciations, gratitude, and compassionate listening. Welcome the students each day with a smile and send them home with a special message. Catch them doing something good and give sunshine calls/notes to parents when their child has done something to warrant it. Use loving kindness meditation (see Chapter Eight). Celebrate successes. Use all of the elements of cooperative learning to ensure effective group work (see Chapter Seven). Watch the Rita Pierson TED Talk, *Every Kid Needs a Champion*. This talk is one of TED's most watched videos! The following ten activities are ones we have borrowed from Jeanne Gibbs (2014):

♥ *Boasters*: This activity allows students to get to know each other on a deeper level and provides an opportunity to build inclusion and community while also allowing students to appreciate themselves and others. Prepare a silhouette of each student (or have them create their own) and have them put their name on the drawing. In small groups, have each student write a positive affirmation for each other on their silhouette. Once everyone has had an opportunity to write on all silhouettes, hold a class discussion about the difference between bragging and affirming. After the discussion, each student will write an affirmation about themselves. It is a good idea to connect this activity with teaching on Growth Mindset (See Chapter Five).

♥ **Community Circle:** The very nature of this seating arrangement builds openness and connection. It builds inclusion and community as you create the atmosphere and the opportunity to share deeply. Students will sit in a large community circle for the purpose of sharing ideas, reflecting, creating a space for attentive listening, sharing cares, concerns and compliments or any activity where you would like the students to be able to interact more intimately. Ensure that the students are heeding the alliance that you have created as a class. You can begin the community circle with a question or a statement. As the teacher, you will always go first to model what the student contributions will look like. Some teachers will use the community circle daily and others may limit to once or twice per week.

♥ **Extended Name Tag:** This strategy provides a graphic organizer for students to explore themselves and others as they build inclusion. Provide each student with a sheet divided into four sections. Have them place their name at the top. The categories in each section of the paper will depend on the objectives you are trying to achieve. For example, the students might write and share about their favourite hobbies, subjects in school, tv shows and music - or you could go deeper as they share their strengths and challenges. The

teacher would create a prompt for each of the four sections based on the topic selected. For example, if the focus was 'favourite things I like to do', the sheet could have the following prompts regarding this topic: "At recess, I like to....", "When I am by myself, my favourite thing to do is...", "The first thing I do when I get home is....", If my family won the lottery, I would like to go to....".It is essential to wait until you know that inclusion has been built before you get the students to share more personal ideas.

♥ **Milling to Music with Huddles:** This activity is well-suited for having your students mix up and talk to a variety of their classmates as you guide them to talk to as many different people as possible. Turn on some upbeat music and have the students mill around as they smile and greet each other. Pause the music, have the students stop, huddle, and talk to one, two or three other people about a topic of your choice. It's fun to encourage them to dance and really move. Milling to Music is a great mental set for lessons or a brilliant way to bring closure to lessons.

♥ **Name Wave:** In every classroom, it is important for you and the students to get to know each other's names. Name Wave is a fun way to do that. It allows everyone to hear all of the names and to hear the correct pronunciation. Have all of the students stand in a community circle. You will start by modeling your name and an action to go along with it. For example, I might say "Jackie" and tug on my right ear. The person on my right will repeat my name and action, and then all the other students will continue my name and action until it goes around the circle. Then the next person will say their name and do an action and that gets waved around. Everyone in the class will get a chance to have their name and action waved around the circle.

♥ **One Ball/Three Ball Pass:** This kinesthetic activity has many possible uses. Everyone stands in a circle and the teacher starts by calling someone's name and throwing that person a koosh ball/bean bag (select something that will be easy to catch and will not roll if dropped). The catcher then selects a different person, calls their name, and throws the ball. Once a student has had a turn to catch the ball and pass on to someone else, they then place their hands behind their back, so that the other members of the circle can see who has had their turn. The goal is to have everyone in the circle have their name called out, receive the ball, and pass on to another student. The last student to catch the ball will then call out the person who started the activity, pass the ball, and then the task is complete. Some examples of prompts are names, story stems, patterns, multiplication questions, etc. You can start them with one ball and when this skill level is mastered, you can add one or two more balls, again following the same pattern around the circle - so it is important for each participant to remember who they threw the ball to. It's really fun to add a rubber chicken into the mix! When used at the beginning of the year to get to know names, it is important to play the game several times in a row so they can put names to faces.

♥ **One Minute History:** One Minute History can be done as a whole community or in small groups. For younger children, small groups are recommended. Each person in the group will have one minute to give an overview of their history. It is important that you model for the students before they start so they hear what is important to say. You might set them up the day before by brainstorming and having them write down some prompts to help them. The idea is to have them learn as much as they can about each other.

♥ **Partner Introduction:** Ask the students to partner with someone they do not know and have them sit together. They will then letter themselves off A and B. Partner A will start by telling Partner B all of the things they would like to know about that person. For example, "I'd like to know where you were born, your favourite colour, your favourite tv show, your favourite computer game, how many brothers and sisters you have." You will give the questioner about one minute to speak while Partner B attentively listens without answering...just listening. When the signal is given, Partner B will respond. It is important to note that each partner can pass on something they are not comfortable talking about. You will give the pairs about 3 to 4 minutes to chat. Then, a signal is given and this time, Partner B will tell Partner A what they would like to know. Again, Partner A is only listening and will not answer until the signal is given. When both partners have asked and answered, you will give the pair one minute to check with each other about one piece of information that is ok to share with the whole community. Once permission is given, you will choose a pair to start. The sharing will sound like, "This is my new friend...and she...".

♥ **What's in My Name?** In the whole community or a smaller group, each person will share their birth name and any variations of it. For example, the meaning of the name, someone after whom they were named, nicknames, shortened forms, etc.

Jackie Eldridge and Denise McLafferty

♥ ***What's in My Wallet/Cell Phone/Backpack?*** In the whole community or a smaller group, each person will share an item that is important to them or something that is symbolic. It might be a photo, a card, a song, a touchstone, a favourite pen, etc.

Self-Esteem Needs

♥ ***Esteem-Building:*** Give meaningful and authentic praise and feedback. Use a strategy like Two Stars and a Wish for feedback (see Classroom Resources). Offer next steps for improvement and encourage students to work from their strengths. Allow choice, and work/ assessment opportunities so they can produce strong work. Use Howard Gardner's Multiple Intelligences in your teaching and allow students to do the same with their work. Chunk material so they can take baby steps. Directly teach about self-esteem, e.g., use quality literature that teaches self-esteem (see Literature Resources  at the end of each chapter). Have them articulate their strengths. Model your own self-esteem strategies and talk about them. Expect appreciations and forbid put-downs - do not tolerate any bullying! Encourage reflection on thoughts and feelings. Utilize classroom dialogue to do group problem solving when issues arise. Teach students about the importance of emotional intelligence and resilience. Use strategies that help them develop these skills (see Classroom Resources).

♥ ***All About Me Book:*** Have the students create a book that is all about them. It can be electronic or in hard copy. The book should include a personal history of themselves and their family. You can tie this activity into learning about culture and heritage. The book can be created by them with their own choices of what to include or you can provide guidelines such as family, hobbies, favourite subjects, etc. Following the completion of the book, the class could do a Gallery Walk where each book is viewed. Include an appreciation sheet to deepen the experience and to validate the hard work. Another option is to have an Author of the Day where the students read their book to the class.

♥ ***Daily Intentions:*** Intentions are meant to encourage people to act and follow through on their actions. It is a way of holding oneself accountable. It is an aim for the day. Encouraging students to set daily intentions allows them to plan and then have you or their teammates check in to see how it is going. You can also add a helping element by having the students check in to see if their friends need any help reaching their goal.

♥ ***Appreciations/No Put Downs:*** Put Downs are rampant among students and it is constantly modeled for them on radio, tv and in movies. It is important to break them of this habit. You can insist that there are no put downs in your classroom by building it into your alliance or agreements. You will always model for the students and hold them accountable when they slip. One way to ensure appreciations is to build it into their teamwork. After they have completed any group work, provide them with an opportunity to give appreciations. When appreciations become a regular occurrence, they will start giving them naturally.

♥ **I Am:** In this activity, you will get students to list all the things that make up who they are. It can be done in a simple list or turned into a poem or spoken word poetry. For example, the list might include such ideas as "I am strong, I am happy, I am smart, I am funny". The list can be posted for all to see. It can also be taped to the student's desk as a daily affirmation.

♥ **I Used to Be, and Now I Am; We Used to Be, and Now We Are:** We want our students to see that they are continually growing and improving. You can ask your students to do this activity individually or in a small group. You might consider having them think about how they were last year in their previous grade and how they have changed over the summer. It might also be done each term to show growth.

♥ **Letters to Myself:** This activity is a great one to start and end the year. In the first few weeks of school, each of the students can write a letter to themselves about their hopes, dreams, wishes, intentions, etc. The letters can be filed away and opened at the end of the year to see what has been accomplished, changed, or achieved. It can be a reminder of how well they have done and/or where they need to keep practising.

♥ **Portfolio for Growth:** Portfolios can take many forms. They are an excellent tool for showing growth and strengths and can be used by the students to conduct student-led conferences with parents and teachers. The creation of a portfolio is very individual, and teachers are encouraged to make them in such a way that it works for them and their class. An excellent resource is *The Portfolio Organizer* by Carol Rolheiser, Barbara Bower and Laurie Stevahn (see Classroom Resources). In addition, Susan Schwartz and Mindy Pollishuke have portfolio resources in their book, *Creating the Dynamic Classroom.* Their use of retell, relate and reflect as reflection tools is an exemplary addition to a portfolio.

♥ **Role Play:** Children love drama and role play. It is part of the curriculum objectives and it is also fun. When we encourage role play with our students, we are offering them an opportunity to explore how others think, feel and act. We can encourage them to take on roles in order to build their esteem, or to see how their character lacks self-esteem. We can encourage them to take on the role and then reflect on its meaning afterwards.

♥ **Visualization:** This powerful tool allows us to create a new world or a new way of being for ourselves. It allows us to imagine and create, to visualize what might be and to see ourselves in a different light. It opens us up to different possibilities instead of repeating previous habits of being and doing. We can help students change their mindsets when we help them see what can be.

Self-Actualization Needs

♥ **Self-Actualization:** Encourage inquiry and creativity. Use materials and teach content using their interests. Promote reflection on future self and personal goal setting. Model your own self-actualization and talk about your own continuous learning journey (courses you have taken, hobbies, interests, favourite books and movies, etc.).

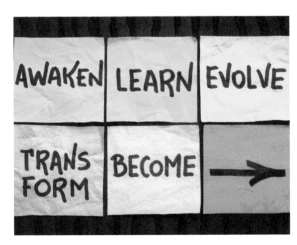

♥ **Acrostic Poem:** These poems have been used in classrooms forever. The students will use their name or a word that best describes them and write it vertically so that each letter can be used as a word starter to describe them. They might use this word or name to create an image of who they want to become or where they want to head in life. In other words, it is a visual self-actualization map to inspire them.

♥ **Career Days:** Many students have ideas about what they want to be when they grow up, but they may not get a chance to speak with people in those roles in the work world. You can take a poll in your class to see what careers/occupations they are interested in, and then invite speakers reflecting their choices to describe the job and to answer questions. In advance of this event, the students could create a list of what they already know about the selected careers/occupations.

♥ **Creativity Choices:** Creativity is one of the most neglected areas in a child's day at school; yet it is one of the most important in helping children self-actualize. When they are allowed to be creative, their self-esteem is boosted, their academic achievement increases, and their problem solving skills are maximized. As a teacher, it is important to allow students to use their creativity as often as possible. Instead of always relying on structured assignments for assessment and evaluation, you can allow the students to think more critically, with more breadth and depth, by allowing them choice and creativity to demonstrate what they know. It can be tied to Gardner's multiple ways of knowing (verbal-linguistic, logical-mathematical, visual-spatial, bodily-kinesthetic, musical-rhythmic, interpersonal, intrapersonal, naturalist, existential) where the students explore their strengths and offer their work in different ways. For example, they can draw, write poetry, perform skits, sing songs, paint pictures, make quilts - the list is endless. When students are always asked to contribute using traditional paper and pencil tasks, they may tune out and turn off.

♥ **Human Library:** The human library is an interesting concept where the teacher will invite human beings into the classroom to be the books. The traditional human library was intended to have people explore diversity. People from different races, cultures, religions, abilities, etc., would be invited to share their stories. The students would sign up to listen to the storyteller with the intention of learning more about each topic from a human perspective. The human library could also look like a career day or any other ways the teacher wants to define it. It is a powerful experience when done through the diversity lens.

♥ **If I Were A…:** This story stem can get the students thinking about who or what they want to be. Perhaps they can research what is involved in becoming a parent, police officer, teacher, astronaut, doctor etc., and then write a story from that perspective. They can also be creative and make up a new career or profession.

♥ **Life Map** (Jeanne Gibbs, 2014): Life map is a powerful activity that can help your students build inclusion and community, increase self-esteem, and look at their self-actualization. Give the students a large sheet of paper and crayons or markers. They will draw their life map from the beginning to the present. They need to know ahead of time that they will be presenting their map to a group or the class, so they feel safe in including whatever is important to them. They can also choose to put down everything but only share certain things. Another way of making it safe is to structure it so that the map is showing their school life or their life with friends. This activity should not be done with highly personal information unless you are sure the environment is safe and that all students are abiding by the designed alliance. It is also a good idea for the teacher to model life map by sharing their own.

- ♥ **Look at Me** (Jeanne Gibbs, 2014): This activity can be done using drawings or photographs at various ages and stages. Students will use the pictures to explore and explain how far they have grown and developed since they were babies. They might also invite their parents to help them with descriptions and necessary information. The purpose is to have the students see how far they have come.

- ♥ **This is Me** (Jeanne Gibbs, 2014): Each student will produce their own poster that outlines who they are. The teacher can create the template including such categories as: name, wants, needs, likes, dislikes, values, words to live by, hobbies, etc. Following the poster-making, the students could do a gallery walk, presentation, video, etc.

- ♥ **Three Step Interview:** In triads, the students will letter themselves off A, B and C. Person A will be the interviewer, Person B will be the interviewee and Person C can be the recorder or videographer. Each interviewer will ask the interviewee questions that will help the person explain important ideas about themselves. The questions can be scripted ahead of time. If there is a video, the students can watch each others' interviews. Another suggestion would be to have the interviewer introduce the interviewee to the class. Ideally, each student would rotate through each of the three roles.

- ♥ **Time Capsule:** Have the students write predictions about where they will be, what they will be doing, studying, perfecting, etc., by the end of the school year. Have them place their predictions and any items of importance to them in a container that can be easily stored until the end of the year. At that time, have the students try to remember their predictions and then do a big reveal!

 Literature Resources

Picture Books

Amazing Grace by Mary Hoffman

Ballerino Nate by Kimberley Brubaker Bradley

Calvin Can't Fly by Jennifer Berne

Chrysanthemum by Kevin Henkes

Exclamation Mark by Amy Krouse Rosenthal

Flight Schools by Lita Judge

Giraffes Can't Dance by Giles Andreae

Jackie Eldridge and Denise McLafferty

Good Little Wolf by Nadia Shireen

How to be a Good Elephant by Jackie Eldridge and Beth Parker

I Like Me by Nancy Carlson

I Like Myself by Karen Beaumont

I Want Your Moo by Marcella Baker Weiner

I'm Gonna Like Me: Letting Off a Little Self-Esteem by Jamie Lee Curtis and Laura Cornell

I'm Not by Pam Smallcomb

It's Ok to be Different by Todd Parr

Junkyard Wonders by Patricia Polacco

Leo the Late Bloomer by Robert Kraus

Not Your Typical Dragon by Dan Bar-El

Spoon by Amy Krouse Rosenthal

The Crown on Your Head by Nancy Tillman

The Dot by Peter H. Reynolds

The Girl Who Never Made Mistakes by Mark Pett

The Spyglass by Richard Paul Evans

The Story of Ferdinand by Munro Leaf

Chapter Books

American Born Chinese by Gene Luen Yang

Fatty Legs by Christy Jordan-Fenton and Margaret Pokiak-Fenton

George by Alex Gino

The Absolutely True Diary of a Part-Time Indian by Sherma Alexie

They Both Die at the End by Adam Silvera

The Hate U Give by Angie Thomas

The Namesake by Jumpa Lahiri

The Skin I'm In by Sharon Flake

CHAPTER TWO

Culturally Relevant and Responsive Pedagogy

What Does the Research Say?

As discussed in chapter one, we must provide safe learning spaces where children's needs and wants are integral to all areas of their growth and development. When children experience exclusion, they cannot realize their maximum potential. Keeping Maslow's concepts in mind, we must remove discriminatory biases and barriers to student achievement and well-being that relate to ethnicity and race, faith, family structure and socio-economic status as well as to sexual orientation, ability and mental health.

In this chapter, we explore:

- ✓ Culturally Responsive Teaching
- ✓ Culturally Relevant Teaching
- ✓ Culturally Relevant and Responsive Pedagogy
- ✓ Culturally Relevant and Responsive Pedagogy Mindset
- ✓ Stages of Curriculum Transformation
- ✓ Equity Frameworks

Through the Ontario Ministry of Education's Policy/Program Memorandum No. 119, released in 2013, all schools are required to develop an equity and inclusive education policy. The goal is nothing less than the provision of equitable learning opportunities for all students in all Ontario schools. These kinds of policies are important for all school districts to consider.

This document emphasizes how crucial it is to acknowledge our students' multiple social identities and positionality and how they intersect with the world. It is designed to spark conversation and support educators as they seek to give life to equity strategies and policies. Its intent is to deepen understanding of teaching practices that engage student populations with a full range of differences in learning background, strengths, needs and interests.

Culture is about ways of knowing ...

Culture goes much deeper than typical understandings of ethnicity, race and/or faith. It encompasses broad notions of similarity and difference and it is reflected in our students' multiple social identities and their ways of knowing and of being in the world. In order to ensure that all students feel safe, welcomed and accepted, and inspired to succeed in a culture of high expectations for learning, schools and classrooms must be responsive to culture.

Gloria Ladson-Billings (1994) introduced the term "Culturally Relevant Teaching" to describe teaching that integrates a student's background knowledge and prior home and community experiences into the curriculum and the teaching and learning experiences that take place in the classroom. There are three central tenets underpinning this pedagogy: (1) holding high expectations for all students, (2) assisting students in the development of cultural competence, and (3) guiding students to develop a critical cultural consciousness. In this student-centred framework, the uniqueness of each student is not just acknowledged, but nurtured.

Other theorists, among them Gay (2000) and Villegas and Lucas (2002), use the terms "Culturally Responsive Teaching" or "Culturally Responsive Pedagogy" to describe teaching that recognizes all students learn differently and that these differences may be connected to background, language, family structure and social or cultural identity. Theorists and practitioners of culturally responsive pedagogy more than acknowledge the "cultural uniqueness" of each student; they intentionally nurture it in order to create and facilitate effective conditions for learning (Brown-Jeffy & Cooper, 2011). They see student diversity in terms of student strengths; they orient to it as presenting opportunities for enhancing learning rather than as challenges and/or deficits of the student or community.

Culturally responsive pedagogy is not about "cultural celebrations," nor is it aligned with traditional ideas around multiculturalism. It involves careful acknowledgement, respect and an understanding of difference and its complexities.

 Theorists write about three dimensions which comprise culturally responsive pedagogy:

1. Institutional
2. Personal
3. Instructional

The *Institutional Dimension* refers to the administration and leadership of school systems, including the values developed and reflected in school board policies and practices. It highlights the need to critically examine the formal processes of schooling that may reproduce patterns of marginalization. Educators need to consider which patterns need to be intentionally interrupted and changed. According to the Alberta Civil Liberties Research Centre (2020), "It may seem easier to recognize individual or interpersonal acts of racism: a slur made, a person ignored in a social or work setting, an act of violence. However, "individual" racism is not created in a vacuum but instead emerges from a society's foundational beliefs and "ways" of seeing/doing things, and is manifested in organizations, institutions, and systems (including education)."

The *Personal Dimension* encompasses the mindset of culturally responsive educators and the practices in which they engage, in order to support the development of all students. Not only are culturally responsive educators self-aware, but they also have a deep knowledge of their students and how they learn best. Henry & Tator (2006) explain that an individual's racist assumptions, beliefs or behaviours are "a form of racial discrimination that stems from conscious and unconscious, personal prejudice".

The *Instructional Dimension* includes knowing learners well and considering the classroom practices which lead to a culturally responsive classroom. It involves choosing instructional design that calls everyone in and opens the door for authentic dialogue.

All three dimensions are foundational to the establishment of an inclusive school culture (Richards, Brown, & Forde, 2006).

Here are some inquiry questions for educators to consider:

- ♥ *What does a school look like, sound like and feel like when we promote reflection, honour the community, and support authentic collaboration among staff, students and parents?*

- ♥ *What does a classroom look like, sound like and feel like when it is inclusive and when instruction is responsive to the full range of student diversity?*

- ♥ *What further information would be helpful in considering cultural relevance and cultural responsiveness in our school?*

- ♥ *How do we work with our communities to help everyone appreciate the importance of culturally responsive teaching?*

- ♥ *What is the impact on our students when we do not acknowledge the complexity of culture and difference?*

Across Ontario and other jurisdictions, it is strongly believed, and well supported by research, that there is a strong correlation between school leadership and student achievement. According to Leithwood et al. (2004), leadership is second only to teaching regarding impact on student outcomes. Although principals are not as directly involved with students as classroom teachers are in terms of day-to-day instruction and learning, they do make a difference. Further, as outlined in Ontario's Leadership Framework, it is the responsibility of school and system leaders to be responsive to the increasingly diverse nature of learning communities by ensuring that schools are inclusive and welcoming of diversity, as reflected in both school climate and the classroom learning environment.

The institutional dimension of culturally responsive pedagogy underscores the significance of education policy and the way schooling is organized. At the school level, it means paying attention to school budget priorities, the relationship between parents and the community and how curriculum and instruction impact the conditions for student learning and student experience. While Ontario is highly regarded internationally as a leader in improving student achievement and supporting student well-being, there is still much work ahead.

The Mindset of Culturally Responsive Educators

Culturally responsive teachers share a set of dispositions and skills – a mindset that enables them to work creatively and effectively to support all students in diverse settings. Outlined below are the six characteristics as outlined by Villegas and Lucas (2002).

1. **Socio-Cultural Consciousness**

   Canadian research continues to affirm that "membership in the white middle-class group affords individuals within this group certain privileges in society," while those outside of this group experience challenges (Dei, et al., 2000). This is because society is influenced by the norms established by the dominant group (Gay, 2002; Dei et al., 2000). Culturally responsive educators understand their position in our present social, historical and political context; through questioning their own attitudes, behaviours and beliefs, they come to terms with forms of discrimination which can affect the experiences of students and families in multiple ways.

   Self-reflection is foundational to the examination and identification of one's own implicit biases. This critical process includes understanding the issues related to the distribution of power and privilege and the relationship of power dynamics to one's own social experience. Self-reflection also allows us to recognize how our own social identity is constructed and to think about how social identities are positioned and shaped by society. This is what it means to possess socio-cultural consciousness.

2. **High Expectations**

   The perceptions we hold of students' abilities have a significant impact on student achievement and well-being (Ladson-Billings 1994, 2001, 2011). However, historically, some social identities – particularly those linked with disabilities or intersecting with race and low socio-economic status – have been deemed as contributing to notions of "at-risk-ness" in students (Dei, 1997; Portelli, Vibert & Shields, 2007).

   Culturally responsive educators hold positive and affirming views of their students and their ability to learn and achieve academic success. They demonstrate genuine respect for students and their families as well as a strong belief in their potential. They consider the social identities of students as assets rather than as deficits or limitations.

3. **Desire to Make a Difference**

   Educators who are culturally responsive see equitable and inclusive education as fundamental to supporting high levels of student achievement (Ladson-Billings, 2001; Gay, 2004). Consistent patterns of underachievement found in groups, such as those students with special education needs or those with students from low socio-economic circumstances, need to be seen as created by deeply problematic systemic and institutional barriers. Culturally responsive educators are committed to being agents of social change, ultimately working to remove barriers and creating conditions for learning that are beneficial for all students (Ontario Ministry of Education, 2009).

4. **Constructivist Approach**

Culturally responsive educators build upon the varied lived experiences of all students in order to bring the curriculum to life. Through this approach, they integrate locally situated learning into daily instruction and learning processes.

Constructivist approaches promote inquiry-based learning – they support students asking questions and creating new knowledge based on their natural curiosity about their own experiences. Knowledge building is reciprocal because students play an active role in crafting and developing learning experiences for themselves and their peers. This results in making learning relevant and accessible for all students in the classroom as they can see themselves in the curriculum.

5. **Deep Knowledge of Their Students**

It is important for educators to recognize that parents, caregivers and families know their children best (Kugler & West-Burns, 2010). Therefore, in an effort to know their students, culturally responsive educators work to build strong relationships with their students' families. They promote mutual respect between home and school and embrace a collaborative approach to teaching and learning.

> " Get to know your students...How do they self-identify and what community do they originate from? What types of print, audio and other experiences motivate them?
> ~Tolouse, 2013~

Deep knowledge, not just of content, but of one's students as individual learners, enables educators to integrate lived experiences into the daily learning of the classroom. Drawing on students' experiences provides teachers with the opportunity to represent their knowledge in the curriculum so it is meaningful, and students see themselves reflected in the learning that takes place in the classroom (Villegas & Lucas, 2002).

> "Take an asset-based approach...The knowledge children bring to school, derived from personal and cultural experiences, is central to their learning. To overlook this resource is to deny children access to the knowledge construction process.
>
> ~Vegas & Lucas~

6. **Culturally Responsive Teaching Practices**

A wealth of research is available both nationally and internationally on culturally responsive instructional strategies. At the core of these strategies is a) holding high expectations for learning while b) recognizing and honouring the strengths that a student's lived experiences and/or home culture bring to the learning environment of the classroom. As Villegas and Lucas observe about culturally responsive educators, "they use what they know about their students to give them access to their learning" (2002, p. 27). Learning experiences are designed to be relevant and authentic, enabling students to see themselves in the daily learning of the classroom. This sends a message to students and the community that student, parent and community knowledge and experiences not only have value, but that they are also important to the learning in school.

Stages of Curriculum Transformation

There are several conceptualizations for equity and diversity education as to what constitutes curriculum transformation ranging from slight curricular changes to a fully revised social awareness and action conceptualization. James Banks (1993), Peggy McIntosh (2000), Randall B. Lindsey (2009), and others have formulated continuums for curricular reform that help move transformation efforts from the former toward the latter. They are conceptualizations that are widely used in schools committed to this important work.

Jackie Eldridge and Denise McLafferty

Included below is a table comparing the three continuums of Lindsey, Banks & MOE.

Randall B. Lindsey	James Banks	Ministry of Education, Ontario
Cultural Destructiveness: Seeking to eliminate references to the culture of "others" in all aspects of the school and in relationship with their communities. **Cultural Incapacity:** Trivializing other English-learning communities and seeking to make them appear to be wrong. **Cultural Blindness:** Pretending not to see or acknowledge the socioeconomic status and culture of English-learning communities and choosing to ignore the experiences of such groups within the school and community. **Cultural Pre-competence:** Increasingly aware of what you and the school don't know about working with English-learning communities. At this key level of development, you and the school can move in a positive, constructive direction. Or you can vacillate, stop, and possibly regress. **Cultural Competence:** Manifesting your personal values and behaviors and the school's policies and practices in a manner that is inclusive to English-learning cultures and socioeconomic communities that are new or different from you and the school majority. **Cultural Proficiency:** Advocating for life-long learning for the purpose of being increasingly effective in serving the educational needs of various socio-economic and English- learning cultural groups. Culturally proficient school leaders hold the vision that they and their school are instruments for creating a socially just democracy.	**Stage 1: Curriculum of the Mainstream** The curriculum of the mainstream is Eurocentric and male centric. It ignores the experiences, voices, contributions, and perspectives of non-dominant individuals and groups in all subject areas. All educational materials, including textbooks, films, and other teaching and learning tools, present information in a Eurocentric, male-centric way. This stage is harmful both for students who identify with dominant culture and those from non-dominant groups. **Stage 2: Heroes and Holidays** Teachers "celebrate" difference by integrating information or resources about famous people and the cultural artifacts of various groups into the mainstream curriculum. Bulletin boards might contain pictures of famous people from their race/culture, and teachers might plan special celebrations for Black History Month or Women's History Month. Student learning about "other cultures" focuses on costumes, foods, music, and other tangible cultural items. **Stage 3: Integration** Teachers transcend heroes and holidays, adding substantial materials and knowledge about non-dominant groups to the curriculum. The teacher might add to her or his collection of books those by authors of color or by women. She or he might add a unit which covers, for example, the role of women in World War I. A music teacher might add slave hymns or songs from Africa to her or his repertoire. At the school level, a course on African Canadian History might be added to course offerings. **Stage 4: Structural Reform** New materials, perspectives, and voices are woven seamlessly with current frameworks of knowledge to provide new levels of understanding from a completer and more accurate curriculum. The teacher commits to continuously expand her or his knowledge base through the exploration of various sources from various perspectives and sharing that knowledge with the pupils. Students learn to view events, concepts, and facts through various lenses. "Canadian History" includes African Canadian History, Women's History, Asian Canadian History, Latino Canadian History, and all other previously differentiated fields of knowledge. **Stage 5: Multicultural, Social Action, and Awareness** In addition to the changes made in Stage 4, important social issues, including racism, sexism, and economic injustice, are addressed explicitly as part of the curriculum. The voices, ideas, and perspectives of the students regarding these and all other topics are brought to the fore in the learning experience. The students themselves becoming yet another multicultural classroom resource. The textbook is viewed as a single perspective among many, and the relevance of its limitations, along with those of other educational media, are explored and discussed.	**Characteristic #1** **Socio-cultural consciousness** An awareness of how socio-cultural structures impact individual experiences and opportunities. **Characteristic #2** **High expectations** Hold positive and affirming views of all students of all backgrounds. **Characteristic #3** **Desire to make a difference** See themselves as change agents working towards more equity. **Characteristic #4** **Constructivist approach** Understand that learners construct their own knowledge. **Characteristic #5** **Deep knowledge of their students** Know about the lives of students and their families; know how students learn best and where they are in their learning. **Characteristic #6** **Culturally responsive teaching practices** Design and build instruction on students' prior knowledge in order to stretch students in their thinking and learning.

Recognizing Diversity as an Intrinsic Feature of Community Life

Diversity is part of the fabric of everyday life. Even in a community where diversity is not evident, there exists diversity among families and neighbourhoods, among histories, lived realities and faiths. If we were going to live in an unfamiliar culture, we would have to learn cultural and spiritual protocols and practices in order to respect and honour them and in turn become comfortable in that new setting. The question then, is not whether there is diversity, because diversity exists in every context. The real question is, "What we are doing with it?" We may be trying to wish it away, we may be simply tolerating it, or, we may be engaging with it as an integral part of our day-to-day process and seeking ways for it to enrich our work and our lives.

Making Connections with Student Achievement

Achievement is informed by students' backgrounds, and the aspirations and interests they bring with them to school. On one hand, this prior knowledge and experience may be of great benefit. On the other hand, it may actually cause students to feel anxious about or resistant to some of our teaching approaches and what we expect them to learn. While we understand that we need to be sensitive to and aware of unique differences among students, our human tendency to be drawn to people who are like ourselves can often become an obstacle. When our teaching doesn't resonate with our students, there may be a tendency to start labelling students' behaviours in negative ways rather than stopping to consider that it may in fact be our behaviours that need to change. We also need to keep in mind that achievement is not only about cognitive skills and their application. It is also about the development of social-emotional skills, emotional intelligence, character, altruism and resilience which are central to creating classrooms, schools, and communities that value, reflect, and draw on diversity.

Making Connections with Equity

Equity is a condition of fair, inclusive, and respectful treatment of all people. Equity does not mean treating people the same without regard for their individual differences. Equity acknowledges that we should not do the same thing for every student. Equity levels the playing field so that all children and youth have what they need to thrive at school. It advocates for the unique treatment of unique people. Equity is also about addressing and taking action to remove systemic barriers to achievement. It is about democracy in education. Students should not have to choose between getting a first-class education and retaining their culture, language and heritage. They should be able to enter, achieve, and graduate from a system without sacrificing their identity and self-esteem. They should experience a system which respects and nurtures their uniqueness and in which their self-confidence, their hope, and their sense of meaning in life can thrive.

Making Connections with Well-Being

Well-being is inextricably linked with both equity and achievement. Children who are hungry will not be able to learn well. Educators who are angry or upset will not teach well. Leaders who feel they have no power to make a difference will not be effective in supporting teaching and learning. Cognitive, emotional, social, physical and cultural well-being is an essential foundation for success. If students feel that they are "other" or "less than," they are likely to have difficulty thriving and succeeding. They may believe, even unconsciously, that "achievement is for someone else, someone different than me". Every child and youth need to come into the school and have a sense of belonging, a sense of being recognized and supported. Every school and every school system need to uphold these values.

Knowing our Children and Youth

When we interact with children and youth, we interact with the entirety of who they are, even if we do not always realize it. The children we see in front of us have a whole story – where they come from, who their parents are, the communities in which they live, the life experiences that influence their perspectives, their personal aspirations and their disappointments, their dreams and their fears, their gifts, and their struggles. They may be living in poverty. They may be members of a racialized group. They may be dealing with trauma or experiencing anxiety or mental health concerns. If we are to truly support students, we cannot rely on pre-conceived notions based on race, gender, and country of origin or other factors. We need to get to know the real person. We need to listen honestly and sincerely. We need to be curious. We need to show that we care and be committed to meeting students where they truly are as a first and essential step toward empowering them and moving them forward.

Knowing Ourselves

Just as fish don't know they are wet, we don't recognize our own unconscious biases, beliefs, and perspectives. They are largely invisible to us and can have a negative impact, not only on ourselves as leaders, but also on those we lead. Introspection and self-awareness are necessary if we are to be successful, engaged and empowered leaders. We need to reflect on what drives us, what motivates us and what we care about, and how and why others may differ from us including their values and beliefs. We often need to leave the safety of our expert stance in order to do this and instead ask questions with a beginner's mindset. Imagine how much greater our impact would be if we were aware of our own biases and preferences and had tools to mitigate any negative effects. We would certainly have the capacity to create school and system cultures in which participants are not limited by the culture but rather, feel free to bring their full selves to the endeavour.

Creating the Inclusive School

In order to have a sense of belonging, children and youth need to see themselves reflected in every aspect of school life and the learning environment. They should not feel the need to hide any part of themselves, their identity or their uniqueness in order to gain acceptance. This begins with the physical school setting. What we see on the school grounds and in the school must reflect the cultures and the cultural teachings of our diverse society. It includes what we see in the curriculum. For example, are students left with the impression that Canada is only 150 years

old? It includes the ways in which we integrate students' interests and backgrounds in how we teach mathematics, science and other subjects. It includes the diversity of staff in all roles and at all levels in the school and system. Such diversity matters in all schools and systems including in those communities where diversity may not be evident or visible. It matters because our children and youth need to see how we function effectively in a world of diversity.

Empowering the Educator

In recognizing that culture is not static, educators and all school staff need to acknowledge that their information about students may be incomplete and that reaching students where they are is constant and ongoing work. They need to develop comfort with sometimes being wrong and with corrective action. In order to understand students, educators and all school staff need to be a part of the school community. In the classroom, the empowered educator must engage with courage and curiosity, and understand that competence involves more than simply ticking off boxes on a standard checklist. The most powerful tool educators have for leveraging and empowering diversity is their personal self and their capacity to approach teaching with a learner's mindset.

Educators must be problem solvers but more importantly they must be healers. They must meet students where they are and ensure that their interactions result in elevating and empowering all students. Teachers must open their hearts to reach children with love and empathy. Teaching does not only happen as a cognitive or mind activity. We must remember that the heart plays a particularly important role.

Elevating the School Leader

Leadership is about the courage, capacity, curiosity and commitment to working with, learning from, and giving voice to those across lines of difference. Authentic leaders see themselves as enablers of the progress of others, and see others as being the vehicle through which organizational purpose is fulfilled. This entails considering the complexities and complications of diversity. It requires recognizing, understanding, and interrupting inequities. It means accepting that while we endeavour to create safe space, conflict and instability are inevitable. An effective and courageous leader will engage with conflict and use it as a vehicle for building relationships and for community growth.

Leadership requires examining school policies and structures that cannot be applied equitably, and therefore may disadvantage some students, families, or staff members. It includes accepting the importance of the school leader as a role model for others. It calls on the school leader to dedicate time to explicitly help others learn how to effectively engage in dialogue in the process of creating a culturally responsive school and culturally responsive classrooms. It demands that we are willing to feel uncomfortable as we face constant change.

Strengthening Community Relationships

Building community relationships involves creating conditions in which all participants in the community not only feel welcome, but also are physically present. For example, we may need to be more thoughtful and persistent in finding new ways to ensure that a diverse group of people participates in school councils. We should not be surprised if we hold a meeting or event on a holy day and find that families for whom this observance is important feel excluded. Similarly, at the district level,

Jackie Eldridge and Denise McLafferty

relationship building is not only about community engagement and involvement, but also about sharing power within the school system. At both school and system levels, consideration should be given to moving meetings out into the community, and to creating space on the agenda for open community dialogue and relationship building. We must enter new territory with each other even if we make mistakes along the way.

Challenging the Dominant Perspective

In a diverse society, we need to become acutely aware of the ways in which the dominant culture, approach, and perspective exert a powerful, and often invisible, influence both within the classroom and across the wider community. We must explore how the dominant culture has shaped the countries we live in. At the system level, we need to identify and examine biases about what is valued, where power lies, whose voices are present, and whose voices we need to hear. We further need to identify and address the systemic barriers that stand in the way of change and improvement. In the classroom, we need to be mindful of the experiences of students so that we teach in a way that genuinely resonates and reflects their backgrounds and identities.

Observing and Assessing

In order to be useful, formal data gathering must move beyond the system level and take place at the school level. From an equity perspective, we must ensure that the data we collect reflect multiple dimensions of student achievement such as the intersections between gender, class, race, ethnicity, ability, and language. Our measurement of progress must move beyond academic achievement to include qualities such as integrity, empathy, kindness, and caring. In this way we act on the assumption that we measure what matters to us and to those we serve. At a personal level, we should consider more intuitive forms of feedback such as the quality of learning experiences which can powerfully inform our practice. For example, as leaders in conversation with educators and educators in conversation with students, we need to dig deeper. We need to learn about who feels a sense of belonging, who is being served, who is being left behind and, equally important, what concrete steps we can take together to address any concerns that emerge.

Equity Continuum

Utilizing the core components of Culturally Responsive and Relevant Pedagogy (CRRP) as the base, Karen Murray and Nicole West-Burns, PhD, created a tool for examining equity work in K-12 educational environments. Their text, the *Equity Continuum: Action for Critical Transformation in Schools and Classrooms* (2011) relies upon the theoretical foundations of CRRP as a guide for change. The continuum indicators ask educators to reflect upon high expectations for students, representative of all social identities; to broadly define culture and support cultural competence within the classroom and teaching environment; and to build students' critical consciousness and questioning of the status quo.

This tool was developed to help assist educators in rethinking the work we all do in schools in order to create more equitable experiences and outcomes for students. It extends the discourse to whole-school pedagogical approaches and practices.

The Framework covers seven areas of equitable practice:

1) Classroom Climate and Instruction,

2) School Climate,

3) Student Voice and Space,

4) Family/Caregiver-School Relations,

5) School Leadership,

6) Community Connections, and

7) Culture of Professional development.

These seven areas ask key questions regarding the thinking/practice of equity. They encourage educators to develop a critical consciousness when examining all aspects of the school community. This type of conscious thinking explores the teaching learning environment using well-designed assessment worksheets that will help identify the strengths and areas of need for all stakeholders involved in the education of the children in the school. The worksheets use key indicators and "look-fors" so that all seven areas are clearly addressed. Some examples outlined by Murray and West-Burns (2011) are:

♥ Students see their lives and others represented in the materials, books, pictures, teachers, administrators, etc., within the classroom and school (e.g., First Nations, Metis & Inuit, African Canadian, etc.). The curriculum speaks to the lives of the students in the classroom and does not mandate a "one size fits all curriculum," based on a white, middle-class societal view.

♥ Schools are places where there is intentional outreach to include the voices from non-dominant group members. Collectively, student ideas, opinions, perspectives, wants and needs are the basis for all that happens in the school building.

♥ Schools recognize and acknowledge that the parent community knows a great deal about their own children and there is a model that allows for true collaboration based on mutual respect.

When we authentically explore our learning environments through the culturally responsive and relevant pedagogy lens, we are more equipped to build inclusive schools where every child knows they belong.

What Does it Look Like in the Classroom?

The quality of the instruction and the expertise of the teacher considerably outweigh the challenging circumstances that some of our students bring to the classroom (Callins, 2006; Willis & Harris, 2000). Effective instruction also

Jackie Eldridge and Denise McLafferty

ensures academic rigour which is essential in a culturally responsive framework; high expectations need to be coupled with the appropriate supports to scaffold new learning (Gay, 2002; Ladson-Billings, 2000).

Some strategies to implement a culturally responsive framework are suggested below. They are adapted from the work of Jeff Kugler and Nicole West-Burns (2010):

- ♥ Expand upon what is considered as the "curriculum" – recognizing both the informal and the subtle ways in which the curriculum defines what is and what is not valued in our schools and society.

- ♥ Use inquiry-based approaches to student learning to develop engaged and self-directed learners. Support students in making decisions about their learning that integrate who they are and what they already know with their home and community experiences.

- ♥ Use a variety of resources, including community partners, to ensure the learning environment and pedagogical materials used are accessible to all learners and that the lives of students and the community are reflected in the daily workings of the classroom. Resources, materials and books should present both local and global perspectives.

- ♥ See the curriculum as flexible and adaptive to the lived experiences of students so they see themselves and their lives reflected in daily learning opportunities.

- ♥ Know and build upon students' prior knowledge, interests, strengths and learning styles and ensure they are foundational to the learning experiences in the classroom and the school.

- ♥ Ensure that learning engages a broad range of learners so that varied perspectives, learning styles and sources of knowledge are explored.

- ♥ Differentiate instruction and provide a wide range of methods and opportunities for students to demonstrate their learning, ensuring both academic rigour and a variety of resources that are accessible to all learners.

- ♥ Work to ensure that the socio-cultural consciousness of students is developed through curricular approaches, emphasizing inclusive and accepting education, to inform critical examination and action regarding social justice issues.

Preparing to Teach all our Students ...

Those engaged in the work of culturally responsive pedagogy are "committed to collective, not just merely individual empowerment" such that the impact of this approach to teaching is directed towards making change for all members of society (Ladson-Billings, 1995, p. 160). As educators, we must be prepared to teach all students while also being committed to preparing students for the reality of a diverse and global society.

The journey towards equity and inclusivity in schools seeks to empower everyone in the learning environment. Such an approach validates and affirms the cultural capital that our students bring to the classroom each and everyday. This journey also brings us closer to reaching our goal in Ontario – providing relevant and authentic learning opportunities every day for every student in every classroom.

Some ways to think about your next steps in the journey towards equity:

What will our school conversation focus on?

How might a process of inquiry among staff further this conversation?

If we implement specific strategies to support a culturally responsive approach to teaching and learning, how will we assess the impact on student learning and achievement?

Classroom diversity: Tips for teachers on how to foster inclusivity

In the context of increasing acts of intolerance and rising diversity in schools, how can teachers create an environment inclusive to all students (Lindsay Craig, OISE, September 7, 2017)? Given the current political climate, a rise in racist incidents playing out in news headlines, and an increasing number of new immigrants in classrooms, teachers in already diverse schools need to teach lessons far beyond regular assignments. Imagine the conflicts that could arise in a class of Christian, Muslim, Jewish, black, Indigenous, white, gay, straight, transgendered, immigrant and refugee students or those whose native language is other than English or French? What is a teacher to do in the face of a racial slur? Or when a child is ostracized for his or her religious beliefs, clothing or language? What can a teacher do to create a classroom space that is not only respectful of difference but an environment that celebrates it?

Given the power of education to fight intolerance, experts at the Ontario Institute for Studies in Education (OISE), say that even in a country generally known for respect of individual differences, it's crucial for teachers of growingly diverse classrooms to create an environment inclusive to all. Below, OISE Professors Ann Lopez and Richard Messina, give nine tips for teachers on how to create an environment that celebrates equality in an increasingly diverse world.

Honest Self Reflection

Before teachers can make a commitment to truly being inclusive of the knowledge and experiences of those who are different from themselves, they must engage in critical reflection about what they themselves need to unlearn and learn. For example, a teacher might think they are "embracing diversity" but may hold stereotypical views of some students, often manifested in excessive discipline or low expectations of certain students. This could be a teacher that has different cultures or languages displayed on the walls in the classroom, but who also becomes quite impatient and aggressive in tone when re-directing a black boy who has become disengaged with the class. This is known as unconscious or implicit bias, which are stereotypes about certain groups of people that individuals form outside their own conscious awareness. That is, some teachers don't realize they treat some students differently based on stereotypes they may hold.

As teachers start the new school year, it's important for them to think about practices and perspectives that might be a blind spot and consider proactive strategies to overcome them. These could include reviewing one's approach to classroom discipline, talking to a critical friend to discuss challenging issues, and searching out additional resources to support him or her on their journey. For example, if not currently offered, teachers and educational leaders should also ask for workshops to assist with this critical self-reflection (Lopez, OISE).

Write a Letter

Teachers could start the year by writing to the families of the kids in their class, asking for information that would help them understand the individual differences of each student. Since not all forms of diversity are visible, the letter from the family helps teachers learn more about the story or identity of the child. It gives the teacher ways to "mirror" that identity in the curriculum and resources (books, activities, etc.) so the child can see him or herself there. For Example:

> Dear parents,
>
> Getting to know each student as an individual and as part of your family is an important aspect of our work with your child. We enjoy learning more about parents, grandparents, your traditions and celebrations, your child's preferences and gifts, your goals and hopes. Please feel free to write me a letter at any time to deepen your communication of these important aspects of family life and identity. I welcome an email or a written letter.

You may want to indicate whether your letter can be shared with other teachers who teach your child. These letters will be received in confidence (Messina, OISE).

Forget Food, Fun and Festival......
and leverage resources

Take advantage of the resources in your school's community. Create activities or assignments that require students themselves to learn about diversity. Be mindful not to focus on "food, fun or festival." While it's often a well-intended tactic, diverse people can do more than cook. We need to break this stereotype. For example, a great resource for teachers in this regard is *Beyond Heroes and Holidays*. Parents have valuable knowledge to

human
resources

share. Find professionals from diverse groups to engage with students. It will help break down stereotypes as to who can be a pilot and who cannot (Lopez, OISE).

Curriculum Check

Diversity must be reflected in the curriculum and pedagogy. Teachers should review texts and other materials to see whose voices and experiences are left out and make efforts to include them in lessons. For example, when teaching history, teachers should carefully examine the content to ensure it's an accurate representation. We must be careful not to re-write history by promoting a war, in which some fought to keep slaves, that appears as something heroic. We need to heed the Calls to Action like that of the Truth and Reconciliation Commission in Canada, ensuring we capture the devastating effects of residential schools on Indigenous children, and their families. Professional development days, workshops and inviting representatives of diverse backgrounds into the schools can help provide tools to assist with this. If teachers do not currently have these available to them, they should ask for such support (Lopez, OISE).

Idea Diversity

It's important that a classroom supports the notion that "idea diversity" is essential to knowledge advancement. To understand an idea is to understand the ideas that surround it, including those that stand in contrast to it. Idea diversity creates a rich environment for ideas to evolve into new and more refined forms. This pedagogical approach may help students to appreciate and value all forms of diversity and how diversity enriches learning. For example, when teaching about scientific concepts like "seasons" or "evolution" it is important to recognize that there are many interpretations of these concepts. For example, Indigenous communities have their own explanations. It is vital that they are presented in non-judgmental ways that enrich the students' learning experience (Messina, OISE).

Model Respect and Care

A positive classroom environment models inclusion and respect for all students. This means teachers ensure they treat all students and their families with respect. For example, if a student whose first language is not English (or French) joins a class, teachers must ensure the child is given time to speak and process his or her thoughts. The teacher must also teach the rest of the class to respectfully listen. How the teacher speaks and interacts with students, models respect and care. Students know when their teachers care about themselves or others, and when they do not (Lopez, OISE).

Challenge Stereotypes

Disrupt narratives and stereotypes in the classroom that position diverse people as lacking in valuable knowledge or unqualified. For example, teachers of more senior grades might discuss with their class a newspaper article about certain organizations trying to recruit more diverse staff. Some students might think that is not fair and only "qualified" people should be hired. Implicit in this notion is the idea that some people from diverse backgrounds are not qualified. The teacher might use this as a teachable moment to talk with students about why it is important for organizations to reflect diversity (Lopez, OISE).

In chapter four, we describe a highly effective activity for helping students eliminate stereotypes, called Funeral for Put Downs/Stereotypes. This experience helps participants immediately see how many stereotypes they hold, see and hear, and provides a platform for setting intentions to eliminate them in their classrooms.

See Colour

In understanding and dealing with racism, it is not enough for the teacher to simply be "non-racist". Educators must be "anti-racist", which means that they actively address racism and its effects. "Active" is the key word. Claiming to be non-racist and/or to "not see race in others" passively allows racism to continue. This may mean  moving beyond celebrations of diversity. That is, teachers should look at ways for the invisible to be made visible. For example, a teacher might create opportunities in the classroom in which it's safe for students to talk about how they experience unfairness and discrimination, how they see these experiences in others, and how to be advocates.

This is important since issues of racism, discrimination or sexism often go unnoticed. Unless there is an established forum to bring these issues into the open, children may simply accept them without realizing there's a way to share and address them (Richard Messina, OISE).

Take Action.....Never Ignore

Even if after putting into practice many of the tips above, if a teacher witnesses a racist or discriminatory remark or behaviour, he or she must always address it, no matter how difficult. However, it must be done in a manner that supports student learning. A few words of advice for how to handle such situations:

- ♥ Stop the class and in a caring and kind manner ("We should chat about this, because I assume you did not mean to hurt….") let the student who uttered the discriminatory remark know that what was uttered was not appropriate.

- ♥ Explain that such words hurt feelings of other people – adjust conversation to grade level as appropriate.

- ♥ Speak to the parents of the child to support that the child learns why those comments are hurtful. Including parents in the dialogue is important.

- ♥ If the comment is heard outside of the classroom, for example, in the gym or the lunchroom, the teacher must immediately speak to that student,

but also follow-up with guidance counsellors and the student's teachers – not to punish, but to continue the process of learning and unlearning.

- ♥ As discussed previously, weave these topics into the curriculum on an ongoing basis. These issues cannot be challenged only when we hear discriminatory remarks.

- ♥ Bring in resources such as storybooks, particularly in the lower grades, that deal with these issues.

- ♥ In addition, in every case, a call home to chat with parents or guardians is essential. This is to reinforce actions taken by the school and ensure everyone – including both the student and his or her family – understands discrimination in any form is unacceptable (Dr. Lopez, OISE).

 # Literature Resources

Picture Books

Brave Girl by Michelle Market

Four Feet, Two Sandals by Karen Lynn Williams

Last Stop on Market Street by Matt de la Pena

Mama Miti by Donna Jo Napoli

One Green Apple by Eve Bunting

The Other Side by Jacqueline Woodson

The Snowy Day by Ezra Jack Keats

Those Shoes by Maribeth Boelts

Trombone Shorty by Troy "Trombone Shorty" Andrews

Whistle for Willie by Ezra Jack Keats

Chapter Books

Anna Hibiscus (series) by Atinuke

Bobby the Brave (Sometimes) (series) by Lisa Yee

Book Uncle and Me by Uma Krishnaswami

Children of the Longhouse by Joseph Bruchac

Clara Lee and the Apple Pie Dream by Jenny Han

Clubhouse Mysteries (series) by Sharon Draper

Dog Days: The Carver Chronicles (series) by Karen English

Indian Shoes by Cynthia Leitich Smith

Juana and Lucas by Juana Medina

Lola Levine is not Mean (series) by Monica Brown

Meet Yasmin! (series) by Saadia Faruqi

My Name is Maria Isabel by Alma Flor Ada

Precious Ramotswe Mysteries (series) by Alexander McCall Smith

Rickshaw Girl by Mitali Perkins

Sherlock Sam and the Missing Heirloom in Katong (series) by A.J. Low

Simply Sarah (series) by Phyllis Reynolds Naylor

The No 1 Car Spotter (series) by Atinuke

The White Elephant by Sid Fleischman

The Year of the Book (series) by Andrea Cheng

Zapato Power (series) by Jacqueline Jules

CHAPTER THREE

The Brain and its Effects on Learning

What Does the Research Say?

Through many years of research on the brain, we have a much clearer understanding of the importance of how physical, emotional and environmental factors influence what happens to the brain's ability to focus, make connections, store information in meaningful ways, and create memories. The amount of research on the brain is massive, as is the literature on the subject, and it is equally fascinating. If we are to be effective teachers, it is important to understand the elements of brain-compatible learning. This ensures we are creating safe places for students, but also, for grasping the ways the brain fosters and maintains information that is learned.

In this chapter, we explore:

✓ *The connections between the brain and the ways people learn*

✓ *Reasons why the brain operates more effectively in safe spaces*

✓ *The connections between the brain, and our physical and emotional response*

✓ *The elements of lesson design*

✓ *The importance of reflection*

Given our knowledge of the human brain, it is our responsibility as educators to consider the learning environment in order to create the most conducive setting for every child in the classroom. As researcher and education consultant Patricia Wolfe demonstrates: "Everyone agrees that what we do in schools should be based on what we know about how the brain learns. Until recently, we have had few clues to unlock the secrets of the brain. Now, research from the neurosciences has greatly improved our understanding of the learning process, and we have a much more solid foundation on which to base educational decisions. We know now that we can effectively match teaching practice with brain functioning." There is also a strong connection between the way the brain functions, and the way our bodies interpret that information. Given all of this awareness, we are going to focus on four critical areas that are fundamental in creating learning environments where students can, and will, learn to the maximum of their potential when given the right set of circumstances.

These include:

- ♥ A safe, inclusive learning community

- ♥ Connections between the brain, and emotional and physical well-being

- ♥ Lesson design and the brain

- ♥ Reflection and processing of information learned

♥ A Safe, Inclusive Learning Environment

To begin, it is important to self-reflect on your teaching and the environment you are creating for your students. Ask yourself:

   ♥ Do your students feel emotionally safe in your classroom?

   ♥ Do they feel that they are valued and belong?

   ♥ Does the classroom climate respect, celebrate, and encourage individuality and diversity?

In order to build a classroom where there is emotional safety, we must first understand the anatomy and physiology of the brain, and the mind-body connection. Evolution has developed our brains to be co-dependent on our senses and the messages they send to us. This body-brain relationship receives sensory information from our world through our sight, hearing, touch/feel, smell, and taste.

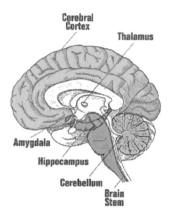

In a learning environment where we feel safe, the brain gathers this sensual input in a calm and thoughtful way. Through this normal pathway, the sensual information we receive travels to the *thalamus* (sensory relay station), and then, on to the *hippocampus* (regulator of learning and memory), and finally, to the most important part of our brain, the *cerebral cortex* (the centre of long-term memory and thinking). Understanding these pathways allows us to see how the learning is taking place so it can be thoughtfully processed and stored in a meaningful way. Ideally, this process is the one we want to occur in the classroom, but unfortunately, this is not always the case. When the normal pathway is interrupted because of a real or a perceived threat, the mechanism for survival (fight, flight, or freeze) is triggered.

In this scenario, the journey through this pathway is accelerated, even short-circuited. It still travels first to the *thalamus,* but at a faster rate, and then, "zings" to the *amygdala* (centre of fear, threat, and passion), and finally, to the *hypothalamus* (the command centre of the brain). The results of this hurried response involve the pituitary and adrenal glands, which secrete the chemical (cortisol) that triggers all the body systems into fight, flight, or freeze mode. This "survival" trigger is responsible for the outward physical reactions most people associate with stress, including increased heart rate, heightened senses, rapid breathing, the rush of adrenaline, and a possible emotional hijacking.

Threats that create a trigger do not have to be an actual event; like someone with a weapon. It can simply be something perceived by the students as a threat, e.g., if the student anticipates that the teacher is going to yell at them or humiliate them in front of their peers, or times when they wonder when the bully is going to start picking on them again. It is also important to note that the threat does not have to be directed at any one person. Students may be living vicariously through their classmates and absorbing the threat, even if it is directed at someone else. Children of trauma are particularly vulnerable to these kinds of threats.

Given the interconnectedness of the various parts of our brains to stimuli around us, it is our responsibility as teachers to be aware of those influences in the learning environment. Every child should feel comfortable and safe, ensuring that the brain operates free from stress as much as possible. If not, students are unable to absorb and learn the information we are teaching. Success in school depends upon a student's ability to decrease their stress. The inclusion of stress-management techniques into the curriculum is an obvious application of neuroscience in education. Such techniques can improve learning, emotional well-being, and physical health.

♥ Connections: The Brain and Emotional/Physical Well-being

Cortisol functions as part of the natural process of the body. In moderation, this steroid hormone is perfectly normal and healthy, with functions such as regulating blood sugar levels and other physiological needs. Under the right circumstances, cortisol is what restores balance to the body after a stressful event, and normalizes the hippocampus, where memories and learning are stored and processed.

When we endure chronic stress, however, the body overproduces cortisol, and the extra cortisol cannot be entirely released. Such long-term activation of the stress-response system and, the overexposure to cortisol and other stress hormones, can disrupt almost all your body's processes. This hormonal increase can lead to illness, anxiety, depression, and it prevents the brain from functioning properly. It will also mean:

♥ Loss of sociability and the avoidance of interactions with others

♥ Shrinkage in the area of the brain responsible for memory and learning

♥ Elevation in stress levels to the point where we downshift to the lower brain

Parasympathetic Versus Sympathetic Nervous Systems: Fight, Flight or Freeze: For us to function at our maximum potential, we need to find ways to stay in the *parasympathetic nervous system* (PNS). This is where we access feelings of love and calm. Operating here, regulates the immune system; reduces stress, enhances healing, and helps regenerate and nourish our bodies. There are various ways for us to activate parasympathetic activity. The emotional content of the PNS is activated by feelings of calmness, love, peacefulness, contentment, satisfaction and being appreciated. The PNS itself is stimulated by rest, sleep, meditation, and relaxation therapies. Laughter and tears are both signs of parasympathetic activity. In this state, the mind can see the bigger picture and is able to turn inward for introspection, reflection, and receptivity.

However, when we are stressed, feeling excluded or fearful, we immediately engage the *sympathetic nervous system* (SNS). The SNS is activated by challenging emotions and thoughts, including fear, sadness, anger, worry, resentment, and aggressiveness.

When teachers make connections between the brain research, safe learning environments, effective instruction, and classroom management, they begin to realize that everything fits together like the pieces of a puzzle. We cannot simply teach content to students when we do not understand the effects on the brain and the need for emotional safety.

Lesson Design and the Brain

In the following section, we demonstrate the connections to the brain by breaking down the essential elements of lesson design as explained by Madeline Hunter. The template is our adaptation of Hunter's model. We use it to teach lesson design at the Ontario Institute for Studies in Education (OISE). It is very thorough and sets our candidates up for success when practice teaching.

Jackie Eldridge and Denise McLafferty

Topic:	
Grade: Subject: Time:	
Resilience Factors: Caring Relationships, High Expectations, Opportunities for Meaningful Participation Emotional Intelligence Skills: Self-perception, Self-expression, Interpersonal, Decision-making, Stress-management	
OBJECTIVES: Curricular Expectations: Lesson Goals: Social Objectives:	
MENTAL SET: Estimated time: Check for understanding (if needed):	
STATED OBJECTIVES AND PURPOSE: Estimated time:	
INPUT/ MODELLING/ DEMONSTRATION: Estimated Time: Check for understanding:	
PRACTICE: Estimated time: Check for understanding:	Materials: Tactics: Examples: Think, Pair, Share 4 Corners Round Robin 3-Step Interview Inside/Outside Circles Paraphrase Passport Placemat Other
CHECKS FOR UNDERSTANDING (Throughout):	

CLOSURE:		
CONSIDERATIONS		
Multiple Intelligences: verbal linguistic logical/mathematical musical/rhythmic bodily/kinesthetic visual/spatial interpersonal intrapersonal naturalist existential	Accommodations: Who: How - kind of assignment - breadth - depth - pace - grouping - time - place - other	Assessment: - self-evaluation - group evaluation - teacher evaluation - observation - anecdotal notes - quiz/test - checklist - rubric - interview - discussion - learning log/journal

Madeline Hunter's Eight-Step Lesson Design

Dr. Madeline Hunter's research shows that effective teachers have a methodology when planning and presenting a lesson. She found that no matter what the teacher's style, grade level, subject matter, or student demographics, a properly taught lesson contains eight elements that enhance and maximize learning. She labeled the elements and began decades of teacher training that continues to this day.

1. **Mental Set (focus, hook): A short activity or prompt that focuses the students' attention before the actual lesson begins.** Used when students enter the room or in a transition (moving between classes). A picture book, music, a game, a handout given to students at the door, review question written on the board, "two problems" on a chart, are all examples of the mental set. You want to engage the students!

2. **Objectives (various): Curriculum objectives** are indicated in the curriculum of the board or district; **learning goals** are for the teacher and make a connection to the unit of study (if applicable); **stated objectives** are what the teacher tells the students they will be doing in the lesson using "kid friendly" language (e.g. Today we are going to read a story and then you will draw a picture about your favourite part); make stated objectives meaningful by telling them why they are learning this content; have a visual of the stated objectives; and **social objectives** (e.g., mutual respect, attentive listening, sharing resources). In planning the objectives part of the lesson, the teacher needs to be clear about the purpose of the lesson, why the students need to learn it, what they will be able to "do", and how they will show learning as a result.

3. **Input (vocabulary, skills, and concepts the teacher imparts to the students:** This is the "stuff" the students need to know in order to be successful in the lesson. It might be a concept that is taught, a video or book. The pupils might also use the inquiry method to explore the input on their own through learning centres or a web quest.

4. **Modeling (show):** The teacher shows in graphic form or demonstrates what the finished product looks like. It's the idea that a picture is worth a thousand words.

5. **Guided Practice (follow me):** The teacher leads the students through the steps necessary to perform the skill using the tri-modal approach of "hear/see/do".

6. **Checking for Understanding (a variety of questioning strategies to determine "Got it", "Not yet" and to pace the lesson):** In other words, move forward/back up. The teacher also needs to know if the students know how to practise. Ensure the questions are open-ended. You should include as many students as possible in the checks. It is important to note that checks for understanding are sprinkled throughout the lesson because the teacher must be constantly aware of their understanding.

7. **Independent Practice:** The teacher releases students to practise on their own based on the input and the checks for understanding. While the students are engaging in independent practice, the teacher is always assessing through observation, questioning, facilitating, and helping.

8. **Closure (A review or wrap-up of the lesson):** "Tell me/show me what you have learned today." The teacher always brings it back to the objectives and includes as many of the students as possible (e.g., community circle, think, pair, share and then random selection of students).

Making the brain connections to the elements above.

Element One: Laura Wenk, professor of cognition and education, explains: "When someone asks you a question or you have a new problem to solve, the knowledge that you bring forward into your working memory to formulate an answer or explanation, is the knowledge that you have already integrated into your understanding of the subject. The greater your expertise in that domain, the more pre-knowledge you have on that topic. This, in part, explains why someone with greater expertise is more likely to consider multiple sides of an issue and come to a reasoned response 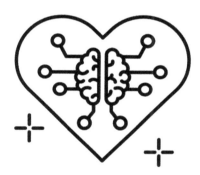 than a novice. We increase the likelihood that our students will be able to recall and use what we teach, by helping them engage their prior knowledge and connect new information to their prior understanding."

At OISE, we teach candidates to design lessons that make use of a ***mental set*** which sets the students up for linking to prior knowledge or gaining new learning that connect to something they already know or want to know. As Eric Jensen, cofounder of the USA's largest brain compatible learning program, explains, "Dendrites in the brain communicate with other dendrites via synaptic connections. The more connections you have in your brain, the better you can create mental models."

Think about a time when you watched a Netflix series and before the show begins, you glimpse the title of shows you also might want to watch. That is a mental set! Or remember the times you have gone to a movie and watched with anticipation a trailer for an upcoming film. Or look at how many times when you are playing a game, ads pop up on your phone trying to entice you to download a new app. These are all examples of mental sets encouraging you to get ready for something new that is coming. The brain can be primed to engage in the new learning in the same way because of the motivating effect of mental sets. It is important for teachers to understand what prior knowledge and experience are brought into the learning environment by their students. Not all of our students have the same experiences and not all are going to understand prior knowledge in the same way. When we are able to make connections for students, they are not left wondering what we are referring to, and this increases their feeling of safety.

Additionally, we must **check their understanding** (assess) throughout the lesson in order to determine whether they are keeping up with us or not. Checking for understanding does not just come at the end of a lesson when students hand in the work. It must be done before, during and after the learning. These checks are also a means of ensuring safety so that the students know you are going to help them if they need it. The Ministry of Education in Ontario (MOE) has an excellent document called, *Growing Success,* that links checks for understanding to the wider frame of assessment and evaluation. The document proposes that teachers use a range of assessment strategies to ready the students for the lesson, called assessment **for** learning. Next, teachers examine the learning while it is happening, called assessment **as** learning. Finally, we begin the process of evaluation, called assessment **of** learning, where we are moving towards reporting.

Surprising students with tests and unfamiliar material can be threatening for some. The above shows the importance of communicating to your students the ways they are going to be assessed and including them in the development of the success criteria. This helps them prepare themselves for what is coming.

Element two in Madeline Hunter's methodology refers to **expectations** and objectives. We must understand where we are going in each lesson. This is why we draw the expectations from our curriculum documents. This information is not necessarily communicated to our students because it is written in teacher-speak. We do, however, tell students (in language they understand) what the **learning goals** and **social objectives** are so they know where they are going today and what they are going to learn. This piece alerts the brain that new information is coming. It is also helpful when the goals and objectives are written down for students because they are able to refer back to them if they forget.

For example, a teacher may tell the students: Today we are going to be learning about residential schools by:

- ♥ Working in groups to read a chapter of a novel called *Fatty Legs*
- ♥ Discussing the content of the chapter and cooperatively filling in a story web
- ♥ Developing a creative way to present our chapter (e.g., mind map, skit, rap, poem, newscast)
- ♥ Presenting our chapter to the whole class

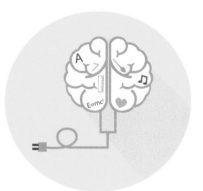

Our *social objectives* for today will be:

- ♥ Attentive listening
- ♥ Cooperation
- ♥ Appreciations

There are two additional key connections to remember regarding brain-compatible learning and the statement of learning goals. Once you state the goals, you must let the students know you are holding them accountable for their attainment of the goals, and you must make it clear why they have social objectives. First, if they are not being held accountable, it signals the brain that the goals are not important. Second, the social objectives are key to helping the students learn the skills of emotional intelligence (discussed in chapter four) and cooperative learning (discussed in chapter seven). Social objectives also assist you in creating a harmonious learning environment and reduce classroom management challenges.

Elements three to seven must connect brain-compatible learning to the ways students learn content. The instructional strategies we use to teach this new knowledge must engage our students and help them make associations to prior knowledge. The "sit and git" or "kill and drill" methods of teaching do not reach many students, and even if some learning occurs, it does not make its way to the cerebral cortex of the brain where it is stored as long-term memory. Brain-compatible research offers us a myriad of understandings for effective pedagogy. When lessons are designed well and the needs of students considered, everyone wins. In 2001, Bennett and Rolheiser reflected on great teachers as being the ones who can integrate solid pedagogy with their "extensive understanding of how students learn *and* an instructional repertoire that allows them to respond meaningfully to what is known about how and what students must learn".

Reflection and Processing of Information Learned

This understanding of brain-compatible learning is also the reason it is important to give students an opportunity to meaningfully **reflect** on what they have learned in the lesson (**element eight**). As mentioned before, our work with teacher candidates and lesson design encourages them to check understanding throughout their lessons and to bring *closure* when finished. As the understanding is continually being checked, it gives the teacher an opportunity to see what the students are learning or what they may need to add to the learning in order for it to be fully integrated.

Bringing **closure** to the lesson in a reflective way enables the teacher to make decisions about learning (assessment *of* learning). In other words, can the teacher move on with next steps, or do they have to back up and re-teach something or teach in a different way so that students are not left behind? Perhaps there are only a handful of students who need review and so the teacher can adjust based on that information. As Bennett and Rolheiser submit:

"Action without reflection and reflection without action are both unacceptable stances in education—students are too important. When teachers use closure in their lessons, they are facilitating reflection so the brain can take over and send the new learning along the neural pathways to the centre of long-term memory and thinking."

The Brain and Focused Attention

Two of the biggest challenges that new teachers face when learning to teach is timing and classroom management. They actually go hand-in-hand if we examine the research on attention span. If a teacher stands in front of a class and talks for long periods of time, they will find they have lost their student's attention and as a result, students may begin to fidget, or misbehave. Instead, we encourage our new teachers to be aware of the attention span rule, i.e., *the brain can only attend for our age plus two minutes, with most of us maxing out at twenty minutes.* If we understand the brain, we know that students are easily distracted, but regular, short breaks can help them focus, increase their productivity, and reduce their stress. Regular breaks throughout the school day—short brain breaks in the classroom to the longer break of recess—are not simply downtime for students. Such breaks increase their productivity and provide them with opportunities to develop creativity and social skills. It can be something as simple as asking them to turn to a partner and share a thought or idea, or it could actually be a "brain break" where students stand up and move in order to reactivate their brains.

What Does it Look Like in the Classroom?

Note: The following suggestions are related to the development of safe classroom environments.

♥ *Saving Face*: Humiliating, intimidating and threatening students is never acceptable. Understand the difference between classroom management and discipline. Discipline is reactive while effective management is proactive and encouraging for students. Allow students to save face by talking to them privately and providing constructive feedback and next steps.

♥ *Teacher Behaviours to Avoid*: Stay away from any anxiety-producing activities like pop quizzes, trick questions and unrelated topics. Make it a habit of reassuring your students by letting them know they can succeed, and you are there to support them and scaffold their learning. Let your students know that it is all right to make mistakes and take risks. It is helpful to point out your own mistakes and to model your problem solving strategies and risk-taking.

♥ *Add Good Stress, Eliminate Bad Stress*: Research on stress explains that there is good and bad stress. We can, in fact, learn in low or moderate stress situations. When the stress levels are appropriate, students learn resourcefulness and resilience. Good stress triggers a rush of adrenaline that prepares learners to rise to the challenge of the situation, evoking their most efficient alert state. Jensen (2004) explains that, "You can achieve this state by ensuring the learners have all the resources needed to complete the task; experiment with appropriate levels of resources, e.g., time and materials, too much support can produce no stress at all—not enough prevents tasks from being completed; avoid irregular or unattainable deadlines. Set realistic expectations so that success is achievable."

♥ *Healthy Mind/Healthy Body*: It is important for teachers to make a concerted effort to ensure that students have proper nutrition and adequate sleep. These practices are essential to learning. It is not always within their control to do so, but they can teach lessons on the importance of healthy habits. They can keep healthy snacks on hand and offer a place to rest when needed. Teachers can ensure students are getting regular exercise through DPA (daily physical activity) within the classroom and timetabled physical education. Without these essential habits, student's brains do not work as effectively as possible and learning is diminished. Additionally, they can provide a calming space by using a variety of mindfulness practices (See Chapter Eight) and creating a mindful atmosphere in the classroom.

♥ *Focus on the Positive*: Students need clear expectations and boundaries. When we identify what we want them to do, rather than what we don't want them to do, we build safety. When we consistently identify the behaviours we would prefer to see happening, e.g., "keep your hands to yourself" as opposed to "no hitting", we have a greater chance of developing positive behaviours over time. Telling students what you don't want them to do, does not identify the replacement behaviour. Instead, tell them what they are to do and why. Positivity always prevails over negativity.

♥ ***Create A Safe-Haven***: Classrooms can be the safe-haven where academic practices and classroom strategies provide students with emotional comfort and pleasure in addition to knowledge. When teachers use strategies to reduce stress and build a positive emotional environment, students gain emotional intelligence and resilience, and learn more efficiently at higher levels of cognition. MRI that measures brain activity, supports this connection.

Note: The next set of suggestions connect learning and the brain:

♥ ***Understand the Connection Between Learning and Emotion***: Learning is more fully integrated when there is emotion attached to it. As often as possible, encourage feelings by asking the students how they felt about lessons. Some instructional strategies are excellent at bringing emotion into the equation. Debates often invoke discomfort, even some anger, but if held responsibly, they are not a bad thing. When students can laugh or cry at stories, the messages are remembered. When they experience complex emotion in our classrooms, we can help them cope through strategies such as compassionate dialogue, drawing, art therapy and journal writing.

♥ ***Make Patterns Obvious***: The brain is constantly looking for patterns and seeks to repeat these patterns when possible. Whenever ideas and concepts link together in a pattern, it is remembered. This is the reason behind the use of music in classrooms. Music uses patterns that greatly enhance memory.

♥ ***Make Meaning Explicit***: Since our brains search for meaning and relevancy in lessons, include real-life connections whenever possible. We pay attention to and remember information that is relevant to our experience, interesting to us, and useful for our lives.

♥ ***Use a KWL Chart***: When a lesson or unit is about to begin, teachers can use a chart that assesses what the students know (K), what they want to know (W), and at the end, a place to let the teacher know what they have learned (L). A KWL chart is a good assessment "for" and "of" learning. This activity can be done in small groups or as a whole class. The charts can then be displayed throughout the lesson/unit (see Classroom Resources).

WHAT I KNOW	I WANT TO KNOW	I LEARNED

♥ ***Use Interest Inventories***: It is crucial to meet the students' interests so you continue to engage them in their learning. Interest inventories allow you to explore what students like and don't like so you can tailor your content whenever possible. When the students realize you are showing concern for their learning, they feel safe and heard (see Classroom Resources).

♥ ***Student Voice***: Children have a need to be seen and heard, and often feel the opposite in some classrooms. When we give students these opportunities, they feel valued and become more comfortable opening up and sharing in your classroom. This is why we often refer to Jeanne Gibbs (2014) tactic of *Cares, Concerns and Compliments* to begin the class so that students have an opportunity to voice a care about themselves or someone else, a concern about something happening in the class and an opportunity to give compliments to each other so that the parasympathetic nervous system is activated. Perhaps someone is feeling sick or has had something happen in their family and would like to express empathy. Or maybe they don't feel ready for the upcoming test or there is a problem happening within the classroom. By sharing, cares and concerns can be voiced and dealt with. It is also a way for students to practise their problem solving skills. Schools are rife with "put downs". In an effort to deter negative messages and offer chances to compliment each other as often as possible, we help students hone their interpersonal skills (see Classroom Resources).

♥ *Give Students the Option to Pass*: If the topic/question is somehow threatening to students or challenging for them, always give them the *right to pass* when it is their turn. Some students may not be comfortable sharing their personal thoughts or there may be another reason why they are not ready to answer. You can always return to those who passed and give them the option to contribute before the activity is completed. Often students engage the next time because listening to other responses makes them feel safer and more confident in expressing their own thoughts and feelings.

♥ *Provide Processing Opportunities*: Give students sentence starters such as "Today I was curious about….", "I was stressed about….", or "Today I learned….", "3, 2, 1" is also an important processing strategy, where students reflect on "Three things I learned today; two things I found interesting; and one thing I still need to know". These activities can be done with the whole class, in a community circle, or in smaller groups with the teacher as facilitator.

♥ *Use Graphic Organizers*: Much of the curriculum taught in today's schools is geared toward verbal-linguistic learners (Gardner, 2019) despite the fact that there are many students who are visual learners. To ensure that we reach these students and tap into their best ways of knowing, we can use a range of graphic organizers (e.g., placemat, Venn diagram, fishbone) so they are able to visually organize their thoughts. A list of graphic organizers is found in Classroom Resources.

♥ *Music, Quotes and Drama*: Provide famous quotes to inspire learning and meaning. Have students re-write song lyrics to demonstrate learning or to describe what they are feeling about content or social skills. Students love music and drama and the use of these strategies, motivates them and engages their creativity.

♥ *Personal Journals/Learning Logs*: These are ways of communicating that allow students an opportunity to express themselves without doing so out loud to the whole community. Journals and learning logs are often used in today's classrooms and as such, they can become boring for students. Try to find a variety of ways for students to reflect on their learning and social experiences. Get creative in this area by having the students draw, act out, or create graphic organizers as a means to reflect.

♥ *Student Portfolios*: This way of documenting learning is common in schools. It is a meaningful and safe way for students to document their academic and social growth; set their own intentions and next steps; and provide reflections and exemplars of their work. Students gain a sense of control when using portfolios, unlike what can happen when assessment is continually forced on them. Portfolios are often used in student-led conferences and are a way for students to present their learning and identify next steps to their parents and teachers (see Classroom Resources).

♥ *Utilize Guest Speakers*: Arrange for experts or guest speakers to come in to speak or show a visual presentation in lessons or units. Guests often elicit an emotional connection that helps to intensify learning. It also provides variety from the regular classroom routine.

♥ *Make Use of Glossaries and Fun Ways to Teach*: Wherever possible, provide students with vocabulary, key ideas and concepts, and concrete examples to link to the new learning. You can play word association games to trigger old thoughts and inspire new ones. All of this can be helpful to activate curiosity, inspiration, and anticipation for lessons. The more fun students have during lessons, the more motivated they are going to be. The use of drama, storytelling, role-play, music and/or movement is also a solid way to engage the brain (see Classroom Resources).

♥ *Use Your Halls and Walls to Teach*: Display murals, pictures, and charts to trigger memory and learning. Always ensure your displays represent diversity in all of its forms. You want students to see the people of the world clearly represented. While teaching, use the chalkboard or white board, digital presentations, and Smart Boards to provide a visual reference for students. There is additional value when tests are taken in the same location where the material was learned. As students are glancing around the room while thinking, they often find clues that trigger memory.

♥ *Teach Students to Prioritize Information*: Teachers can facilitate learning and memory by teaching their students to prioritize information. To do so, they use modelling and guided practice so students understand what they should be prioritizing and judging as worthy. While modelling and guiding are important, it is also important to remove this assistance at some point and encourage students to develop independence.

♥ *Chunk Material*: It is often challenging for students to absorb large amounts of information all at once. Chunking information into smaller and meaningful segments makes it easier to remember. Allow processing and settling time with partners or small groups in order to integrate learning.

♥ *Plan Weekly Reviews*: Conduct weekly discussions about lesson content to help students put the material into perspective. Graphic organizers such as mind maps and concept maps facilitate this learning for visual-spatial learners.

♥ *Develop Social Skills*: Longer breaks, such as recess or playtime, provide opportunities for children to learn important social skills. We know through the research that when children play together they learn how their own emotions and behavior are fundamental skills for life, so dropping recess is a mistake. According to the American Academy of Pediatrics: Recess is a "crucial and necessary component of a child's development" and sacrificing it for more academics is counterproductive.

♥ **Incorporate Brain Breaks in your Classroom**: If students are getting fidgety or bored, a few minutes of exercise, e.g., standing beside desk and touching their toes, can reset their attention. Use short activities that stimulate curiosity to boost students' motivation and improve their mood. Sometimes the best learning happens from informal instruction, with an insight or inspiration. Set aside time for creativity, e.g., brain challenges, art projects, etc.; all can help boost kids' imaginations.

Note: The following strategies have been borrowed from the work of Eric Jensen (Brain Compatible Strategies, 2004):

♥ **It's in My Bag**: A fun strategy to use with reflection/processing. Have the students find a bag at home (any bag), and then tell them to fill it with one (or two-depending on time) item(s) that remind them of how they feel about what they are learning and/or how they are feeling socially in the classroom. They can share their bag items with a partner, in a small group, or with the whole class.

♥ **On-line Discussion Groups**: Using a moderated on-line platform, have students create a dialogue with their peers and the teacher regarding their learning and pertinent content. Students write weekly summaries and identify key concepts learned and indicate areas where additional clarification is required. For older students, rotate the role of moderator so that all participants have an opportunity to take on a leadership role. Perhaps as moderator, they would select the discussion topic for the following week's e-mail discussion session.

♥ **Unstructured Playtime**: This provides an opportunity for imaginary and creative play and allows children to practise divergent thinking. Children benefit from the freedom to explore new ideas without fear of failure or the stress of grades. Regular exposure to new experiences can increase their cognitive flexibility, preparing them for academic challenges.

♥ **Commercial Breaks**: In pairs or small groups, have students choose a concept or topic, then prepare a brief commercial to perform in front of the class. Give them 30 seconds for presentation and encourage them to be silly, funny, (within appropriate norms) to "sell" the information.

♥ **Write your Name with Body Parts**: Using arms, elbows, hips, head, trace the letters of names.

♥ **Stretching**: Have students take turns leading stretches. You can choose to include music where students can stretch in small groups or as a whole class.

♥ **Creative Active Breaks: Getting to Know you Charades**: In pairs, students communicate three personal facts to their partner without using words. Only charades gestures and movements are allowed.

♥ **Instant Replay:** In pairs, students take turns to act out an idea (for five seconds) and mimic (from memory) their partner's gestures. Add subject matter content to increase academic connection.

♥ **March the Brain**: One of the quickest ways to improve blood circulation and mental focus are short marching activities. Marching comes with plenty of fringe benefits; its rhythm can enhance learning. What students learn while they are marching is more likely to be remembered later because: 1) marching adds a kinesthetic element to learning, 2) sounds and rhymes are catchy and easy to remember, 3) a change of location triggers spatial-episodic memory, and 4) it stimulates the senses in a fresh, visceral way.

♥ **Brain Laps**: In the gym or outside, warm students up by having them run a quick lap to get the circulation going, and then each student tells ten different people what they think the three most important words were from the previous lesson. Be sure the behaviour norms are established before you begin this activity (e.g., noise level, respectful behaviour, etc.).

♥ **Follow the Leader**: Put students in teams to brainstorm a topic and send them out for a walk. The team leader dramatizes or says something about the topic content, and the team members follow along and repeat it.

♥ **Hook and Linking Games**: Players match words to definitions or identify opposites or similar pairs. Have fun with pictogram games like *Pictionary* or word completion games like *Scrabble*. Try seek-and-find games like *Concentration, I Spy* or *What's Missing from this Picture?*

♥ **Listening Games**: Try *Simon Says, Telephone,* or reciting tongue twisters. Students always benefit from practising auditory skills.

♥ **Balancing Game**: Have students walk along a painted or taped line on the floor, challenge them to try it with their eyes closed.

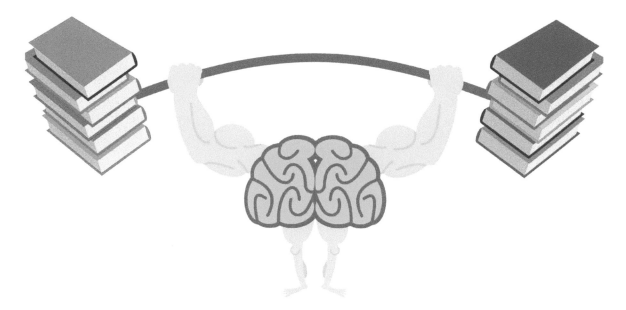

Note: The following activities are effective brain breaks.

♥ **Clap-Slap:** This fun and engaging brain break is done in a circle where everyone can see each other. The teacher will begin by clapping their hands together and sending the clap/slap to another person in the circle by pointing it at them. The pace should be quick and energizing.

♥ **Elephant**: Also done in a circle with the teacher in the middle. The teacher will twirl around and point at one person. That person becomes the elephant's trunk with an arm outstretched. The people on the left and right become the elephant's ears holding their hands like the letter C to the person who is the trunk. The last person to do their action is "out" but nothing really happens to them; the game simply continues.

♥ **Fork and Spoon** (Jeanne Gibbs, 2014): For many groups, this game takes practise as the students might get frustrated at first. However, it is fun to challenge them to see how far they can get each day. The teacher will start by turning to the person on their right saying, "This is a fork!" The person says, "A what?" The teacher says, "A fork" and the person takes the fork and responds, "Ah a fork!" They then turn to the person on their right saying the exact word sequence from before. The exchange continues until about five people have received the fork at which time the teacher turns to the person on the left and introduces a spoon. The teacher says, "This is a spoon." The person says, "A what?" The teacher says, "A spoon." The student says, "Ah, a spoon!" as they take the spoon and begin to pass it to the left. The students soon begin to realize that there will be a cross-over in the middle and they have to problem-solve to get both the fork and the spoon around the circle!

♥ **Four Up** (Jeanne Gibbs, 2014): This activity is a fun way for the students to focus and get some energy. Have the students sit in a circle. The rule is that only four people can be standing at any one time. They must watch their classmates and decide whether to stand up or not.

♥ **I Like My Neighbour** (Jeanne Gibbs, 2014): Students will sit on chairs in a circle with one fewer chair than students. One person will stand in the middle and say, "I like my neighbour who…". They will fill in the blank with a descriptor of any kind. For example, "I like my neighbour who has a pet", or "I like my neighbour who eats ice cream." Every student for whom that idea applies, gets up and moves to another chair while the person in the middle also tries to find a chair. The person left without a chair becomes the person in the middle. The students must move beyond the chair immediately next to them.

♥ **That's Me** (Jeanne Gibbs, 2014): Every child will begin by sitting down. When the teacher calls out a descriptor, e.g., "I walk to school", the students who agree with that statement will stand up saying, "That's me!". Other examples may include, loves math, doesn't like liver, enjoys soccer, loves summer, etc.

♥ **This is a Scarf** (Jeanne Gibbs, 2014): As the students stand in a circle, the teacher will start by holding up a scarf and saying, "This is a scarf. It's not really a scarf, it's a skipping rope". The teacher will then imitate that movement with the scarf. The idea is to get the creativity flowing. The teacher then passes the scarf to the next student in the circle and they will continue the activity with a different action for the scarf.

♥ **Traffic Jam** (Jeanne Gibbs, 2014): Have each student find a partner and stand one behind the other facing in the same direction. One pair is selected to be the bumper car. The object of the game is that each pair will try to stay away from the bumper car. If the bumper car touches them, the role of bumper car is now with the new pair. The game is really fun when the car is told to close their eyes and is steered by the driver.

♥ ***Vehicle:*** Have the students stand in a circle and select four students or have four volunteers who will sit in the "make believe" car, made up of four chairs, two in front and two behind. The driver (sitting on front left chair) then calls out the type of vehicle it is and each person in the car must do the actions of that vehicle. For example, if "roller coaster" is called out by the driver, all of the passengers act out that item, e.g., wave their hands in the air and squeal with delight. Each new driver gets to call out a vehicle. For each rotation: the front passengers move to the right, then backwards to back row and then left; the new driver moves into the driver's seat (front, left); the other three students move over or back and the person in the back left seat leaves the vehicle and rejoins the circle.

♥ ***What are you Doing?*** (Jeanne Gibbs, 2014): In this brain break everyone stands in a circle and the leader begins by doing an action, e.g., brushing their hair. The person on the leader's right will say their name and ask, "Denise, what are you doing?" The leader responds by saying a different behaviour, e.g., "I am flossing my teeth". The new person then does the new action (flossing teeth) and the next person asks, "John, what are you doing?" Again, they are told an action other than the one being done, e.g., "I am putting on my socks". This continues until everyone in the circle has had a chance to participate.

 Literature Resources

Picture Books

A Walk in the Rain with the Brain by Edward Hallowell

Bob the Brain by Cassaday Synnestvedt

Falling Through the Cracks by Carolyn Sollman

How Does Your Brain Work by Don L. Curry

My First Book About the Brain by Patricia J. Wynne and Donald M. Silver

The Journey Through the Brain by Ayla Duckett

Think Tank: The Human Brain and How it Works by Baby IQ Builder Books

Understanding Your Brain: Lifting the Lid on What's Inside Your Head by Rebecca Treays

What Goes on in My Head: How Your Brain Works and Why You Do What You Do by Robert Winston

You Can't Use Your Brain if You're a Jellyfish by Fred Ehrlich M.D.

Young Genius Brains by Kate Lennard

Your Fantastic, Elastic Brain: Stretch It, Shape It by JoAnn Deak

Chapter Books

How Do We Think? by Carol Ballard

It's All in Your Head: A Guide to Understanding Your Brain and Boosting Your Brain Power by Susan L. Barrett

101 Questions Your Brain Has Asked About Itself but Couldn't Answer ... Until Now by Faith Hickman Brynie

Inside the Brain by Eric H. Chudler

The Great Good Thing by Roderick Townley

Why Do I Laugh or Cry? And Other Questions About the Nervous System by Sharon Cromwell

CHAPTER FOUR

Emotional Intelligence

What Does the Research Say?

Today, we hear more and more about emotional intelligence (EQ). It is now considered more important than the previously "hallowed" intelligence quotient (IQ); a measurement often thought to set the standard for excellence in life. Peter Salovey and John Mayer, the first to coin the term "emotional intelligence" in 2000, define it as "the ability to monitor one's own and others' feelings and emotions, to discriminate among them and to use this information to guide one's thinking and actions." Another way to describe its importance is: "Emotional intelligence is involved in the capacity to perceive emotions, assimilate emotion-related feelings, understand the information of those emotions, and manage them."

In this chapter, we explore:

Brain- compatible
Emotional   Learning
Intelligence   Culturally Relevant &
Responsive Pedagogy
Resilience   The Resilient
Child   Human Needs
& Wants
Mindfulness
Inclusion &
Caring Relationships

✓ *The five components of emotional Intelligence and the fifteen sub-components*

✓ *The importance of social-emotional learning and today's classrooms*

✓ *The connections between emotional intelligence and success in life*

✓ *The many ways to teach content while also helping your students to develop their emotional Intelligence*

✓ *The connections between emotional Intelligence and work-life or school-life balance*

✓ *The five components of emotional Intelligence and the fifteen sub-components*

Internationally known psychologist, Daniel Goleman, popularized the term, "emotional intelligence" in the mainstream. He is now considered one the world's leading authorities on the subject. Goleman divided emotional intelligence into five main components:

Self-awareness: The ability to recognize and understand personal moods and emotions and drives, as well as their effect on others. Hallmarks of self-awareness include self-confidence and a realistic self-assessment. Self-awareness depends on one's ability to monitor one's own emotional state and to correctly identify and name one's emotions.

Self-regulation: The ability to control or redirect disruptive impulses and moods, and the propensity to suspend judgment and to think before acting. Hallmarks include trustworthiness and integrity, comfort with ambiguity and openness to change.

Jackie Eldridge and Denise McLafferty

Internal motivation: A passion to work for internal reasons that go beyond money and status, which are external rewards, such as: an inner vision of what is important in life; a joy in doing something; curiosity in learning; a flow that comes with being immersed in an activity; and a propensity to pursue goals with energy and persistence. Hallmarks include a strong drive to achieve, optimism in the face of failure, and organizational commitment.

Empathy: The ability to understand the emotional makeup of other people. A skill in treating people according to their emotional reactions. Hallmarks include expertise in building and retaining talent, cross-cultural sensitivity, and service to clients and customers. In an educational context, empathy is often thought to include, or lead to, sympathy, which implies concern, or care or a wish to soften negative emotions or experiences in others.

Social skills: Proficiency in managing relationships and building networks, and an ability to find common ground and build rapport. Hallmarks of social skills include effectiveness in leading change, persuasiveness, and expertise building and leading teams.

The importance of emotional intelligence spans education, families, and intimate relationships, and is widely used in the corporate world. People understand the need to hone the skills and to ensure it is taught or coached when the skills are not as strong as they could be. It is, therefore, critical for educators and students to work on their emotional intelligence so that a lack of EQ does not interfere with learning and getting along with others.

Emotional intelligence takes on many forms in the field of education. The skills are most often referred to as social and emotional learning or SEL. Goleman shares the reach and importance of this work: [Tens] of thousands of schools worldwide offer students SEL. In the United States, many districts and even entire states currently make SEL curriculum a requirement, mandating that just as students must attain a certain level of competence in math and language, so too should they master these essential skills for living.

Around the world, Singapore has undertaken an active initiative in SEL, as have some schools in Malaysia, Hong Kong, Japan, and Korea. In Europe, the U.K. has led the way, but more than a dozen other countries have schools that embrace EQ, as do Australia and New Zealand, and here and there countries in Latin America and Africa. In 2002, UNESCO began a worldwide initiative to promote SEL, sending a statement of ten basic principles for implementing SEL to the ministries of education in 140 countries.

Canadian schools are following suit with boards around the world by integrating social and emotional learning into their curriculum expectations. Similar to what the other Canadian systems are saying, in 2014 the Ministry of Education and Training in Ontario made the following recommendation:

Daily activities present opportunities for direct instruction and practice of social-emotional skills. Use literature, sharing circles, real-life experience, and community meetings to develop knowledge and skills to: a) identify and manage emotions; b) pursue positive and reasonable goals; c) communicate caring for others; d) initiate and sustain positive relationships; and e) demonstrate respect for self and others.

In order for teachers to best understand a range of approaches for meeting curriculum expectations, Hearts and Minds Matter has built an understanding of the important components of emotional intelligence, using comprehensive sources designed to assist teachers in their understanding and teaching of emotional intelligence. Our purpose was to give a comprehensive look at the assessment of emotional intelligence and the strategies to teach these important skills in the classroom. We took the work of Salovey, Mayer and Goleman and blended them with assessment tools developed by Multi-Health Systems, a leading publisher of scientifically validated assessments in Canada. Unlike some assessments, Multi-Health Systems takes a more in-depth look at emotional intelligence, identifies its five main components, and then includes fifteen subcomponents to further explain the concepts (MHS - EQ-I 2.0). This analysis allows educators to connect their teaching strategies to emotional intelligence.

Teachers are often overwhelmed by the amount of new content they are asked to teach, and yet, we know these components of emotional intelligence are already embedded in effective instruction. Simply by teaching with instructional intelligence, teachers can give students the opportunity to practice their EQ skills. If we couple instruction with effective and on-going feedback, the impact we can make on the ways students become emotionally intelligent can be significant.

In this chapter, we help teachers see that there are no add-ons; instead, it is simply about good teaching.

As we develop emotional intelligence skills in children, we are able to see the strong connection to motivation, classroom management, lesson and unit planning, and differentiated instruction. When students possess solid emotional intelligence, they become highly motivated to learn, are not inclined to seek attention through misbehaviour, and actively want to participate in lessons and units designed to meet their needs. We also notice that classrooms run more smoothly and we can cover significantly more curriculum content.

Emotional Intelligence and Brain Health

There are additional correlations between effective instruction, emotional intelligence, and good mental health, as well as a strong relationship with the brain research and Maslow's hierarchy of needs (See Chapter One). Emotional intelligence is learned and can be improved. Teachers, therefore, can make a difference in the ways they teach their students. Emotional Intelligence has to do with the neuroplasticity of the brain, where stimuli, continuous practise, and systematic learning creates changes and helps us make connections. In terms of moving up the hierarchy of needs, it is evident that once our basic physiological needs are met, we can employ our emotional intelligence to achieve the higher levels. For example, when the classroom is safe, students can further develop their sense of belonging, self-esteem, confidence, and relationships as they strive to self-actualize, reach their potential and higher creativity.

Emotional Intelligence, Career Success and Balanced Lives

As previously mentioned, emotional intelligence is thought to be more important than IQ, but why is it so important in today's world? If we explore the classified ads for current jobs, the first qualifications we notice are the so-called "soft skills". These are the ones directly associated with emotional intelligence. Leaders value these skills over the ones necessary to do the job. They know they can train people to develop the job competencies; however, they need people to arrive with emotional intelligence so they can fit into the already existing teams and organizations. The following advertisements were taken from *Indeed*, an international job site. Notice the emphasis on what we'd define as emotional intelligence!

City of Toronto

Excellent interpersonal skills with the ability to communicate effectively, both orally and in writing, and ability to develop solid professional internal and external work relationships with various levels of staff within the City, other organizations, and the public.

Hospital for Sick Children

Excellent interpersonal and communication skills; ability to work with clients in a professional manner. Ability to work well independently as well as part of a team.

Roger's Communications

Connect and build rapport with a variety of customers by actively listening to our customers, asking the right questions, and offering solutions (products and services) which cater to customer needs.

It's no wonder that *the Center for Creative Leadership*, a global provider of leadership development programs, reports that:

"75% of careers are derailed for reasons related to emotional competencies, including an inability to handle interpersonal problems; unsatisfactory team leadership during times of difficulty or conflict; or inability to adapt to change or elicit trust."

While emotional intelligence skills are exceedingly important for getting and maintaining a career, they are also important for leading a balanced life. This is an area where many people are seeking help. Those who write about productivity, business success, gratitude, and life balance, report the following important connections to emotional intelligence:

Physical Health: The ability to take care of our bodies—especially, manage our stress—has an incredible impact on our overall wellness and is heavily tied to our emotional intelligence. Only by being aware of our emotional state and our reactions to stress in our lives, can we hope to manage stress and maintain good health.

Mental Well-Being: Emotional intelligence affects our attitude and outlook on life. It can also help to alleviate anxiety and avoid depression and mood swings. In short, a high level of emotional intelligence directly correlates to a positive attitude and a happier outlook on life.

Relationships: By better understanding and managing our emotions, we are better able to communicate our feelings in a more constructive way. We are also better able to understand and relate to those with whom we are in relationships. Understanding the needs, feelings, and responses of those we care about leads to stronger and more fulfilling relationships.

Conflict Resolution: When we can discern people's emotions and empathize with their perspective, it's much easier to resolve conflicts or possibly avoid them before they start. We are also better at negotiation due to the very nature of our ability to understand the needs and desires of others. It's easier to give people what they want if we can perceive what it is.

Success: Higher emotional intelligence helps us to be stronger internal motivators, which can reduce procrastination, increase self-confidence, and improve our ability to focus on a goal. It also allows us to create better networks of support, overcome setbacks, and persevere with a more resilient outlook. When we are able to delay gratification and see the long-term, we directly affect our ability to succeed.

Leadership: The ability to understand what motivates others, relate in a positive manner, and to build stronger bonds with others in the workplace, inevitably makes those with higher emotional intelligence better leaders. An effective leader can recognize what the needs of the people are, so that those needs can be met in a way that encourages higher performance. An emotionally savvy and intelligent leader is also able to build stronger teams by strategically utilizing the emotional diversity of their team members to benefit the team as a whole.

Nurturing EQ Skills

It is important to note that nurturing emotional intelligence in our students means that we also need to take a serious look at ourselves and our own emotional intelligence. Our emotional intelligence is contagious; we can only help our students if we have solid EQ skills ourselves. For example, if we expect students to practise emotional self-regulation and we are regularly yelling at them, our efforts are going to be lost. If we expect them to be positive and engaged and yet we are always complaining, they are going to adopt our mind set. However, if we are modeling emotionally intelligent skills, we can then expect students to follow our lead. To begin, let's look at the comprehensive scale created by Multi-Health Systems and work from there. The following are identified as the components and sub-components of emotional intelligence. The main component is hi-lighted and the sub-component is in the brackets beside each one:

Self-Perception (self-respect, self-actualization, emotional self-awareness)

Self-Expression (emotional-expression, assertiveness, independence)

Interpersonal (interpersonal relationships, empathy, social responsibility)

Decision-Making (problem solving, reality-testing, impulsivity)

Stress Tolerance (flexibility, stress tolerance, optimism)

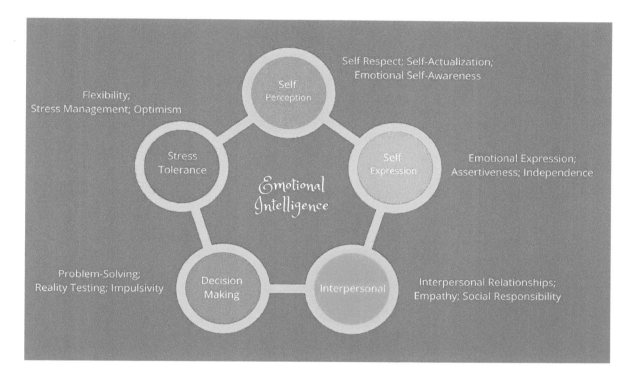

Let's break each component down, and then find ways of exploring the categories for ourselves and our students. As you review the components, take a moment to reflect on your own emotional intelligence. What are your strengths and areas of challenge? Do you see yourself as strongly exhibiting these characteristics or are there some you need to build and hone? Make a list of your strengths and areas of challenge and set your intention to work through them so you can be the best teacher possible.

Self-Perception

- ♥ **Self-respect** is respecting yourself and accepting your strengths and weaknesses—your inner strength and self-confidence.

- ♥ **Self-actualization** is your willingness to try to improve yourself and to engage in relevant and meaningful objectives to live a rich and enjoyable life.

- ♥ **Emotional self-awareness** is about recognizing and understanding your emotions. Do you understand the cause of your emotions and the impact they have on your thoughts and actions and how they affect others?

Self-Expression

- ♥ **Emotional expression** is about the ways you express emotions (verbally and non-verbally).

- ♥ **Assertiveness** involves communicating your feelings, beliefs, and thoughts openly and defending personal rights and values in a socially acceptable way.

- ♥ **Independence** is the ability to be self-directed and free from emotional dependency on others. You can make your own decisions, plan, and carry out daily tasks without supervision.

Interpersonal

- ♥ **Interpersonal Relationships** is about developing relationships that are mutually satisfying and characterized by trust and compassion.

- ♥ **Empathy** is about recognizing, understanding, and appreciating how other people feel and being able to support them in a way that respects the person's feelings.

- ♥ **Social Responsibility** is about willingly contributing to society, to the welfare of others. You have a concern for the greater community.

Decision-Making

- ♥ **Problem solving** means working to solve problems when there are emotions involved. Can you stick with it? Do you understand how emotions affect decision-making?

- ♥ **Reality-testing** means staying objective and seeing things as they really are. Are you thinking clearly and seeing both sides?

- ♥ **Impulse control** is the ability to delay or resist an impulse, decision, or rash behavior. Are you stopping and thinking?

Stress Tolerance

- ♥ **Flexibility** is the ability to adapt emotions, thoughts and behaviours to unfamiliar, unpredictable circumstances or ideas.

- ♥ **Stress management** involves coping with stressful or difficult situations and believing that you can manage or influence situations in a positive way.

- ♥ **Optimism** is a positive attitude and outlook on life. It involves staying hopeful and resilient, despite setbacks.

Jackie Eldridge and Denise McLafferty

Working on Your Own Emotional Intelligence

Teachers can find themselves in stressful situations. Their actions impact students' learning, so developing their own emotional intelligence helps them deal with such challenges in more understanding ways. In the January 2019 issue of *Exploring Your Mind*, the benefit of emotional intelligence was described as something that helped teachers: deal with new challenges that come with problematic groups of students and crowded classrooms or a lack of motivation. We live in a society where values education and dealing with students' problems in a more understanding way are important. Teachers have more influence than we think. Being a teacher isn't easy. Too many lessons, too many students, and anxiety define a teacher's day-to-day life. In order to examine and work with your own emotional intelligence here are some suggestions:

♥ **Pat Yourself on the Back**

Examine your teaching practice and ask yourself whether you are confident in what you are doing or whether you are "scared to death!" The art and science of teaching takes a long time to master and confidence levels are naturally low at the beginning of your career. Some say it takes as long as five years to really develop confidence; however, one must develop confidence in order to be successful. Students are excellent detectives. They are quick to spot your uncertainty. As a result, you must give yourself credit where credit is due and work hard on the areas that you find challenging. It is also important to know that it is all right to ask for help. Many people view this request as a sign of weakness; however, it is actually a sign of strength to recognize when you can't do it alone. After all, we want our students to learn to work together, so why shouldn't we?

♥ **Be Honest. Reflect on Your Own Emotional Awareness and Expression**

Ask yourself how aware you are of your own emotional expression. What emotions are you feeling and expressing? Are they well-received or do you send mixed messages? This area of emotional intelligence can be tricky for some teachers because there are so many emotions that pop up during the day, in ourselves and in our students. Try asking yourself the following questions to get a read on where you are on the continuum:

- ♥ How effective are you at self-regulation?
- ♥ Can you read your students/other staff members and understand when their emotions are affecting them?
- ♥ Can you stay calm in most situations or are you prone to flying off the handle?
- ♥ Do you have a means of calming down or do you carry your emotions with you?
- ♥ Can you identify what behaviours are triggering you and what emotions are the result of those triggers?
- ♥ Can you work with these emotions to overcome them?

When you are able to identify your own emotions and reactions, you become more mindful. You are then able to start the process of building control over yourself and maintaining control in your classroom. In this way, you create an environment that is caring and nurturing.

♥ Get Perspective

We don't always see ourselves clearly or in the way others see us. Perceptions are different among people and there are times when our own vision is clouded. Of course, we want to do the right thing, but sometimes we are simply fooling ourselves. It happens to all of us. By authentically asking those close to us, our colleagues, friends, family members and even our students, we can learn more about ourselves. It is especially helpful to our emotional intelligence work when we are not aware that we are doing or saying certain things. The key to this suggestion is to be willing and able to accept the feedback. Feedback is meant to help you grow. It is not criticism!

You might ask people how they see you when you are with your class and how they view your interactions with your students? Does their perception match yours? Are they able to give you feedback on your emotional awareness and expression? Are you able to accept that feedback?

♥ Be Observant

You might adopt a "witness attitude" as you are working with your students and other staff members. Try to make candid discoveries about yourself. Try writing things down and focusing on the way you feel and how you think others are feeling in response to you. You might explore the facial expressions and body language of others so you can get a read on how they are reacting. If you notice that they are uncomfortable, take

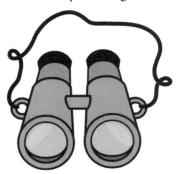

note, ask them how it could have been different or simply adjust your behaviour with them the next time.

You might also observe how you are thinking and feeling in your encounters with others. Make note of the pleasant and unpleasant experiences you are having. Adjust accordingly. It is a good idea to understand that you can only change yourself and not others. You can model for them and give feedback, but ultimately individuals must make their own decision to change.

♥ Develop Authentic Relationships

Teaching is a relational experience. We are not isolated as teachers. Instead we have many people with whom we must interact, i.e., students, other teachers, administrators, parents, etc. Solid relationships are at the core of what makes people good teachers. If this area of emotional intelligence is lacking, it is going to be a long and strenuous career. Everyone wants to be respected and included, so it is important to understand the ways to do this with everyone you encounter.

When you have a good rapport and meaningful relationships with your students, learning happens regularly, and classroom management issues are reduced. When you have strong bonds with your colleagues, you garner support when needed and your time at the school is much more enjoyable. When you connect with parents, you have their support and assistance when needed. Teachers who fail to see the importance of cooperation and collaboration are setting themselves up for failure. Their relationships become adversarial and a great deal of stress ensues. It all speaks to the high value of relationships and open communication.

Jackie Eldridge and Denise McLafferty

♥ **Mindful Moments**

Taking a mindful moment is an effective strategy when we are uncertain of what to say or do next. It might be as simple as taking a moment to stop, take a breath and think before we act or speak. It is not easy because most of us are accustomed to jumping in and getting on with things. However, a little mindfulness makes an enormous difference, especially if strong emotions are starting to well up. The stress and fast pace of teaching can create situations where we are feeling anxious or we feel we need to be first to jump in. When you are in this situation, it can be challenging to self-regulate. Instead of doing or saying something you might regret, take a breath, and then act. The more you practise this skill, the more chance you have of developing the habit of thinking first. The topic of mindfulness in schools and classrooms is explored in Chapter Eight.

♥ **Explore Your "Why"**

In the Hearts and Minds Matter professional development program, we begin our journey by asking our participants to reflect on why they have chosen to become educators. The answers are varied:

"I love working with children."

"I want to make a difference in kid's lives."

"I want to inspire children."

"I want to encourage my students the way I was encouraged."

It is not going to be phrased:

"I want to make sure kids toe the line".

"I want to discipline children because there is not enough discipline out there."

"I want to tell students what they should know."

Most teachers would agree that working with children is a true gift and we have a lot to offer them, especially when we can help them to become good global citizens. This work requires empathy and compassion. According to the Merriam-Webster dictionary, empathy is, "the action of understanding, being aware of, being sensitive to, and vicariously experiencing the feelings, thoughts, and experience of another of either the past or present without having the feelings, thoughts, and experience fully communicated in an objective manner". From the same source, compassion is "sympathetic consciousness of others' distress together with a desire to alleviate it".

One would think these definitions are the hallmarks of teaching and that every teacher understands these concepts. However, many teachers find it a challenge to put themselves in the shoes of some children since they come from vastly different demographics. If we don't examine our own empathy and compassion, we will never be able to reach the children who need us the most. It is especially true of those children who have learning and social-emotional challenges.

Psychologist Adam Grant calls this phenomenon, "the perspective gap". He purports that it is extremely difficult to put ourselves in another person's shoes. We may forget how specific situations feel, even if we've experienced similar circumstances. You hear it a lot when people talk about "kids nowadays". It's as if they have totally forgotten what it was like to be a child themselves. Or, if we've never experienced something similar to what our students are going through, our perspective is limited or perhaps skewed. This lack of understanding is especially true when we are working with children who come from trauma. It is difficult, if not impossible, to understand what these children are going through. Given that we want to be able to see the experience through the eyes of another, we must go further than our own experiences, especially if they are different. This is the power of empathy. Showing true empathy means exploring the "why" and asking ourselves questions like the following:

- ♥ Why does this student feel the way they do?
- ♥ What are they dealing with that I don't see?
- ♥ Why do I feel differently than they do?

In a popular social media meme, author L.R. Knost says, "When little people are overwhelmed by big emotions, it's our job to share our calm, not join their chaos". Oftentimes, the behaviour we are seeing in children is not misbehaviour but a cry for help. If we possess empathy, we are more likely to see the reasons instead of simply getting stuck on the so-called "bad kid".

♥ Empathize

Struggling children need our help. Empathize, see the child through a "Beginner's Mind". In other words, instead of fretting over the child's behaviour each and every time it presents itself, look at the child as though you have never met them before. It makes it a lot easier than holding on to the same baggage every day. We might also adopt a trauma-sensitive approach. This is where we can safely assume that someone in our classroom has experienced trauma, and we are careful not to re-traumatize them or unintentionally provide triggers. This topic is explored in Chapter Six.

♥ Uncover the Learning

Teachers are often at the receiving end of criticism, especially in the media. This unwanted feedback is mostly unwarranted, and yet, there are times when we can learn from what people are saying. The choice is to take the feedback and work with it, or let it eat away at us to the point where we shut down and are unable to move forward. It is up to each of us to decide. When we hear this information, we can either put our feelings aside and try to learn from the situation, or we can get angry and let emotion overtake us, thereby creating more stress.

In developing our emotional intelligence, we might consider the following:

- ♥ Putting personal feelings aside, you can ask, what can I learn from this alternate perspective?
- ♥ Instead of focusing on what was said, ask yourself, how can I use this feedback to help improve my teaching and/or my relationship with my students?

Of course, there are times when criticism is harmful or vengeful. We must be strong in this case and consider the source. We must also be prepared not to allow it to get to us. However, if it is valuable, it is worth your attention. If your goal is to truly be the best teacher you can be, don't let emotion close your mind to negative feedback. Instead, embrace the learning and move forward.

♥ Develop Your Decision-Making Skills

Today's schools are filled with students who have difficulty making decisions and problem solving. These challenges are the result of not having enough practise. Many children have grown up in homes where everything is done for them, decisions are made for them, and someone else solves their problems. This catches up with them when they leave school and find themselves unable to exercise these much-needed skills. If you find yourself in this position, it is necessary to realize how important such skills are, and how much resilience results from being able to carry them out. Start small and work your way up to more difficult decisions. Learn to trust yourself and to realize that mistakes are opportunities for growth. It is also good practice for working with your students. Make mistakes welcome!

♥ Find a Balance

Teaching is considered one of the most stressful professions. One in five teachers actually resign within the first five years. There are many reasons for such stress. Some are internal, stressors we create and can control ourselves; some are external, those that are beyond the scope of a teacher's sphere of influence. It is important for educators to understand what they can and cannot change so they develop an element of influence over their lives. It is also important to understand ways to cope with the stress and to find balance in our lives. Finding a balance is one of the keys to a successful career. Chapter Eight is devoted to mindfulness and the ways we can ensure that our stress is kept in check.

♥ Practise

We are human and we make mistakes. That's okay. Learning to improve our emotional intelligence is a process on which we must continually work. Like anything else, we need to practise our skills in order to improve them. In terms of developing our emotional intelligence, we must understand that it's impossible to have complete control over our emotions. You might start by setting some intentions for working with one or two areas at a time. "Play" with them before moving on to the others. It is easy to get overwhelmed, so be gentle with yourself. Remember, you are the role model for your students. They are watching you all the time. The more you develop your emotional intelligence, the more they will too!

Why Teaching Emotional Intelligence Is Important

It is easy to see how emotional intelligence can contribute to positive classroom environments created by pro-active teachers. Emotional intelligence enables students to have positive interactions with others, anticipate their feelings, and experience appropriate levels of empathy. As we have already seen, emotional intelligence is also extremely important when students are looking for part-time jobs or ready to embark on a career. Teaching emotional intelligence does not have to be an add-on. Using effective instructional strategies that put students in the position of working with others gives you the perfect opportunity to allow students to practise their skills.

What Does it Look Like in a Classroom?

♥ *Embed Social-Emotional Learning into Your Daily Teaching Practices*: Whenever you are teaching any subject area, consider using the strategies that are offered throughout this book to help your students build relationships with classmates. The use of cooperative learning strategies, tactics and skills is an excellent way to encourage students to work together, listen to each other and to share ideas and resources. It is also important to use literature that represents strong emotional intelligence as a complement to any other materials you are using. The classroom resources section connects strategies to emotional intelligence by exploring the component of EQ and the role it plays in the strategy. You might also pause videos or stories whenever there is conflict present and ask the students to tell you how they might resolve it using their emotional intelligence. Think about engaging your students in discussions about social problems and the ways they can be handled. This way, the lesson becomes about literacy, history, and social and emotional learning. You can integrate your expectations so you do not feel like you are having to plan additional material.

♥ *Engage Students in Problem solving and Decision-Making*: Whether it's helping solve a difficult math or science problem or designing an alliance with your students at the beginning of the year, engage them in all types of problem solving. For instance, if the children are having trouble including other students, have them brainstorm ideas and agree to work on one or two of them as a class. Often the best ideas for dealing with issues come from the students themselves. Ask students to give you their input on anything that happens in the classroom, as well as on issues outside the classroom, e.g., class trips, recess issues, bullying, etc. They know each other and they know themselves. Group inquiry projects are another useful way to teach students how to work together and how to solve conflicts when they arise; skills they need in many areas of life. It is helpful to teach good communication and conflict resolution strategies early on in the year so they can rely on these skills when the needs arise. As adults, we must make a myriad of decisions all of the time. These skills must be nurtured from a young age. Allow children to make decisions about the choices they make while problem solving. Choices could be about units of study; about books to read for literature circles, etc.

♥ *Instill Perseverance, Determination, and the Value of Intrinsic Rewards*: Self-motivation is a key component of social-emotional learning, and a necessity for students to learn in order to accomplish what they want in life and to become resilient. While there are many students who naturally strive to better themselves in some way, there are other students who need a little more encouragement in this area. You can talk to students about the ways to experience success and allow them to understand that they must put forward effort and perseverance. In this fast-paced world, it is easy to give up and move onto something else as there are so many options; however, giving up is not helpful. We need to inspire our students to "stick-with-it" so they can learn perseverance. When students keep trying, praise them and encourage them even if they are still struggling. Model your own ways of sticking with experiences. Talk to them about hurdles you have crossed. Let them see there is a way! Encourage all of your students to set goals and/or intentions so that they can feel a sense of accomplishment. At the same time, we want to help them see the possible positive outcomes of their determination, instead of always looking at the negative.

Jackie Eldridge and Denise McLafferty

♥ *Openly Teach Respect*: Respect is something that teachers used to be able to count on from students and parents; unfortunately, that no longer seems to be the case. As a result, teachers must be aware that respect needs to be taught and students need to take responsibility when they are not respectful. It is also the responsibility of teachers to model respect. Children and/or parents do not respect a disrespectful teacher. We must view respect as a life-lesson, something that holds us in good stead in all areas of our lives. There are no bounds to respect. We must learn to respect each other in terms of race, gender, culture, language, sexuality, ability, socio-economic background, etc. We must encourage our students to do the same, and when they slip, we must hold them accountable. When we instill respect in our students, our classroom management challenges disappear, bullying is reduced and the business of learning follows naturally.

It's a good idea to introduce the concept of respect the first day of school in September. Make it an essential component within your classroom expectations/alliance and ensure that students participate in the creation of this invaluable classroom guide. When they have input, they own it and will be more likely to commit to it. One strategy to help students create the classroom expectations/alliance is through the use of a double-t chart. This tool allows them to dissect each of the behavioural expectations and clearly understand what they "look like", "sound like" and "feel like". For example, with respect:

LOOKS LIKE	SOUNDS LIKE	FEELS LIKE
Working together	Appreciations	Safe
Attentive listening	"Please" "Thank you"	Welcoming

♥ *Character Education*: Many boards have implemented character education. which is meant to encourage the development of ethical and responsible students. While it is important to teach your students the importance of good values, honesty, trustworthiness, and taking responsibility for their actions, it is also important that students demonstrate these traits and be accountable. We can give our students many opportunities to develop and hone these skills in the classroom on a daily basis. Provide learning experiences in every subject area where students can examine the values of people they are learning about. For example, have them look at historical figures and decide whether they acted ethically or not; while reading a short story or novel, pause and ask the students to tell you what the character may or may not do.

You can encourage your students to think about ways in which they are contributing to the overall caring culture of their classroom. Have them self-reflect about the ways they are demonstrating and becoming more responsible, honest, and trustworthy. Whenever you see this behaviour enacted, it is an opportunity to show praise and gratitude for their actions.

♥ *Give Students a Voice*: When children are not allowed to share opinions and ideas in safe spaces, they get the feeling that they do not matter. In order to build their emotional intelligence, we want them to share, question and debate many issues, remembering we want them to do so in socially appropriate ways. If they are to develop their self-expression, interpersonal and decision-making skills, they must be able to practise them. Teachers should ask for their students' opinions and allow them to listen to and respect the ideas of others. They need to develop their perspective-taking, so they learn to respect different points of view. We must teach them that we do not have to agree with everyone, but if we disagree, we do so in an agreeable way. When we provide this kind of platform for students, they learn to trust themselves and others, and ultimately, they develop confidence in this area.

♥ *Provide Resiliency Skills*: In education, there is a great deal of research about the importance of resilience and its connection to emotional intelligence. This research also applies to academic success. Students are not afraid to make mistakes when they understand that making mistakes will help them grow. When students are able to bounce back, are mindful of their opinions, and understand their beliefs, they gain a strong sense of who they are and where they can go.

♥ *Encourage a Caring-giving Consciousness and Empathy*: One way to encourage a care-giving consciousness is to openly discuss the importance of caring for others and the need to develop empathy. You can do so by frequently challenging your students to put themselves in the shoes of their classmates. During lessons, you can ask the students to think about what is going through their minds when they are learning about specific literature or historical figures. What are they feeling? You can discuss the importance of developing positive relationships, and how this affects them and their classroom environment.

♥ *Use the Emotional Intelligence Intention Cards*: A companion resource to this book is a deck of emotional intentions cards that can be used to teach the individual components of emotional intelligence. The intentions on the 30 cards in the deck are grounded in the five major components, with two cards for each of the sub-components. There are various creative ways that teachers use the cards. For example, each day, the teacher can pull a card for the class or each child can pull their own. One school chose to include the day's intention in their morning announcements! There can be a brief brainstorming session on how best to work with the designated skills throughout the day. The key with this exercise is to set the students up for success and hold them accountable; for instance, there can be a reflection at the end of the day. The teacher can also model and do a think aloud throughout the day to ensure the students see that the teacher is willing to work on the skills as well.

♥ *Create a Good Deeds (Mitzvah) Jar*: Children can practise doing good deeds. When they do one, write it on a piece of paper and put it in the jar so that these deeds can be acknowledged at the end of the day. An excellent way to introduce the use of the jar is the book, *Have You Filled a Bucket Today*, by Carol McLoud. This book is an amazing resource to share with your students in order to help them understand the value of friendship and looking after each other.

♥ ***Client/Consultant*** (Jeanne Gibbs, 2014): Letter each student off A and B. Have the A's form a line and the B's form a line facing the A's; now each person has a partner they are meeting face-to-face. Partner A will start by telling Partner B a challenge they are having. It could be something to do with school, at home or with their friends. Partner B attentively listens until the teacher gives a signal. Partner B will then paraphrase back what they heard their partner say and if they have all of the details, they will proceed to give a suggestion, idea, or piece of advice. The partners then switch, and Partner A will now attentively listen to Partner B followed by their suggestions. Once the two partners have helped each other, the teacher will have all of the B's take one step to the right, so they now have a new partner. You will now repeat the exact same steps. The new partners share the same problem, getting new advice from their new partner. You can have the line move as many times as necessary.

♥ ***Funeral for Put Downs/Stereotypes*** (Jeanne Gibbs, 2014): This activity is a powerful reminder that put downs and stereotypes are rampant and that we must bring awareness to them in order to eliminate them. Have the students sit together in small groups (3 or 4 students). Provide each group with a blank piece of paper. Ask the students to write down all the put downs or stereotypes they have heard or used themselves. It is helpful if each student uses their own colour pen or marker so that the teacher can check at-a-glance that everyone is participating. They will all be writing at the same time without talking. After a few minutes, the teacher will give the signal and the students will read their contributions aloud using a round-robin format. Once the put downs or stereotypes have been read, the students will go back around and state an intention for how they will work to eliminate these behaviours from their day-to-day interactions. As each one states their intention, they will rip the paper a little bit at a time. When each person has taken a turn, the last person to hold the ripped paper will place it in the "fake" fire or shredder to symbolize their intentions.

♥ ***Inside/Outside Circles:*** Letter each person in the class A or B. All of the A's will form a circle facing the outside and the B's will form a circle facing the inside, each lined up with a partner. If there are odd numbers, create a group of three. You can use this activity in the same way you did for Client-Consultant or you can use it for content review, a mental set or closure to a lesson (see Classroom Resources).

♥ ***Making a Choice:*** Students often have trouble making choices or decisions. It is important to offer them many different situations in order for them to practise the skills involved in making choices/decisions. They need to know that with choice comes responsibility. You can have the students brainstorm together, then prioritize their choices, followed by sticker voting for the final choice. You can also encourage choice through reading and writing where each student is the author of their own choice.

♥ ***On My Back*** (Jeanne Gibbs, 2014): Have each student write their name on a piece of paper and tape it to their back. As you play some upbeat music, students will mill around. When the music stops, they will write an appreciation on each of their classmate's papers. In this activity, you want to make sure the students understand the concept of mutual respect so that only positive, respectful comments are written down.

♥ ***Put Yourself on the Line/Fold the Line/Paraphrase Passport*** (Jeanne Gibbs, 2014): In this activity, you want students to place themselves on a line in response to a prompt from the teacher. Before the prompt is made, the teacher would indicate where the strongly-agree and strongly-disagree ends of the line are. Students would then place themselves on the line related to their feelings re: the prompt. When deciding where to place themselves on the line, students may have to negotiate with other students in order to decide where they will place themselves. Prompt examples, "Put yourself on the line according to whether you believe all students should be allowed to carry cell phones or not." "Put yourself on the line according to whether you are a junk food junkie or a health food fanatic." The students must form the line without clumping, thus the need to negotiate with others about their place. Once the line is formed, you can fold the line or split the line and have them stand in front of a partner to discuss their position. When they meet their partner, they will letter themselves off A and B. Person A will begin by stating their point of view, while Person B attentively listens. When the signal is given Person B will paraphrase what they heard. It might sound something like, "What I heard you say was…" or "The problem for you is…". Each person gets a chance to share and be heard.

♥ ***Snowball Poetry:*** Students will sit in a circle holding an 8x10 piece of paper and a pen. Put a hula hoop or empty box in the centre. Have the students fold the paper into four sections. Each student will write one line of poetry in the top left and then scrunch their paper into a ball. The teacher will call out: "Snowball" and all the students will throw their paper ball at the box/hula hoop. When  the teacher gives the signal, they will take a snowball that is not their own. They will then write a second line of poetry in the top right section. This practice is repeated until all four sections of the paper ball contain a line of poetry. The class can then share their poems or the teacher can create a class anthology.

♥ ***Suggestion Circle*** (Jeanne Gibbs, 2014): This activity is similar to Client-Consultant except the students will sit in a circle and one volunteer will sit in the middle. That person is willing to share a problem or challenge they are having. They proceed to give their explanation while the class attentively listens. Once the details are provided the volunteer will go around the circle and give each classmate an opportunity to ask a question for clarification. Note that during this phase, only clarification is allowed, no suggestions. Once the questions/clarifications have been asked, the volunteer will go back around the circle to receive the suggestions. Once the suggestion is given, the volunteer simply says, "Thank you" and moves to the next person. The teacher/recorder will write down all of the suggestions and give to the volunteer.

♥ ***Teaching Attentive Listening:*** A must-have skill to further develop a care-giving consciousness and empathy is the critical skill of attentive listening. As children become more entrenched in the world of social-media and limited attention spans, their listening skills are diminishing. While brain-research tells us that we can listen "for our age plus two minutes, maxing out at twenty minutes," this time may even be less if children are not taught the skills of attentive listening. Students need to learn how to listen and they need to be held accountable throughout the day. Of course, you as teacher also must model your own attentive listening. This skill should be taught at the beginning of the school year and be one of the expectations in your classroom alliance. In addition, it should be built into lesson plans as a social skill. There are several strategies for teaching listening listed

Jackie Eldridge and Denise McLafferty

in Classroom Resources. One effective strategy that can be used to build all the expectations within the classroom alliance is the double T chart. Have the students first do a think, pair, share about what they think listening "looks like", "sounds like" and "feels like". After they have had the opportunity to discuss, the teacher will ask them to contribute their ideas to a double-t chart. The chart will be posted in the room for the rest of the year so the students can see it and refer back to it when listening is not happening (see Classroom Resources).

LOOKS LIKE	FEELS LIKE	SOUNDS LIKE
Nodding heads	Respectful	"I understand"
Eye contact (if culturally appropriate)	Appreciations	One person talking

♥ **Unfinished Fantasies:** Have the students review or write their own fantasies. They can share with a partner and have them offer support or suggestions on how to make them real.

 # Literature Resources

Picture Books

After the Fall by Dan Santat

Benji, the Bad Day and Me by Sally J. Pla

Have You Filled a Bucket Today by Carol McLoud

How to Be a Good Elephant by Jackie Eldridge and Beth Parker

I'll Root for You and Other Poems by Edward van de Vendel

Life by Cynthia Rylant

Me and My Fear by Francesca Sanna

My Heart is a Compass by Deborah Marcero

My Heart by Corrina Luyken

The Day You Begin by Jacqueline Woodson

The Feeling Flower by Leah Dakroub

The Feelings Book by Todd Parr

The Lying King by Alex Beard

The Name Jar by Yangsook Choi

The Rough Patch by Brian Lies

They All Saw a Cat by Brendan Wenzel

Wallpaper by Thao Lam

What Do You Do When You're Feeling Blue? by Andi Cann

Wings of Change by Franklin Hill

Zen Shorts by Jon J. Muth

Zen Socks by Jon J. Muth

Chapter Books

Dumplin by Julie Murphy

El Deafo by Cece Bell

Ghost by Jason Reynolds

Hatchet by Gary Paulson

Malala's Magic Pencil by Malala Yousafzai

Out of My Mind by Sharon M. Draper

The Outsider's by S.E. Hinton

Speak by Laurie Halse Anderson

The Red Tree by Shaun Tan

Under the Mesquite by Garcia McCall

CHAPTER FIVE

Resilience

What Does the Research Say?

According to Bonnie Benard, a renowned researcher in the area of resilience: "The most powerful and informative studies in human development are those that are longitudinal, that follow individuals from infancy and childhood into adulthood and later adulthood. These prospective long-term human developmental studies serve as the final judge as to what really happens to people over the course of their lives and what really makes a difference in terms of their inner well-being and external life success. Especially instructive to the process of human development and adaptation are the studies that follow what happens to children facing adversity and challenge in their families, schools, and communities".

This line of research, now called resilience research, offers the most compelling evidence that all people have the capacity or human potential for healthy development and successful learning throughout their lives, even when faced with environmental risk. Furthermore, this body of research has identified the human strengths associated with healthy development and successful learning as well as the environmental supports and opportunities that facilitate the development of these strengths.

In this chapter, we explore:

✓   *Resilience theory and practice*

✓   *The strong need to facilitate the development of resilience in today's world*

✓   *The ways resilience can be fostered in classrooms and schools*

What is Resilience Theory?

Resilience is the ability to bounce back in the face of adversity. According to Ann Masten, psychologist, child development researcher, and professor, "Resilience theory is a set of ideas that discuss the impact of challenging events on individuals and families and how well they have adapted to that traumatic experience".

Research surrounding resilience is driven by these questions:

♥ What is the difference for children whose lives are threatened by disadvantage or adversity?

♥ How is it that some children successfully overcome severe life challenges and grow up to lead a competent and well-adjusted life?

Exposure to adverse events can put mental health at risk, but not all people at risk fall prey to the risks associated with trauma. In fact, some people may use their trauma to propel them forward into higher levels of Maslow's hierarchy of needs as they work towards self-actualization.

For 40 years, Masten studied children around the world and how they adapted to challenging circumstances. Over time, Masten discovered several common traits among those considered resilient, and concluded that resilience is a combination of factors such as relationships, family, individual differences and personality. In 2011, she defined "resilience theory" as follows:

The Characteristics of Resiliency

Besides documenting that resilience is innate to all human beings, resilience research has also identified the personal strengths associated with healthy human development. These individual assets do not cause resilience but are the positive developmental outcomes demonstrating that this innate capacity is engaged. Each of these skills are also present in emotionally intelligent people. These strengths fall into four categories:

> **Social Competence or Relationship Skills**
>
> **Problem Solving Skills or Cognitive Skills**
>
> **Autonomy and Self-Awareness or Emotional Awareness**
>
> **Sense of Purpose, a Bright Future and Meaning**

While researchers and writers often use differing names for these personal strengths, this core set of competencies appear to transcend ethnicity, culture, gender, geography, and time (i.e., the writings of Masten & Coatsworth, 1998; Eccles & Gootman, 2002; Snyder & Lopez, 2002; and Werner, 2004).

Social Competence skills are the social, emotional, cognitive, and behavioral skills needed to get along with others. When one is socially competent, we can say they are also emotionally intelligent. In classrooms, social competence leads to inclusion-building and fewer classroom management issues. When a classroom operates from this place, the teacher can get on with the business of teaching because they don't have to worry about conflict and behaviour problems. Social competence, however, becomes one of the biggest challenges for classroom teachers if they do not work on them with their students.

Problem Solving skills are necessary for developing independence. They are required in every career, and in our personal relationships. Without them, children cannot develop resilience. They remain dependent on others to work through problems of any kind. In today's classrooms, we frequently see children who have not honed these skills because their lives are prescribed for them. They are told what to wear, what to eat, what clubs to join, what activities to do. Teachers find this type of student challenging to teach because they tend to be very needy.

Autonomy is a highly valuable skill that allows one to act independently, and with agency. An individual is able to make decisions that allow one to live life in the way that is meaningful for them. When children feel they have autonomy, they don't allow others to bully or manipulate them. They learn ways to stand up for themselves and develop the ability to think for themselves. These skills are especially important with current pressures from peers and social media.

Sense of Purpose and Bright Future is a valuable tool that creates positive thinking and a growth mindset. In our Hearts and Minds Matter training, we ask our participants to watch the Simon Sinek video, *How Great Leaders Inspire Action* because we want them to fully understand their purpose in becoming a teacher. We want them to always go back to their "why", so they do not forget the reasons they became teachers in the first place. When children begin to think about their sense of purpose with a bright future, they also become motivated to strive to make that happen.

Bonnie Benard explains that because of our psychological need for belonging, we seek to relate to and connect with others, and thus, develop our social competence/relationship strength. Our psychological need to feel competent drives us to develop our cognitive problem solving skills. This need to feel competent, combined with the psychological need to feel autonomous, lead us to seek people and opportunities that allow us to experience a sense of our own power and accomplishment (our mastery motivational system), sense of autonomy and self-awareness. Our safety motivation system includes the need to avoid pain and maintain physical survival—that drives us to develop not only problem solving but also social competence, sense of purpose, bright future, and autonomy.

When we help students develop their emotional intelligence, we are simultaneously assisting them in working towards resilience. These are extremely important traits. In our work with teacher candidates, we frequently refer to Benard's work as it relates to solid classroom practice. Benard also describes various protective factors that affect one's resilience:

Caring relationships that convey compassion, understanding, respect, interest, listening and a safe environment. These relationships assist children in getting their need for love and belonging met. Nel Noddings, a leader in the ethics of care theory, states, "It is obvious that children will work harder and do things for people they love and trust".

High expectations must be conveyed to children in order for them to have a standard to which they can aspire. If the expectations are too low, the children only reach for the lowest bar unless they are internally motivated to reach higher.

Teachers with high expectations convey the message: they believe in their students and they unconditionally support them in their quest. These teachers positively view their students and encourage them to view themselves in the same way. Instead of having a deficit mindset, students are encouraged to have a growth mindset.

Opportunities for Meaningful Participation and Contribution may take the form of afterschool clubs and sports teams, or inclusive activities within the classroom. Once again, they are opportunities for children to feel like they have influence in their classroom through a range of responsibilities, and involvement in problem solving and decision-making. It is also important that children feel like their voices are heard and respected. According to educator Alfie Kohn, "It is in classrooms and families where participation is valued above adult control that students have the chance to learn self-control. The power of participation to affect these individual outcomes clearly speaks to our deep human need to belong and have some power and control over our lives."

Fostering Resilience: Families, Communities and Schools

In order to develop resilience, it is important that children are included in environments that foster such hardiness. The natural places for this support are families, communities, and schools. When children can find safety in these places, they can develop their personal strengths. Families are the obvious first choice. They can be loving and nurturing, and parents can be good role models; however, not every family has the capacity to give the child what is needed. Some children come from dysfunctional families which are challenging and can teach the wrong kinds of behaviour. This can disrupt the journey towards resilience.

However, the research on resilience is clear. When children have a place to go, that is, community, it may not be necessary for them to have a strong family life. This makes communities valuable places to assist children. These places may include churches, clubs, sports teams, cultural centres, etc. In a video shown during the professional development program known as Tribes, there is a quote from an adolescent that sums up what the power of community means:

> "You can walk around trouble when you have
> somewhere to walk to and someone to walk with."

Schools are the third valuable place where children can learn the skills leading to resilience. The Ministry of Education for Ontario refers to the school environment as the "third teacher". Teachers play an indispensable role with all children in this regard. However, the opposite can be true if teachers do not understand the power of the safe place. If they are constantly yelling, unable to manage the class, or unpredictable and distant, children do not want to be there. When schools are safe places that give children a sense of belonging, where they can predict what their days will be like and where they feel safe and protected, a child's chances of becoming resilient are greatly increased. For this reason, school has a powerful role. It's also a good reminder to teachers as to the reasons they entered the profession.

As we have discovered with Maslow's hierarchy of needs, brain-compatible learning, and emotional intelligence, we do not have to add anything else to our already full plates. It is simply about creating a caring and inclusive classroom environment and making use of effective instructional strategies and classroom management. One important lesson for teachers to understand is that our sphere of influence only extends so far. We cannot "fix" children. When children are really struggling and unable to cope, there are other, more qualified professionals who have expertise designed to help children and families. It is perfectly okay for us to ask for help. We can, however, offer our students the protective factors of **caring relationships, high expectations, and opportunities for meaningful participation and opportunities** (see Classroom Resources).

Context, Connectedness and Modelling

Long term studies of successful human development in high risk contexts as well as of successful schools in urban settings, teaches us that it is not *what* we do but *how* we do it that counts. In other words, context matters more than content, process more than program. Michael Resnick, professor at the University of Minnesota School of Medicine, conducted a fascinating study based on surveys of ninety thousand students from grades seven through twelve at one hundred and forty-five schools, interviews with twenty thousand students and their parents, and surveys with one hundred and thirty school administrators. The study found: "Parent/family connectedness and perceived school connectedness were protective against every health risk behaviour measure (except history of pregnancy)".

The three protective factors outlined above, are critically central to what create this sense of connectedness. They are precisely how humans (not just children) meet their basic needs for safety, love and belonging, power, accomplishment, and ultimately for meaning. No matter what subject matter we teach, nor, for that matter, what official role we play in a young person's life (teacher, parent, neighbor, youth worker, etc.), we can do it in a caring and empowering way, and at no extra cost! It is clearly what we model that makes the final difference. When we fully embrace the needs of our students, the research on the brain, emotional intelligence, and resilience, we can and will make a difference. Social learning theorists tell us that most of our learning comes from the modeling around us. Our students will learn empathy, respect, the wise use of power, self-control and responsibility when:

- ♥ We are caring and respectful

- ♥ We help our students discover and use their strengths

- ♥ We give them ongoing responsibilities as active decision-makers

Moreover, when we ourselves model this emotionally intelligent behavior, we are creating a classroom climate in which caring, respect, and responsibility are the behavioral norms. Schools and classrooms have made a difference in the lives of students. Creating these safe havens means building inclusive communities through relationships and responsibilities that invite our disconnected and disempowered young people back to a promising future. Just as teachers can create a nurturing classroom climate, administrators can create the nurturing school environment that supports teachers' resilience: caring relationships with colleagues; positive beliefs, expectations, and trust on the part of the administration; and the ongoing opportunities and time to reflect, dialogue, and make decisions together. A wise administrator once remarked, "If you don't feed the teachers, they'll eat the students".

McLaughlin and Talbert, who have studied learning communities for many years, showed that supporting teachers by providing them the time and opportunity to work collegially, and thus build a sense of professional community, is the critical variable in both sustaining school change efforts and raising students' academic scores. Just as students need the structure of the small group process to reflect and dialogue in relationship to ideas and to each other, so do teachers. Resilience research clearly tells us that when you care and believe in our most precious resource, our students, you are not only enabling their healthy development and successful learning, you are, indeed, "creating inside-out social change and building the compassionate and creative citizenry that will be critical to the 21st century"!

What Does it Look Like in the Classroom?

- ♥ *Loving Support:* Children need to feel unconditional love and support when they are at school. They need to know they matter to the teachers, other students, and the administration. In essence, students need to know you will provide them with their basic human needs and emotional safety. While some students may not behave in the ways we would like them to, they need to know we still love them…we simply do not like their behaviour at that moment in time.

♥ **Mutual Respect**: We want to foster a sense of mutual respect in our classrooms and schools. In other words, we will respect the children and we will earn their respect in return. Respect needs to be explicitly taught and everyone needs to be held accountable. When respect is disregarded, we need to call our students (and ourselves) to task. Mutual respect should be one of the first things taught in our classrooms as the year begins. As previously mentioned, one way to teach mutual respect is to have the students brainstorm what it means, discuss it and then contribute to a double t chart that will remain visible throughout the year. It is important to note that the alliance is fluid and can be modified as the year progresses. If something happens in the classroom that is in violation of the expectations established, use this teachable moment to modify and adjust in consultation with the students.

♥ **Compassion**: Compassionate teachers do not judge. They are aware that each student is an individual with their own unique life experiences and therefore, all of them need to be treated with compassion regardless of personality, behaviour or needs. These teachers do not take behaviours personally and they are not offended when students have unexpected demands. In fact, compassion means that teachers are aware that there may be something going on beneath the surface and they are patient as they wait for the turmoil to pass. Trauma-informed practice (Chapter Six) is an important concept to understand when cultivating compassion. In particular, students need to know they are listened to; their feelings are validated; the teacher is interested in them; and they are treated as a whole child. In this classroom, children know they matter! Keeping compassion in the forefront of our teaching allows us to make it visible.

♥ **Challenge Students with Supportive Messages**: We can never stop challenging our students. They need to know that we have high expectations for them, and that we are always going to support them. We are going to "hold their hands" when needed and we are always going to give them wings to help them fly. These messages are important to students as they show we care.

♥ **Provide a Roadmap for Success**: Make success criteria and curriculum expectations an integral part of the learning environment. Engage students in conversation/dialogue about what the learning looks like and how they can achieve success. We must be explicit in our expectations by giving them a road map of where they need to end up to achieve the outcomes. We can use success criteria, rubrics, exemplars, and samples of high-quality work. We can chunk their learning, giving them feedback throughout the process. We can motivate our students through engaging lessons and effective instructional strategies.

♥ **Growth Mindset**: The work of Carol Dweck on growth mindset emphasizes the importance of helping children develop a growth vs a fixed mindset. It is about focusing on strengths instead of deficits. Fixed mindsets often keep children stuck in believing they cannot do certain things, whereas a growth mindset will open them up to see the possibilities. The language that children use to describe themselves or that we use to describe them can be very limiting. We want to encourage them to believe in themselves. We must help them re-frame negative thinking

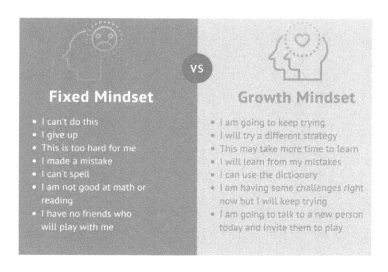

and help them see they each have strengths. They need to know we will support them with their challenges and mirror back their negative self-talk to see another perspective. As a teacher, you have a huge impact if you model a growth mindset and positive self-talk.

♥ **Be Open About the Possibilities and Paths to Resilience**: Teachers can provide a gateway to helping children realize their personal power and abilities to overcome obstacles. We can scaffold ways for them to think differently about and construct alternative meanings to their lives. We want children to understand that:

  ♥ They are not responsible for the adversity in their lives. If they are children of an alcoholic, we want them to know they did not cause the drinking. If a parent is incarcerated, we want them to see that it was the parent who made the decision to break the law and not them.

  ♥ Adversity is not permanent. They can find ways to see a bright future because, "This too shall pass".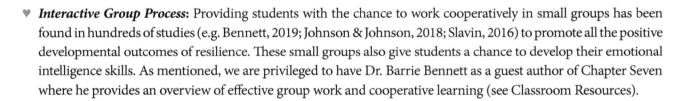

  ♥ They can problem-solve to "rise above" their situation and find other ways to live.

  ♥ They can change their own self-talk of "I am not good enough, smart enough, pretty enough, strong enough". We can model and teach them to always speak about themselves from a growth mindset. They can develop a positive self-image through affirmation, perseverance, and finding people they can associate with who will support them.

♥ **Interactive Group Process**: Providing students with the chance to work cooperatively in small groups has been found in hundreds of studies (e.g. Bennett, 2019; Johnson & Johnson, 2018; Slavin, 2016) to promote all the positive developmental outcomes of resilience. These small groups also give students a chance to develop their emotional intelligence skills. As mentioned, we are privileged to have Dr. Barrie Bennett as a guest author of Chapter Seven where he provides an overview of effective group work and cooperative learning (see Classroom Resources).

♥ **Reflection, Dialogue, and Critical Thinking**: When asked by researchers, young people continually say they want safe places for honest and open reflection and dialogue around issues salient to them, especially those related to challenging topics. Teachers are well positioned to provide this space for their students, especially when they know their conversations will be held in confidence and the space is safe and judgement-free. It is critical to note, however, that teachers are bound by law to report any form of abuse. If a student discloses, ensure the child feels protected, but they must know about your duty to report so they are not surprised when the police or children's aid come to their home. You can explain that you love and care for them, you will be there for them, but, in this case, you are required to make the call. You can reassure them that you will continue to offer support throughout the process.

♥ **Giving Responsibilities**: Children who are given responsibilities are more inclined to develop resilience than those who are not expected to contribute. Taking ownership and responsibility is also a key component to developing a strong emotional intelligence.

♥ **Creative Expression**: Providing children with opportunities for creative expression can facilitate higher-order thinking, problem solving and a movement towards self-actualization. When young people have the opportunity to express their imagination, to tell their story; to connect their inner experience and feelings to their outer world, it is a powerful protective factor. Storytelling, creative writing, painting, drawing, video production, drama, dance, and music, can facilitate healing and potentially prevent negative outcomes because we are providing students with positive channels for expressing themselves.

♥ **Service**: Many secondary schools have included service as part of the core requirements for graduation. When students have opportunities to help others, to give back to the community and to participate in meaningful social justice activities, they develop a sense of social responsibility which helps develop empathy and resilience. The 2019 Climate Action Strike is a great example of how students around the world organized peaceful marches and demonstrations to let the world know they would no longer sit back and watch the environment deteriorate. Other possible service opportunities might include peer tutoring, community service, service learning, cross-age mentoring, visits to seniors' homes, working at food banks and volunteering for charitable organizations.

♥ **Finding a Sense of Purpose**: There are many examples of crises or tragedies that children become aware of through media and simply talking with friends. When these experiences happen, either in the classroom, school or elsewhere in the world, teachers can help students find a sense of purpose that can help them move forward. The first steps would be to have individual, small group, or classroom discussions so that students have opportunities to express their feelings and ask questions. These dialogues are important so students feel supported while teachers clarify any misinformation that may be spreading. A next step might be to invite the class to brainstorm ways to assist those in need. Some examples are fund-raising activities, writing individual or class letters of support, donating time at a local community agency or creating public service announcements.

♥ **Build Strong Social Networks**: We are social beings and have a need to be connected. Children who feel disconnected are at high risk for substance abuse and suicide. All of us need people in our lives with whom we feel connected and can share our feelings. Encourage students to build their social network so they can find peers with whom they can confide.

♥ **Zones of Regulation**: The Zones of Regulation are widely used in elementary classrooms, especially in the primary division. This strategy supports the development of self-regulation in children. Feelings and levels of energy are divided into four colours: red, blue, yellow, and green. Using this tool will help children accept that feelings and the expression of emotions are natural. It also helps them to develop the skills necessary to move to a different zone when needed. While mostly used in early primary, this practice should not be limited to this division. Children of

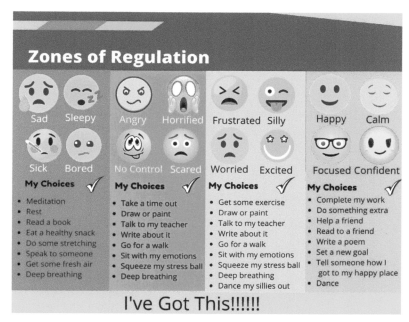

all ages experience challenges with self-regulation and bringing the zones into all grades would benefit every student. The graphic can be altered to meet the needs at each grade level.

♥ *Teach Critical Thinking Skills: Media and Social Media:* It is challenging to limit student access to media, as it is such an important part of their lives. Instead, we need to help them view media and social media through a critical lens, so they learn how to manage the overwhelming information and messaging. Provide examples of the positive side of media and also the destructive potential of this medium.

♥ *Be Aware of Cyberbullying:* According to Public Safety Canada cyberbullying is: Sending mean or threatening messages by email, text or on a social networking page

   ♥ Spreading embarrassing rumours, secrets, or gossip about another person through these sites

   ♥ Taking an embarrassing picture or video of someone and posting to a social media site

   ♥ Posting online stories, pictures, jokes, or cartoons that are intended to embarrass or humiliate

   ♥ Hacking someone's email account and sending hurtful content to others while pretending to be them

   ♥ Using someone else's password to get into their social networking account and post material as them

   ♥ Tricking someone to open up and share personal information and then sharing that information widely

   ♥ Creating online polls and rating people in negative, mean ways

   ♥ In online gaming, repeatedly harming a player's character, or using personal information to make direct threats

♥ *Essential Things to Know About Cyberbullying:*

   ♥ Harassing messages, posts and photos can be distributed quickly to a very wide audience, including strangers, and can be extremely difficult to delete once they've been sent or posted

   ♥ Because cyberbullying happens online, bullies may not witness first-hand the pain they're causing, making it easier for them to continue and even increase the intensity of their attacks

   ♥ Many teens and children have no idea that by sharing messages they've received, "liking" a post or passing it on, they become part of the problem. This behaviour instantly spreads the humiliation and harm far and wide

   ♥ Paying close attention to our students and to the challenges that could befall them is important for teachers. We can provide them with resilient skills to overcome these challenges

♥ *Cyberbullying Facts:*

   ♥ 8% of Canadian teens have been victims of online bullying on social networking sites

   ♥ 35 % of Canadian teens have seen mean/inappropriate comments about someone they know

   ♥ 14 % of Canadian teens have seen mean/inappropriate comments about themselves on social networks

   ♥ 18% of Canadian parents have a child who has experienced cyberbullying

   ♥ 31 % know a child in their community who has experienced cyberbullying

   ♥ 90 % of Canadians would support a law that would make it illegal to use any electronic means to coerce, intimidate, harass, or cause other substantial emotional distress.

Social Competence Tactics

Cooperation

I will cooperate with my friends and family!

Jackie Eldridge and Beth Parker

♥ **Broken Telephone:** This activity is designed to emphasize the challenges of listening attentively. It is a good idea to play with this strategy a couple of times before teaching attentive listening. Once they have learned what listening "looks like", "sounds like" and "feels like", then play the game again. Have the children sit/ stand in a circle. The teacher creates a message (one or two sentences long) and whispers it in the ear of the first child. That person then turns to the next person and repeats exactly what they think they heard. The message is passed to everyone and the final recipient says the message out loud. As the teacher, observe the children as it is possible to see where the message breaks down.

♥ **Bumper Stickers:** Each child will receive a slip of paper and will create a message/quote that identifies what they believe, who they are or what is important to them. Students can also decorate their bumper stickers. When they are finished, use milling to music to have the students show their ideas and talk to a partner about why they used that phrase. Repeat milling to music at least five to six times, so that students get to share their sticker with several others.

♥ **Four Corners:** As a teacher, you can use this activity for any content you need to cover. The students will go to a corner that best describes how they are thinking or feeling. You might have them choose a corner that has a rating scale (agree, strongly agree, disagree, strongly disagree). It might be used to have them think about a character/historical figure they are most like. It could also be used with metaphors. For example, when you are new to a group are you most like drums, trumpet, flute, piano or lion, fox, dove or a deer. When they get to their corner, they will discuss why they chose that spot. It is important to pay attention to how many people are at each corner as you do not want an overly large group. The groups should be no more than 4 or 5. If there are more students, divide the group to make smaller numbers. Once they have had a chance to discuss, choose a person to present on behalf of the others. For example, the person born the farthest/closest to the location where you are, or the person with a birthday closest to that day. Then give the group a few moments to make sure that person knows what to say. That person then becomes the spokesperson for the group. (Also discussed in Chapter Seven)

♥ **"I" Messages:** "I" messages are a valuable communication and conflict resolution tool that you would introduce to your students at the beginning of the year. This strategy is used to help them resolve conflicts with others. To introduce "I" messages, teach the students about feelings and ensure they are able to identify them verbally. There are many great literature and video resources available in this area. When introducing the format for "I" messages, post this chart in the classroom and ensure that students use it when dealing with conflict.

I feel <u>ADD A FEELING</u> when <u>ADD THE BEHAVIOUR OR ACTION.</u>

For example, "I feel angry when my things are taken without me being asked first". "I feel sad when I am left alone at recess." It is important to note that the sentence cannot include the person's name or the word "you", as this may cause them to respond defensively. The sentence must remain neutral.

♥ **People Hunt:** Create a chart of topics relevant to your students' interests/experiences. Each student moves around and asks people about the descriptors. For example, someone who likes ice cream, would put their initials or their name in that box. The expectation is to get a different signature for each item. In this way, students are encouraged to speak with as many of their peers as there are ideas on the chart. This ensures they talk to other students in the class, instead of just their friends. One variation to this activity is to have the students create the different topics.

Likes Ice Cream	Loves School	Doesn't like broccoli
Always wears a helmet on a bike	Collects something	Loves to swim
Has a pet	Wants a pet	Loves weekends

♥ **Please and Thank You:** This game is like Simon Says except the direction must include "Please". Once the action is done, the leader says, "Thank you". For example, "Please jump on one foot", versus "Jump on one foot".

♥ **Round Robin Storytelling:** Have students stand/sit in a circle. Use a talking stick (see below) to ensure the speaker is identified. The teacher will start the story and then pass the talking stick to the person on the right. Once the person has the stick, they will continue the story. The talking stick is passed from person-to-person until the story is finished. It is important to note that no one can speak unless they have the talking stick.

♥ **Treasure Hunt:** This fun and engaging activity can be easily tied to any curriculum content as the students hunt for various treasures. It can also be done inside or outside of the classroom. In order to solve the treasure hunt, the students must work cooperatively as a team. It is a good idea to have the students plan ahead and then reflect afterwards about their cooperation. It is also fun to add an element where the students must ask others for help in order to find the treasure. This component requires students to demonstrate appropriate social competence skills like manners, appropriate questioning, body language and problem solving.

♥ **Talking Stick:** A "talking stick" is an invaluable tool in a classroom when you want to teach your students about turn-taking and attentive listening. Grounded in Indigenous tradition, the talking stick is used to identify the person speaking. Traditionally the talking stick was an eagle feather, but you can use whatever object you like. The object is passed around the circle or the classroom and no one speaks unless they are in possession of the object. It is important to note that when children speak out-of-turn that you hold them accountable.

Autonomy

Independence

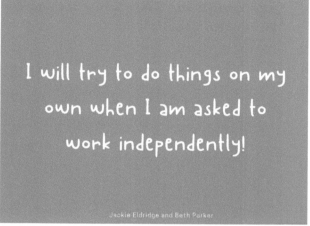

I will try to do things on my own when I am asked to work independently!

Jackie Eldridge and Beth Parker

♥ *Contracts:* Contracts are part of our world and children can learn that they may have to sign contracts when they are adults. Having this experience in school can prepare them for this reality. We can have children sign contracts for behaviour, work completion, collaborative skills, etc. You can create your own contract based on your needs and the needs of the children. It might also be helpful to ask parents to be a witness to the contract, so they are fully aware of classroom expectations. The use of contracts encourages students to be autonomous and responsible.

♥ *Checklists:* A checklist is a way to keep students on track and provides an opportunity to assess the students' work. The checklist can be developed by you or co-constructed with students to give them a sense of responsibility and autonomy. It also provides them with voice in your class that encourages increased participation (see Classroom Resources).

♥ *Intentions:* The setting of intentions is a tool for students to take ownership of where they are headed and how they are going to get there. Encourage students to set their intentions daily or weekly. To ensure clarity, model for them.

♥ *My Strengths are…:* Young people need to talk about their strengths in order to fully believe them, however, many people are uncomfortable talking about these qualities. We do not want our students to become braggarts, instead we want them to know their strengths and to understand they can build on these areas for continual self-improvement. You can provide them with a chart or organizer using whatever descriptors resonate with you and the students.

I am good at...	My strength is...
I know...	My strongest quality is...

♥ ***Ask Three, Then Me:*** Some students require additional attention and asking questions of the teacher is one example. This strategy reduces their dependence on you. The rule requires that they must ask three other students first before they ask the teacher. When this rule is in place, children are more likely to become independent.

♥ ***Retell, Relate, Reflect*** (Susan Schwartz and Mindy Pollishuke, 2019): This reflection tool allows children to reflect on their own learning and make deeper connections to their experiences. It is a skill that can be applied to any curriculum area at any time during the day or week. The following is adapted from *Creating the Dynamic Classroom.*

Retell the Story/Content:

Some sample starting phrases are: This story is about...; It happened...; I noticed that...; I liked the part when...; I especially liked it when...; In this piece...; You mean to say that...

Relate:

Some sample starting phrases are: This story reminds me of...; I remember when...; It makes me think of...; It makes me feel that...; That happened to me, too, when...; When I was younger...; That situation is just like...; This is different from...; This compares to...; It sounds like...

Reflect:

In this section you might: wonder about the cause and effect of an experience; think of another way to deal with an experience; question in order to search out more information; make predictions about what might happen next; make inferences and draw conclusions; explore and share insights; want to investigate further and/or explore other related topics

---

♥ ***Roles and Responsibilities:*** More and more we see children in school who do not have a sense of responsibility and yet this skill is important in helping them develop resilience and emotional intelligence. We want to encourage students to be responsible and to feel like they have ownership of their learning and their classroom. When we assign roles and responsibilities to the students, they will want to participate, take pride and work together to make the classroom an effective learning environment.

♥ ***Self-assessment:*** As part of the curriculum expectations in many school boards, students are asked to self-assess; however, it is not something that comes naturally to students. We must provide them with direction in this area, and we must model and provide them with templates or organizers to help them along the way. There are many examples of self-assessment that can be found on-line and you can create your own templates to suit your needs. The following are some prompts that will be useful for students.

> ♥ One thing I learned; One thing I did well; One thing I still need to work on.
>
> ♥ My strongest area is... My challenge is...
>
> ♥ Use a rating scale using different icons

♥ **Talking/Question "Chips":** The use of talking/question "chips" will help build autonomy by providing boundaries for how many contributions the children can make or how many questions they may ask. The idea is that each child will have a certain number of "chips" (e.g., poker chips, marbles, stickers) and they either must provide that number of comments or they are limited to that number of comments or questions. Some children are reluctant to speak and need encouragement while others want to take over the conversation or they ask too many questions. The use of talking chips is especially effective in group work.

♥ **Two Stars and a Wish:** Like self-assessment is required, peer-assessment is also utilized in many schools. We cannot expect our students to know how to peer-assess if we do not teach them and model what it looks like. We want to ensure our students are practising mutual respect for each other before we give them this responsibility. Providing a framework like two stars and a wish focuses student thinking. The students will express two things they liked about their partner's work and one thing they would like to see for next time. Teachers can also use this idea in their feedback.

Problem Solving

Stick With It

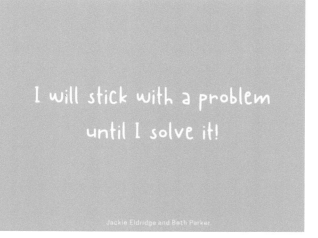
I will stick with a problem until I solve it!

Jackie Eldridge and Beth Parker

♥ **Amazing Race:** This activity is fun and engaging and celebrates teamwork and problem solving. The students will work in pairs or teams to solve clues along the way until they get to the end. The teacher will hide clues around the school or in the classroom and each team must solve a clue, complete a task, or answer questions before they move to the next part. The race is timed and the first group to complete the whole race wins.

♥ ***Brainstorming, Prioritizing, Consensus-building:*** Students will sit together in a small group (no more than 4 people) and brainstorm their ideas. One person will act as the recorder. It is important to encourage the students to write as many ideas as possible. Jeanne Gibbs (2014) uses the following acronym for brainstorming that helps students to focus:

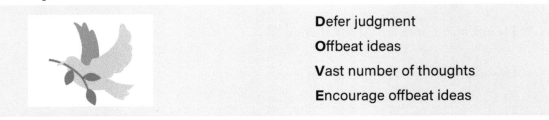

Defer judgment

Offbeat ideas

Vast number of thoughts

Encourage offbeat ideas

Once the students have as many ideas as possible, the teacher will encourage dialogue among the students to allow them to prioritize their top ones. Provide each group with three index cards. The children must select their top three ideas and write each on a card. Following this step, the class then come to consensus on the top choice. This activity provides several life skills that will help the students with problem solving and decision-making.

♥ ***Dream Quilt*** (Jeanne Gibbs, 2014): In small groups or as a whole class, the students will design a quilt square that represents the topic of choice. They will discuss the final product in advance so there is cohesion within the quilt images.

♥ ***Examine Both Sides:*** Teaching the students to look at both sides of an issue or problem provides them with critical thinking skills and helps them to explore different perspectives. Using this skill, students can apply it to all content areas. It is helpful to provide students with a graphic organizer to organize their thoughts (see Classroom Resources).

SIDE A or CHARACTER A	SIDE B or CHARACTER B	MY CONCLUSION WITH EVIDENCE

♥ ***Kitchen Kapers*** (Jeanne Gibbs, 2014): In groups of 3 or 4, students will use the materials provided to invent a brand-new kitchen utensil. Once the groups are finished, they must create an ad campaign to sell the idea to their classmates. The materials are placed in a business-sized envelope and include: two 3x5 index cards, two paper clips, four toothpicks, one pencil. The groups have 12 minutes for their design. Each team member must contribute to the design and be able to explain what role they played. They must also reflect on their process to understand how well they worked together, what they learned and how they can improve their collaboration.

♥ ***Mr. Green Jeans*** (Joanne Meyers): This game is fun and it challenges thinking at the same time. The teacher will start by saying, "Mr. Green Jeans is going on a vacation. In his suitcase he is taking…" The clues are given and when the rule is understood, they respond by giving an example that fits that rule. You will keep playing until quite a few students have the idea. After several children have responded, have a student give the rule. For example, "Mr. Green Jeans is going on a vacation and he is bringing jello, apples, cherries, Skittles, umbrella, bottle". Appropriate responses might be, "kittens, berries, bells". The reason these answers are correct is because the rule is that all items have a double consonant.

♥ **PMI:** Plus, Minus Interesting. This tool is a way of helping children to make decisions. It involves critical thinking and problem solving. Provide the students with the organizer and they will determine what was a good idea or decision (plus), what may not have been a good decision or something that won't work (minus) and what was interesting and can be considered because it is a balance of the plus and minus. It is helpful to have the students brainstorm as many ideas as possible (see Classroom Resources).

PLUS	MINUS	INTERESTING

♥ **Re-frame Game:** Making a game out of learning is highly motivating for students. In this game, provide the students with a perspective or use literature to guide you. The students must look at the perspective and re-frame it to something else. A good example is the story of *The Three Little Pigs* where the wolf is seen as bad and yet in *The True Story of the Three Little Pigs*, we see a different perspective.

♥ **Spaghetti/Marshmallow Challenge:** In small groups (no more than 4) the students will problem-solve to build the biggest free-standing structure using only the materials provided. The materials are: one metre of masking tape, 25 sticks of spaghetti and one marshmallow. Each group has 20 minutes. The team must collaborate, they cannot use any other materials, they can stick masking tape to the table, the spaghetti can be broken into smaller pieces, the marshmallow must remain intact and be placed at the top of the structure. After the structures have been measured, the students should reflect on the skills they used, what worked and what didn't and what they would do differently the next time.

♥ **Two on a Crayon** (Jeanne Gibbs, 2014): Have the students sit with a partner. They have one sheet of paper and one crayon between them. The idea is to lean into each other's energy and work cooperatively to draw one picture. The pairs will hold the one crayon and when one person is ready, they will start to draw. Give each pair five minutes. When the activity is complete, you will have them reflect on the process, similar to the spaghetti/marshmallow challenge.

♥ **Values Line:** This activity is similar to "put yourself on the line" where the students will stand in a line that demonstrates their values about a topic. They must decide about where they stand in relation to others' ideas. Once they get to the line, they will chat with their classmates to negotiate where exactly they fit. You can then fold or split the line and have them talk about their reasoning behind the spot they chose. In this case, they will attentively listen to each other's ideas and then you can do the line again to see if they choose another spot after listening to someone else (see Classroom Resources).

Optimism (Sense of a Bright Future)

♥ **Goal Setting:** Goal setting provides the students with a target to reach. It can be done individually or as a class. Goal setting can include school, personal, relationship goals. It can include any time frame that you deem necessary. It is wise to revisit the goals periodically to recalibrate if needed. You can use the "life map" strategy as a visual to help the students visualize where they are headed.

♥ **Gratitude Journal:** This type of journal helps students to see what they have to be thankful for instead of focusing on the negative and things they perceive they don't have. It can be done daily or once per week. Have the students write spontaneously or provide a template.

> Today I am grateful for: _____
>
> When I think about _____ it makes me feel_____.

♥ **Mental Vacation:** We can all use a little break from time-to-time and this visualization activity provides that time. Have the children sit/lie down in a comfortable location and close their eyes. It is helpful to have some soft music playing. Guide them in an ideal vacation or have them visualize on their own through your prompts. For example, imagine where you are, how you got there, what you see and smell, what you are doing, what you are eating. If you have highly visual learners in the class, they can also draw or paint.

♥ **Wishful Thinking:** Put the students sit in a community circle. Using a Magic Wand as a talking stick, have the students share their wishes. As each child holds the wand, they will say, "I wish…". After each child has shared, have them reflect on the wishes and offer suggestions for how to achieve them or simply draw attention to what they may have in common. Remember to model the kind of sharing you want the children to do.

♥ **My Future Self:** All children have hopes and dream for the future. In this activity, have the students write a letter to their future self, describing what they are like, what they are doing, where they are living, what they needed to do to get there, etc. The letter can be put in a time capsule to be opened at the end of the year or can be put away somewhere safe to be read at a much later time in their lives.

♥ **Something Good** (Jeanne Gibbs, 2014): Much like "wishful thinking", "something good" involves a talking stick and the community circle. It is a great idea to use a small world globe as the talking stick. You will start the circle by holding the globe and saying, "Something good in my world is…". After each child has spoken, you can reflect in the same way you did with 'wishful thinking'.

♥ **Swish, Swish, Make a Wish:** Using the rhyme, children stand in a circle and make a wish. You can also use a talking stick here. The child will say: "Swish, swish, make a wish, I would like to have…". Then the community imitates the sprinkling of fairy dust on the speaker. The speaker responds, "Thank you!" and then passes the talking stick to the next person.

♥ **Time Capsule:** This activity can be done individually or as a class. The children will gather up items that they may need for the next grade, or that they value, or things that symbolize who they are. They could also make respectful predictions about their classmates. At the end of the year, the contents of the Time Capsule are revealed.

♥ **Trust Walk:** This activity can be done in the classroom, gym, or schoolyard. It is done in partners with one of them blindfolded. The partner who can see, guides the other around by the hand or the shoulder reassuring them the whole time so that trust is developed. After a period of time, they will switch roles. It is important to have the students ask permission to touch each other. Children of trauma may be uncomfortable with touch.

♥ **Vision Board:** These are a popular way to encourage people in goal setting and understanding ways to achieve those goals. Each child will have: a sheet of bristol board, old magazines, crayons markers, etc. They will gather or create pictures that represent their hopes and dreams as they create the images. They can also use words. It is a good idea to have them brainstorm ideas before they commit to gluing them on their vision board. The boards can be displayed in the classroom or the students can bring them home and place them in a central location. The more the students visualize their goals, the more likely they are to attain them.

 Literature Resources

Picture Books

A Perfectly Messed Up Story by Patrick McDonnell

Ada Twist by Andrea Beaty and David Roberts

Emmanuel's Dream: The True Story of Ofosu Yeboah by Laurie Ann Thompson and Sean Qualls

Harry Potter by J.K. Rowling

Ish by Peter H. Reynolds

Otis by Loren Long

Pete the Cat by E. Litwin

Rosie Revere, Engineer by Andrea Beaty and David Roberts

She Persisted by Chelsea Clinton and Alexandra Boiger

She Persisted Around the World by Chelsea Clinton and Alexandra Boiger

Sad the Dog by Sandy Fussell and Tull Suwannakit

The Dot by Peter H. Reynolds

The Most Magnificent Thing by Ashley Spires

The Girl Who Lost Her Smile by Karim Alrawi

The Paper Bag Princess by Robert Munsch

You Are Awesome: Find Your Confidence and Dare to be Brilliant at (Almost Anything) by Matthew Syed

Chapter Books

A Long Pitch Home by Natalie Dias Lorenzi

Beverly, Right Here by Kate DiCamillo

Front Desk by Kelly Yang

Genesis Begins Again by Alicia D. Williams

Harry Potter by J.K. Rowling

Holes by Louis Sachar

I, Cosmo by Carlie Sorosiak

Stanley Will Probably Be Fine by Sally J. Pla

CHAPTER SIX

Trauma-Informed Practice

This chapter is based on Dr. Jackie Eldridge's research that has spanned the past two decades. It is also grounded in her own experience as a child of trauma.

In this chapter, we explore:

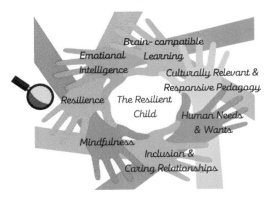

✓ *The importance of understanding trauma-informed practice*

✓ *The incidence of trauma*

✓ *Stories of experience*

✓ *The role of the teacher in trauma-informed practice*

What Does the Research Say?

According to the 2013 Encyclopedia of Social Work, the origin of the term, trauma-informed care, has evolved over thirty years and is now filtering into a range of settings, from mental health and substance-abuse treatment providers to child welfare systems, and even schools and criminal justice institutions. In the simplest terms, the concept of trauma-informed care is straightforward. If professionals were to pause and consider the role trauma and lingering traumatic stress plays in the lives of the specific client population served by an individual, professional, organization, or an entire system, how would they behave differently? What steps would they take to avoid, or at least minimize, adding new stress or inadvertently reminding their clients of their past traumas? How can they better help their traumatized clients heal? In effect, by looking at how the entire system is organized and services are delivered through a "trauma lens", what should be done differently? The answer can be used to guide practice, policy, procedures, and even how the physical caregiving environment is structured.

I was first introduced to the concept by Dr. Deborah Sinclair, a social worker who worked for many years with women who have experienced intimate partner violence. I was immediately intrigued by the power of this method. I saw direct connections to education and the ways teachers create safe places for their students. As the Encyclopedia of Social Work indicates:

> Long before anyone used the term "trauma-informed care", caring professionals and committed volunteers were instinctively acting in a trauma-informed manner. Much of this was influenced by the emergence of the feminist movement and the increasingly influential voice of survivors of interpersonal trauma, as seen in the rape crisis centers and the domestic violence movements of the 1970s (Burgess & Holmstrom, 1974) and the dramatic growth of child-advocacy centers and multidisciplinary teams in child abuse in the 1980s. These natural incubators for trauma-informed innovation and practice were "married" in the 1990s with the growing body of science and trauma-specific empirical research into how human beings respond in the aftermath of traumatic events, and how professionals and concerned activists could help them move toward recovery.

Jackie Eldridge and Denise McLafferty

My original research in the mid-nineties focused on caring teachers. I explored this concept long before I had ever heard the term trauma-informed care. After researching these practices, I now bring this concept into my work as a teacher educator because I know how important it is for teachers to understand the prevalence of trauma and the ways they can help students with whom they work on a daily basis.

As can be seen from the definition of trauma-informed practice, there is no magic formula that must be learned or understood. In 2018, Edutopia conducted a Twitter chat engaging teachers on the topic of trauma-informed care and social-emotional learning (SEL). They discovered that, "Participants asserted that trauma-informed care and SEL practices benefit all children, building critical skills like self-awareness, self-regulation, empathy, and an openness to teamwork and cooperation". They recommend adopting a "universal approach", assuming *all* children are trauma affected and need social and emotional learning instruction and support. In other words, these practices will help to build the emotional intelligence and resilience of all children.

Afterall, what child does not need to learn these skills?

The answer is that every child needs the skills, even those who have never experienced trauma. We can take that claim a step further by emphasizing the world-wide need to have more people who are emotionally intelligent, so that collectively we can build a stronger global community. In today's schools, we are seeing more children who experience mild to severe mental health challenges. It is not uncommon to encounter students as young as four years old who are experiencing anxiety, depression, and more severe behavioural concerns like oppositional defiant disorder. A 2018 Pew Research Center survey of thirteen to seventeen-year-old children found that seven in ten teens experience anxiety and depression. The same survey found that six in ten children feel pressure to get good grades while nearly three in ten are burdened as they try to look good and fit in socially.

Social and emotional learning is a process for teaching children how to manage these challenging emotions, make decisions, and work with others. In 2019, Engoo Daily News reported on a 2018 survey of over five hundred U.S.

school districts that ninety percent of district leaders had already brought in SEL programs and activities or planned to do so over the 2019-2020 school year.

The importance of building strong social-emotional skills is no longer something we might consider an add-on to teaching curriculum content. It is now becoming a crucial part of what students must learn in order to develop into healthy and resilient adults. While this content is necessary for all children, it is even more important for children of trauma so they can learn that the trauma was not their fault and that, with the right skills, they can become resilient, leading healthy and fulfilling lives beyond the ones in which they were born. When teachers are aware of the factors and skills of resilience, they can include them in their day-to-day interactions with students, thereby helping them to move beyond their potential barriers.

In Chapter Five, we explored the meaning and research on resilience and the work of Bonnie Benard. When I first encountered Benard's research, I examined my own experience and realized that while I did not have a strong family model, I mostly had caring school experiences and I was part of a strong community outside of my home. I also had all four attributes that helped me become a resilient adult. Growing up in the family that I did, I had to be autonomous or I could not have survived. I often had to fend for myself and I had to be able to do things on my own because there were times when neither of my parents were capable of looking after me. I had to take control over my life because, in many ways, I was the parent in the family. I had to problem-solve different ways of doing things because I did not always have the guidance of an adult to help me.

I also learned early on that I could associate with others to guide me. While I never asked for help, I always knew it would be provided to me from extended family, friends, and my teachers. With this attribute, came the development of social competence as I frequently sought positive relationships with both adults and peers. I also believe that my sense of purpose was defined early in my development. I was ashamed of my life and knew that I did not want to repeat that cycle. Instead I watched my teachers and I believed that one day I could help others like they helped me.

The following two stories are excerpts from my doctoral dissertation that is an autobiography/biography and includes: my own experiences; the story of two of my teachers (Hope Kohara, my grade seven teacher, and Neil Harris, my grade eight teacher); a classroom teacher; and, a student and her parents. The first story is fictional yet rooted in accounts I have seen and heard over many years as a teacher.

The Unsafe Place

It is Friday again. Most of my classmates are rushing out the door smiling, cheering, and clamouring to get home, "See you Monday. Have a good weekend!" they yell as they brush past me. My friends are off to put their school week to rest so that they can play, have some fun or just watch television. I often wonder where their parents will be taking them this weekend. I watch them admiringly as they disappear into the distance. They seem to have it all. But me, I'm tired, lonely, and consumed by the trepidation which exists in my bones. It is there with me as I shuffle through my so-called life.

Jackie Eldridge and Denise McLafferty

I guess I should go home, although my inner voice is beckoning me to run. The voice is not very loud because it has no idea what it really means to run. It is just something I heard on t.v. once when I watched a show about a kid whose life mirrored mine. But where did she end up? On the street? She was filthy dirty, exhausted, and hungry. I don't think I can do that yet. I am too young, too scared. But I feel like I have nowhere to turn. There is no one who will understand if I do try to tell them my innermost secrets. I am also ashamed. My dad drinks too much and when he does, he always yells at my mom and me. She doesn't do anything. She just sits in the chair with her head down crying. Me, I am filled with rage, but I can't fight back because I am just a stupid girl. At least that's what my dad says. He says all women are stupid. Sometimes I am confused by this because I usually get good marks in school, but he must be right because my mom doesn't say anything to correct him. I can't yell back at him because if I do, he'll be furious and start throwing things around. I am frightened. I don't want to make him mad because when he's mad, he drinks and sometimes he hits my mom. I can't take that chance because it probably is my fault that he drinks. I just sit there and listen, and I try to push the confusing thoughts away.

I try to imagine a place in my mind where I might like to be. This place is a "safe place". It is a place where people understand me, where they smile at me, where they care for me. It is not a place where they will judge me if they did happen to find out about my secret. I can't take that chance though. I can't tell them because if they know my secret, they won't like me anymore. They have to like me. It's really all I have, although sometimes it is hard for me to make them like me. I am always watching. I watch my dad to see what it is that I do wrong to make him drink and hit my mom. I watch my teacher to try to find out why she yells at us. I think I am being quiet and doing my work but still she yells. Sometimes she sounds like my dad. Her face turns red and she slams the metre stick on the desk. It sounds like my dad's fist when he hits the walls or when he hits my mom too hard. Sometimes my teacher sends kids to the corner to face the wall. I don't like it when that happens because they always seem so embarrassed and all of the other kids tease them. I don't tease them because I know how they feel.

Oh well. I guess I'll go home. Everyone else seems to be gone. I walk slowly because I have to carefully check the streets to make sure my dad is not staggering up one of them. I stop at the corner store owned by a kind couple, named George and Maria. I buy a custard square and sit in the park to eat before I have to walk the final block. I put the key in the lock and call out, hoping to hear my mom call back. If she does, it means everything will be ok. If she doesn't, I brace myself for what is to come. When I go in, my mom is laying on the couch in the dark. She's sick again. She hasn't been feeling well for a few days. I ask her what's wrong and she says it's her nerves. I suppose I'll have to cook supper tonight because my mom can never cook when her nerves are bad.

As the evening wears on, I suddenly realize that it's late and my dad is not home yet. My stomach starts to churn as I feel that sinking feeling coming over me. I wonder if he will be home or if he is off on another binge. I fall asleep on the couch and wake up in the middle of the night. I didn't hear my dad come in, so I saunter into my room. When I wake up the next morning, I make myself breakfast and watch television. The rest of the day passes much like any other day. My life seems so useless. I look outside to see the kids and their friends running up the street or playing in the park, but I can't go because I have to stay home with my mom when her nerves are bad.

On Sunday, we have dinner and I go into my room to get some rest. As I lie in bed, I suddenly hear the key scratching on the door. It's him. He's back and the scratching noise means he's too drunk to find the keyhole. My mind races and my stomach becomes hard like a rock. I can't move. I am immobilized, frozen in my bed, listening, waiting. The door finally opens and he comes in staggering, swaying, bumping into the table and knocking over the lamp. A long series of ugly, vulgar cuss words fill the room and I am filled with shame once again. What if the neighbours hear him? What if they saw him staggering up the street? What if he had been in a fight and his face was all bashed in like it was the last time? What can I do? I feel so helpless.

"Helen, where the hell is my supper? What's the matter with you? All you women are alike, you're all so goddamned stupid!"

"Get out here and give me my supper!" There's no sound, no movement, no response. I hear him weave his way up the hall to her bedroom.

Jackie Eldridge and Denise McLafferty

"Get out of bed. Get me my supper!"

"I can't. I'm sick. Get your own supper."

I cringe when I hear this hostile exchange because I know what's coming. I try to get up to make supper, but I am too late. I hear the sudden smack, the lightning quick blow to the body which makes me want to throw up every time I experience it. My heart is pounding. I know I won't sleep very well tonight but I have to because if I don't, I won't be able to stand the pain I am feeling deep within my soul. Suddenly, I hear a thud as my dad misses the bed and hits the floor where he will likely stay until he is sober.

When I get up in the morning, I tiptoe around. I stop and see my mother's silhouette in the shadows. I turn on the light to see the aftermath of the night before. I look at the clock. I want to help but I can't. What can I do? I'm a kid. I have to go to school.

"I'll be all right," she says. "Just go to school and don't worry about me. He won't get up for a while. I 'll be fine. But please come home right after school in case I need you."

I hurry out the door, running up the street so I am not late. My heart beats faster as I trip and my books scatter all over the street. I bend over to pick them up as I hear the school bell ringing in the distance. A lump forms in my throat and I want to cry because I am going to be late for the third time this month. I head for the main office bracing myself for the school secretary who I know will yell at me, telling me that I am always late and I should be smarter than that. I slowly take the late slip and head for my class. I'm not in any hurry because I can hear my teacher from the hallway. "What do you mean you forgot your homework? How many times have I told you? What is the matter with you? I hear the class laughing and I can well imagine that someone is being ridiculed for some reason or other. My head begins to pound.

Here I am back at school on Monday morning and things are no different here than they are at home. The only difference is that my teacher isn't drunk. I doubt if she would hit any of us, but I know she doesn't like us. It's just like at home when she yells though because no one can say anything to her. If they do it will be worse for them. Just before I get to the door, I hear her yell.

"Who is that sneezing? What are you doing at school if you have such a bad cold? Your mother should have kept you home!"

As I walk in the door, I feel her steely stare. Her eyes are like daggers as they pierce through me. I am thankful that she doesn't say anything directly to me, but she makes the whole class sit silently while I go to my desk. I try not to make any noise as I slide sheepishly into my seat. I start my day listening to the lesson but soon my mind begins to wander as I visualize my dad and mom at home alone together. I wonder if everything will be all right when I get home. My mind fades in and out during the day. I am frequently jolted back to reality when I hear the sound of my teacher's voice humiliating another student for talking while they are supposed to be doing their work.

Sometimes I am afraid in this class because I don't know what is expected of me. Sometimes I am afraid to put up my hand when I know the answer because I am stupid, and I don't want anyone else to find out. Sometimes I am so tired that I just want to put my head down on my desk and fall asleep. Sometimes I just want to cry. I struggle through the day and when the bell rings I have mixed emotions. I don't really want to stay here because I don't feel very safe, but I am afraid to go home. Maybe one day I will run away, or maybe one day I will find that "safe place" that right now I can only imagine.

The events of these peoples' stories when fused together paint a chilling and disheartening view of the education landscape. They also reflect the view of Dr. Barbara Muscak, Director of Social Work at the Hospital for Sick Children: Often aware of their own inability to meet teacher expectations, students frequently feel defective. For many, spontaneity is replaced by self-consciousness, curiosity by trepidation, and joy of mastery by fear of failure. Further, this gradual, painful, and costly strangulation of the child's life force does not cease when they exit the classroom. Indeed, it may be a spectre which frequently haunts them and permeates outside activities.

Sadly, this story is the social narrative of many children who are invisible to those who work with them every day. One can only imagine the catastrophic effects that the culmination of the events of this story might have on this child's life.

For me, it is not difficult to envision the educational future of someone like this young girl who feels so alone, so fearful, and so much in need of care. From my own vantage point, I see a need to understand this experience and bring its devastating effects to the fore. I am driven, in many ways, to expose this segment of the educational landscape, not because I want to accuse individual teachers, but because I recognize this narrative's threatening presence and I understand the aftermath.

Psychologist Lestor Havens explains, "the truth cannot make us free unless we are strong enough to face it". As teachers, we must gather our strength and collectively work together to empower each other and, ultimately, our students. In a narrative study, OISE professor Mary Beattie alludes to a "web of relationships" that emphasize an ethic of nurturance, responsibility and care. Beattie suggests that "this way of knowing emphasizes connection over separation, collaboration over competition, and understanding and acceptance over judgement and evaluation". Through my stories and others like them, I hope that teachers will be able to recognize the "unsafe place". I further trust that this acknowledgement will turn the tables so that these teachers can create a "safe place", a place where children are nurtured, accepted, understood, and cared for. As I wrote the "Unsafe Place" story, I was emotionally drawn into it because of the nature of this child's experience. Her story is my story. I was that invisible child. I am reasonably sure that most of my teachers did not know about my home life as was evident by Hope and Neil's testimony in my interviews with them. I feel safe in saying that I did manage to keep my "secret story" just that—a well-hidden enigmatic story which was veiled in the mask of my public life.

My story is not unlike some of the children in todays' classrooms; however, my story veers from the composite because of the teachers I was fortunate to have. Neil and Hope gave me a "safe place". They cared for me and unconsciously protected me from the social narrative that could easily have become part of my story. Like the child in this previous story, there were many times when I thought about running away, and like that little girl, I, too, was afraid. Luckily, I had a "safe place "where I could journey to each day. No one really needed to know about my private life; no one needed to do anything catalytic to change it. They just needed to care.

The following story is also a composite based on facts I included from the interviews I conducted with Hope Kohara and Neil Harris. It is a glimpse at the "safe place", a place where this young girl might find the emotional security she so desperately craves and deserves because, after all, she is a human being and she needs to be cared for (Noddings, 1984).

The Safe Place

It is Friday again. Most of my classmates are rushing out the door smiling, cheering, and clamouring to get home. "See you Monday. Have a good weekend!" they yell as they brush past me. My friends are off to put their school week to rest so that they can play, have some fun or just relax while watching some television. I often wonder where their parents will be taking them this weekend. I watch them admiringly as they disappear into the distance. They seem to have it all.

I hold back. I don't want to leave this place. I love it here. I feel like this is my home. I will miss my teachers, Miss Kohara and Mr. Harris, and I will miss my friends. I feel safe here. Everything is predictable. I can count on them.

Miss Kohara says, "It is important to welcome students and to let them know that I am going to accept them."

Miss Kohara nurtures us. Sometimes she says she "mothers"' us too much. I don't think that is possible. I like her mothering. It makes me feel safe and loved. Mr. Harris says kids need a place where they "want to be, where they feel comfortable". It should be a "safe place" where they get positive reinforcement, good feedback, encouragement, love and plenty of learning opportunities."

At home, things are not like here. My dad drinks too much and when he does, he always yells at my mom and me. She doesn't do anything. She just sits in the chair with her head down crying. Me, I am filled with rage, but I can't fight back because I am just a stupid girl. At least that's what my dad says. He says all women are stupid. Sometimes I am confused by this because I usually get good marks in school. Both of my teachers tell me I'm a good student. They praise my efforts and encourage me. But my dad must be right because my mom doesn't say anything to correct him. I can't yell back at him because if I do, he'll be furious and start throwing things around. I am frightened. I don't want to make him mad because when he's angry he drinks and sometimes he hits my mom. I can't take that chance because it probably is my fault that he drinks. I just sit there and listen, and I try to push the confusing thoughts away.

I try to visualize that place in my mind where I long to be. This place is my "safe place." It is my school, a place where people understand me, where they smile at me, where they care for me. It doesn't matter if they know my secret. They probably don't need to know because they like me for the person I am. At home, I am always watching. I watch my dad to see what it is that I do wrong to make him drink and hit my mom. I don't have to watch my teachers though; they are kind and compassionate. They understand all of us. They seem to know when something is bothering us and they give us a caring look. That look melts the ice in my veins, the ice that threatens to harden me to life's injustices. Sometimes Miss Kohara asks students to stay in for a while, just to talk. She says she finds it "amazing what kids will tell you when you have them on a one-on-one." Sometimes kids will tell you important things that are bothering them (Interview notes, March 1994). She says she wants to know as much about us as she can so that she can help us. Lots of times she tells us stories about when she was

Jackie Eldridge and Denise McLafferty

in school. She says she used to have trouble reading. I think she tells us these stories to inspire us. She wants us to know that if we work hard, we will be successful. I think she genuinely cares about us and how we will do in the future.

Another thing I like about my teachers is the fact that they don't scream at us or humiliate us like some teachers do. They always accept us. They try hard to understand us and they are sensitive and warm. Miss Kohara's smile is infectious. Our class is harmonious and we all feel like we are part of her family. It is almost as if she knows how we feel. It's as if she puts herself in our shoes. I am not the only one who likes being in her class. We all feel the same way. We like Mr. Harris too. He makes learning fun. He gives us different ways of doing our work to keep us interested. We really had fun when he turned the cafeteria and the portables into learning centres so we could explore and experiment with new ideas. Both Miss Kohara and Mr. Harris seem conscious of caring for us and we, in turn, care for them and strive to do our best.

Unfortunately, it's Friday. I guess I have to go home. Everyone else seems to be gone. I walk slowly because I have to carefully check the streets to make sure my dad is not staggering up one of them. I stop at the corner store owned by a kind couple, named George and Maria. I buy a custard square and sit in the park to eat before I have to walk the final block. I put the key in the lock and call out, hoping to hear my mom call back. If she does, it means everything will be ok. If she doesn't, I brace myself for what is to come. When I go in my mom is lying on the couch in the dark. She's sick again. She hasn't been feeling well for a few days. I ask her what's wrong and she says it's her nerves. I suppose I'll have to cook supper tonight because my mom can never cook when her nerves are bad. As the evening wears on I suddenly realize that it's late and my dad has not come home yet. My stomach starts to churn as I feel that sinking feeling coming over me.

I wonder if he will be home or if he is off on another binge. I fall asleep on the couch and wake up in the middle of the night. I didn't hear my dad come in, so I saunter into my room. When I wake up the next morning, I make myself breakfast and watch some more television. The day passes much like any other day. However, I am not going to dwell on my life at this point. My life has purpose. I have hopes and dreams. Miss Kohara and Mr. Harris always talk about the future and the possibilities that life holds for us. Miss Kohara encourages us to believe in ourselves, to give ourselves credit. She reminds us to find our strengths and to understand our weaknesses so that we can overcome them. I would love to be a teacher like her someday. On Sunday, we have dinner and I go into my room to try to get myself ready for Monday. I love Mondays. Mondays are safe.

As I lie in bed, I suddenly hear the key scratching on the door. It's him. He's back and the scratching noise means he's too drunk to find the keyhole. My mind races and my stomach becomes hard like a rock. I can't move. I am immobilized, frozen in my bed, listening, waiting. The door finally opens, and he comes in staggering, swaying, bumping into the table and knocking over the lamp. A long series of ugly, vulgar cuss words fill the room and I am filled with shame, but I block the sounds out as I retreat to the "safe place" in my mind.

"Helen, where the hell is my supper? What's the matter with you? All you women are alike, you're all so goddamned stupid! Get out here and give me my supper!" There's no sound, no movement, no response. I hear him weave his way up the hall to her bedroom. "Get out of bed, get me my supper!"

"I can't, I'm sick. Get your own supper."

I cringe when I hear this hostile exchange because I know what's coming. I try to get up to make supper, but I am too late. I hear the sudden smack, the lightning quick blow to the body which makes me want to throw up every time I experience it. My heart is pounding. I know I won't sleep well tonight but it will be all right tomorrow. I drift off to sleep, blocking out the pain I am feeling deep within my soul. This feeling is replaced by the warmth I feel as I visualize my classroom and my teachers.

When I get up in the morning, I tiptoe around. I stop and see my mother's silhouette in the shadows. I turn on the light to see the aftermath of the night before. I stop and comfort her, telling her it will be all right. I kiss her gently on the cheek as I look at the clock. I know I will be a little bit late, but I know my teacher will understand. I haven't been late too often. I hurry out of the door. As I am running up the street, I feel my body relax, the strain of a weekend at home subsides. I have left the tension behind at my house where the storm may await me when

I get back. Somehow though, I am able to face that storm after a day at school because I always get so much strength from my teachers. They don't even know what they give me on a daily basis. Maybe someday I will be able to repay them. For now, all I can do is try my best each day. I know they will appreciate that.

Sometimes my mind fades in and out during the day but I am gently brought back from the prisons in my mind by Miss Kohara's soft persuasion. I am never afraid to put up my hand in the class because Miss Kohara is never critical. She makes us feel good about our attempts whether they are right or wrong. She encourages us. I think she genuinely likes us.

Mr. Harris always listens to us. He says, "People want to be happy and cared for. If I notice that a child is unhappy, I always try to talk to them, to get to the bottom of it because it is better to get it out in the open than to hold it back. If it is the classroom that is making them unhappy then I would want to change it."

I struggle to hang on to my school days. When the bell rings at the end of the day, I feel a sense of sadness because, for now, I will have to leave my "safe place" behind.

As the story, *The Safe Place,* suggests, teachers can offer caring and support, positive expectations, and ongoing opportunities for participation without consciously knowing they are helping to build resilience in their students. Just imagine what can happen when they do understand and consciously build these protective factors into their everyday interactions with their students! Likewise, teachers can teach and model emotional intelligence simply through the strategies they use to teach content and the ways they interact with their students. When a teacher understands emotional intelligence, and they have a strong EQ themselves, they have the skills to reach all children. They are able to empathize with children who are trauma-affected, thereby creating safe spaces for them.

Also imagine how important it is for children of trauma to have someone they see every single day have empathy for them; someone who actively and compassionately listens to them and has unconditional positive regard for them. Imagine a classroom where the teacher understands their own feelings, can manage their emotions, self-regulate and model that for students without losing control and yelling, or humiliating them on a regular basis. This teacher is one who can manage the class and can get down to the business of teaching content. It is not to say that the emotionally intelligent teacher won't need help from time-to-time, especially with children who have mental health issues or severe learning challenges. It is simply that the emotionally intelligent teacher can problem-solve and understand the importance of asking for help.

As teachers begin to make connections between the needs of their students and their own needs and trauma-informed practice, they begin to fully comprehend the importance of such approaches. They begin to see that we all can and will make a difference. Sharon Salzberg, a renowned spiritual and meditation teacher, explains that,

"When we see the relatedness of ourselves to the universe, that we do not live as isolated entities, untouched by what is going on around us, not affecting what is going on around us, when we see through that, that we are inter-related, then we can see that to protect others is to protect ourselves, and to protect ourselves is to protect others."

Most teachers are familiar with the African Proverb, "It takes a village to raise a child", and so, it does. Together we can build that village for all children, no matter where they are coming from or where they have been.

What Does it Look Like in the Classroom?

♥ **Teach Emotional Intelligence:** The more opportunities children have to develop their EQ, the better they will be able to identify, understand, express and accept their feelings. They will also be able to understand that what happened to them is not their fault. In addition, they learn assertiveness and interpersonal relationship skills that will help them develop a community of support.

♥ **Build Inclusion:** Part of the experience of trauma means that children do not always feel like they fit in. Sometimes they feel different from others because of the nature of their experience. Use the strategies throughout this book to ensure that you are continually building inclusion and community in your class. When children of trauma know they have a friend and a community, it helps them feel safe.

♥ **Model the Expression of Feelings:** It is often the case that children of trauma are not good at expressing their feelings. It could be that they have been conditioned not to show emotion or they are fearful that letting their feelings out will somehow expose them. When teachers model their own expression of feelings, it gives students a glimpse at what that experience can be like and they will see that it is perfectly all right to express emotion.

♥ **Use Quality Literature to Teach:** There is a vast selection of books that explore various forms of trauma and the expression of emotion. Including this literature in regular story time, units of study, or simply putting them in your classroom library will go a long way to providing great resources for children to explore with you or on their own.

♥ **Inside Out** (Disney, 2015): This Disney Pixar movie is a wonderful resource for all children, whether they have experienced trauma or not. The story line demonstrates and validates emotion. It can be used as part of a unit on emotion, self-regulation, etc.

♥ **Teach Emotional Regulation:** There are many children in today's classrooms who do not have strong self-regulation skills. When they feel strong emotion, they do not always know what to do with the feeling and they can get confused. Instead of self-regulating, children can explode in anger, be overcome with fear and anxiety, or suffer with deep sadness. We must support them through the teaching of self-regulating strategies and provide them with the opportunities to practise. Many teachers use the Zones of Self-Regulation to help students with this task. (See Chapter Five)

♥ ***Teach Growth Mindset***: Some children of trauma have a fixed mindset because of the severe nature of their experience or they have not had the opportunity to develop their emotional intelligence to the point where they can see a bright future and believe in themselves. (See Chapter Five)

♥ ***Daily Movement***: For many people, trauma gets stored in the body and if there is no mind/body awareness, the trauma can be perceived as illness. Incorporating daily movement in the classroom can give children a physical outlet to reduce the effects of trauma. Mindful movement or yoga is an excellent way to build activity and brain breaks into the day.

♥ ***Mindfulness***: Trauma is often associated with a mind that is cluttered as it races from one thought or emotion to another. Children do not have the skills to learn to slow that "monkey mind" down. We can teach them the skills through daily mindfulness practices. These exercises include helping children to make a mind/body connection. In other words, we can assist them in noticing where they feel thoughts and/or emotion in their bodies. Several valuable practices are found in Chapter Eight.

♥ ***Using Art as a Form of Expression***: Art therapy is a powerful tool used to help children express their emotions and to get at the core of what their trauma is and how it has affected them. There is a caution here; teachers are not art therapists and so using art must be limited to the expression of emotion. If a child were to become anxious or to disclose an experience of abuse, the teacher must be prepared to seek professional help (see Classroom Resources).

♥ ***Use Music and Dance***: Being able to release emotion through the arts is well known in research. Music and dance can trigger emotion, allowing a student to express feelings that have long been buried. These art forms can also elicit memories so the child can begin the process of tapping into experiences that have not been resolved. However, there is a caution that must be explained when a child is triggered into remembering painful memories or emotions. Teachers are teachers, and even though they wear many hats during the day, they are not trained therapists, psychologists, or social workers. As such, they must seek help from a skilled professional if anything in the classroom adversely affects the child.

When children are expressing strong emotion without being able to self-regulate, resulting in chronic mis-behaviour in the classroom, they could be sending you a message—they are hurting. If your attempts at trying to nurture them or create a safe place for them are not working, they may need more support and additional help from a mental health professional.

Some Additional Tactics

♥ **Dear Abby:** You can encourage students to write a letter to you or a fictitious person describing challenges or difficult emotions they are having. Ensure that they know that no one else is going to read the letter. Remember, if a child makes an abuse disclosure, you will have to make a report to the Children's Aid and your principal.

♥ **Five Tribbles** (Jeanne Gibbs, 2014): This tool has many uses from allowing students to express emotion to having them tell you how well they understand a concept. The students will hold up the image that best represents how they are feeling. The slips of paper can also be coloured and laminated for continued use.

♥ **Imaginary Pen Pals:** Sometimes it is easier for children to express themselves to someone/something they do not know. They can write to an imaginary pen pal sharing how they feel.

♥ **Matching Feelings:** Whenever we work with feelings, it is important to do some pre-teaching as not everyone understands their feelings or are comfortable expressing them. There are many great books available that address feelings. It is also a good idea to have some real-life images of people showing different feelings, so the students have a point of reference. Create a game with faces expressing a variety of emotions and a list of different feelings that the students can match.

♥ **My Sphere of Influence:** The work of Stephen Covey is seminal in understanding what we can and cannot do regarding our sphere of influence. For example, I may not be able to influence someone who is bullying me, but I can choose to avoid their social media feed. I may not be able to change the way my parent talks to me, but I can choose to ignore their words and know that I am a good person.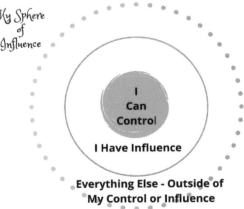

♥ **Paint Centre:** The opportunity to express oneself artistically is a wonderful way to allow children to express their feelings. Unfortunately, many teachers abandon creative centres beyond the early primary years. Instead of limiting this opportunity, have a permanent paint centre set up where students can paint when they need to express themselves or offer it as a choice in an assignment.

♥ **Sand and Water Tables:** The sense of touch is grounding for all people and nature is the perfect way to ground, especially when anxiety is high. Like the paint centres, sensory tables are often missing beyond early primary classrooms. Think about creating this space in your classroom as a place for students to go if they need a chance to ground themselves to calm down.

♥ **Wheel of Choices:** Sometimes children are emotionally highjacked or frustrated and they cannot decide what to do. The Wheel of Choices gives them ideas. When they are upset, they can look at the wheel and decide about what they will do. For example, "I can walk away", use an "I" message or ask the person to stop. It is important for students to make their own decision and not always rely on adults to solve the problems.

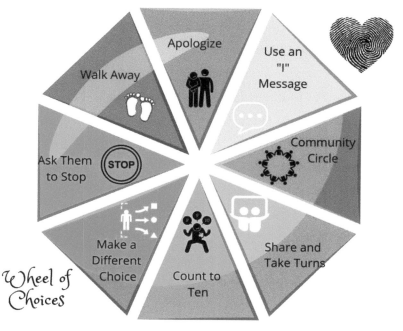

♥ **Zap:** Have the students stand in a circle. As the leader, you can let the students know what they are "Zapping". For example, we are going to zap the bad weather away, or 'put downs' away or negative thoughts, etc. You can also let the students choose. The children rub their hands back and forth together and on the count of five they sweep both hands to the centre as they say, "Zap". You can zap things away and you can also zap positive energy if someone needs it!

Literature Resources

Picture Books

A Terrible Thing Happened by Margaret Holmes, Sasha Mudlaff and Cary Pillo

Always and Forever by Alan Durant

Bubble Gum Brain by Julia Cook

Come with Me by Holly McGhee

David and the Worry Beast by Anne Marie Guanci

Dead Bird by Margaret Brown Wise

Good People Everywhere by Lynea Gillen

How Hattie Hated Kindness by Margo Sunderland and Nicky Armstrong

I Can Handle It by Laurie Wright

I Don't Want to Talk About It by Jeanie Franz Ransom

Is a Worry Worrying You? By Ferida Wolff and Harriet May Savitz

Maybe Tomorrow? By Charlotte Agell

Most People by Michael Leannah and Jennifer E. Morris

My Day is Ruined by Bryan Smith

My Family is Changing by Pat Thomas

Once I Was Very Very Scared by Chandra Ghosh Ippen

Speranza's Sweater by Marcy Pusey

Standing on my Own Two Feet by Tamara Schmitz

The Rabbit Listened by Cori Doerrfeld

The Worry Glasses by Donalisa Helsley

What Do You Do with a Problem? By Kobi Yamada

When Mommy Got Hurt by Ilene Lee, Kathy Sylwester and Carol Deach

When Sadness is at Your Door by Eva Eland

Wilma Jean the Worry Machine by Julia Cook

Chapter Books

Bridge to Terabithia by Katherine Paterson

Easter Ann Peters' Operation Cool by Jody Lamb

Hannah's Suitcase by Karen Levine

Stargirl by Jerry Spinelli

The Diary of a Young Girl by Anne Frank

The Glass Castle by Jeannette Walls

The Bread Winner by Deborah Ellis

The Kite Runner by Khaled Hosseini

The Lost Boy by Dave Pelzer

CHAPTER SEVEN

Effective Group Work and the Connections to Inclusion, the Brain, Emotional Intelligence and Resilience

By Dr. Barrie Bennett
Professor Emeritus: Ontario Institute for Studies in Education

In this chapter, we are privileged to welcome Dr. Barrie Bennett as our guest author.
Dr. Bennett is one of the world's leading experts in the area
of cooperative learning and effective group work.

In this chapter, Dr. Bennett explores:

✓ *The heart and mind connection*

✓ *Levels of cooperative learning*

✓ *Group structures*

✓ *Essential attributes of effective group work*

✓ *Nine types of positive interdependence*

✓ *Ways to invoke safety*

✓ *Framing questions, wait time and thinking skills*

The first educational book I wrote, with two other colleagues, was titled, *Cooperative Learning: Where Heart Meets Mind*. The next book I wrote with a colleague focused on classroom management, *Classroom Management: A Thinking and Caring Approach*. You can see how the idea of "mind" and "heart" merge with the same key themes in each work—as effective teachers, we must focus on both; and then, do more.

This idea of heart and mind and "interacting socially" is not just an educationalist's idea. I was in the doctor's office recently and the information on the wall argued the importance of how talk impacts the brain, and how it impacts learning. Neurologists argue that talk is critical for intellectual growth. Educationalists and thinkers from the last century, B.F. Skinner, Jean Piaget, and Lev Vygotsky, all argued that learning was socially constructed. Each of them valued the power of social learning.

As mentioned in Chapter Four of this text, most job ads in the industrialized world state that the job positions require a person who is a good communicator, highly skilled interpersonally, someone who can work with all stakeholders, and someone who can work as part of a team. Essentially, employers are looking for future employees with strong emotional intelligence. Again, you can see how thinking and interacting with others is so important.

In this chapter, I simply provide an overview of the complexity of cooperative learning, which is one of three basic options to learning. The other two are working individually (individualistic) and working competitively (competitive).

Personally, as I go through life, I find it essential that I continue to develop the skills for engaging in any of those three options (cooperative, individualistic, competitive). I'm guessing that most of us have had moments where we are not that excited about the idea of competition. That said, keep in mind that competition, and the conflict and change that typically comes with competition, is not, by default, good or bad. The determining factors are more aligned to how we choose to deal with them.

From my experience in teaching over almost fifty years, cooperative learning is no different: when done correctly, this belief system is highly effective; when done incorrectly, it is one of the worst approaches in the design of learning environments. Thinking individualistically, if a lecturer stops every five to seven minutes, and has the students quickly discuss the key issue presented (Think, Pair, Share), the exam results almost double in comparison to the class who only listens. So, working alone can be "good" or "bad" (effective or ineffective). Teachers choose.

By the end of this chapter, I hope you have a deeper appreciation of the idea of learning cooperatively and all the intricacies that make it work. I also hope you value the work of a variety of educators in the area of cooperative learning. I've found that merging their voices is critical; there is no one answer or solution.

The Three Levels of Cooperative Learning

In this diagram, I provide an advanced organizer for this chapter and for how I understand the complexity of cooperative learning. There are three levels, somewhat like an old-fashioned wedding cake with the large layer at the base holding up the other two. We'll start with level three and work our way through the attributes of effective group work (level two), and then, building inclusion and safety into the classroom (level one). Creating the safe classroom

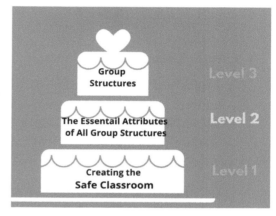

is foundational to all this work. If this piece is not in place, then not much else can be effectively implemented. I've provided a few sample rubrics throughout that you might use to reflect on your own application of some of the key ideas connected to effective cooperative work in each of the three levels.

Level Three: Small Group Structures

Level three refers to the variety of ways groups can be structured. In his 1985 book, *Cooperative Learning Structures*, Spencer Kagan lists around one hundred different structures, making his work the most prolific in this area. Below is a list of ten common structures (from least to most complex). Beside each structure is the last name of the person who designed it.

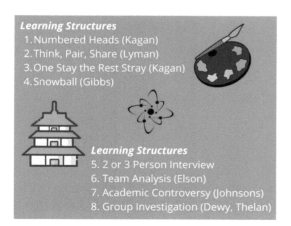

Learning Structures
1. Numbered Heads (Kagan)
2. Think, Pair, Share (Lyman)
3. One Stay the Rest Stray (Kagan)
4. Snowball (Gibbs)

Learning Structures
5. 2 or 3 Person Interview
6. Team Analysis (Elson)
7. Academic Controversy (Johnsons)
8. Group Investigation (Dewy, Thelan)

Think of the range of structures as the colours of paint on an artist's palette. This is a crucial way to differentiate one's instruction in the design of learning environments.

The complexity issue is a key factor to consider when it comes to assessing students' learning. Usually, the more complex the structure, the higher the effect size. Keep in mind that the 'five basic elements' (a focus of this chapter) is also a complex structure. The difference is that the 'five basic elements' connect to, and enhance, the application of the other group structures.

Note that, from my experience, a key consideration comes when applying small group structures. This is when you would be wise to integrate with most structures the Johnsons' 'five basic elements' and the *Hearts and Minds Matter* process. These two areas of inquiry increase the chances the small-group structures work effectively.

Why Small Group Structures Work

Four key reasons explain why most small group structures work:

- ♥ They use effective group work attributes

- ♥ They connect to two-key factors (concepts) of motivation

- ♥ They connect to the idea of differentiated instruction and they invoke Kagan's idea of simultaneous interaction

♥ Effective Group Work Attributes

Individual accountability, face-to-face interaction, and goal positive independence are three of the five attributes from David and Roger Johnsons' research that enable effective group work. Each attribute invokes *individual accountability* (e.g., Think Pair Share, Place Mat and a 2 or 3 Person Interview). Note: not all them do it that effectively (i.e., 4-Corners, Jigsaw and Academic Controversy need additional support to increase individual accountability) (see Classroom Resources).

Each attribute promotes *face-to-face interaction* with students sitting so that they can see each other, talk in group sizes of two, three, or four. Each attribute is designed to achieve a learning outcome, which means they invoke *Goal Positive Interdependence*.

♥ Motivation

Two key factors related to motivation are *novelty* and *variety*. When a teacher is working with a group of students for approximately two hundred days a year, a more extensive instructional repertoire increases the chances that students are going to experience a wider range of ways (novelty and variety) to interact around content learning.

Madeline Hunter, provides an interesting acronym for understanding motivation:

Success—regular feelings of success

Knowledge of Results—feedback and next steps

Accountability—understanding responsibility

Meaningful participation—lessons are meaningful and connected

Positive feeling tone—classroom is a positive place; children know they belong

Interest—lessons are interesting to the students and their experience

♥ Differentiated Instruction

Differentiated instruction, as defined by American educator and author, Carol Ann Tomlinson, refers to a body of writing related to teachers that require a large range of instructional methods to respond to the

Jackie Eldridge and Denise McLafferty

diverse ways in which students learn. Differentiated instruction attends to the different ways in which students can approach learning. Keep in mind that when students work effectively in groups, they are working at invoking interpersonal intelligence (part of Howard Gardner's work on Multiple Intelligence and their emotional intelligence). As you know, students can also work collaboratively to complete Mind Maps, Concept Maps, Concept Attainment, and Venn diagrams, etc. (see Classroom Resources). Small-group structures can connect with a variety of other methods that push other intelligences. For example, when students complete a Place Mat using Venn diagrams, they are integrating logical-mathematical intelligence into the learning process.

Simultaneous Interaction (a Spencer Kagan attribute for his structures)

The research shows that academic-engaged time strongly correlates with increased academic learning. Kagan argues that one of the key attributes of small-group structures is simultaneous interaction. This refers to all students being at work at the same time, which means, they all have something to do. Given they are all involved, you can also see how this connects to classroom management. Simultaneous interaction is similar to, but not the same as, individual accountability. You can have one without the other, but one does not necessarily lead to the other. For example, students may all be involved, but this does not mean they feel accountable to share. The same happens in reverse; just because students feel individually accountable does not mean they are always actively involved. The wise teacher attempts to invoke both.

In addition to the Johnsons' work, research from Elizabeth Cohen informs us about important issues in this area of effective group work. For example, she found that when teachers move into a group to listen, especially if what the students are working on is more complex and unpredictable, the teacher's presence actually reduces group effectiveness. She found the level of thinking drops, the level of collaboration drops, and students defer to the teacher. She does not say, "*Don't interact with groups*"; rather, she says, "*Be judicious about when you go in, how long you stay, and how much you say*". Less may be more.

Teachers can structure groups to engage students in social learning in a rich variety of ways. Four sources of expertise in these areas come to mind:

♥ As introduced earlier, one of the most powerful educators in this field is Kagan, who has collected and designed one of the most extensive lists of group structures (e.g., Think Pair Share, Four Corners, Round Robin, etc.) (see Classroom Resources).

♥ Jeanne Gibbs has created an extensive number of group structures that fit into the three stages of the program Tribes (e.g., Snowball, Graffiti, Gallery Walk, etc.) (see Classroom Resources).

♥ Throughout *Hearts and Minds Matter*, there are varied ways to structure groups as you explore the connections of these activities to emotional intelligence, the brain and resilience. There is no need to view social-emotional learning as something else that needs to be taught. The skills are embedded in the effective instructional strategies you use to teach content.

Note: One would be wise to consider the wisdom of *Level 2* (effective group work) when implementing the structures of *Level 3*. Some structures, like Jigsaw (Aronson's work), Teams Games Tournaments (De Vries work), and Group Investigation (Thelen's work) are complex. They require students to effectively apply a variety of social, communication and critical thinking skills. Failing to intersect the skills of Levels 1 and 2 make it virtually impossible to properly implement these more complex group structures—comparable to the problem of driving a car with one or more flat tires and no gas!

Level Two: The Essential Attributes of Effective Group Work

Level two refers to the engine of group work; those five factors that must be considered and acted on when designing this critical instructional strategy. In other words, they are the essential attributes or basic elements that drive or guide group work. David and Roger Johnson have focused on this area since the 1960s. As educators, researchers, and writers, they have won international awards for their work. The Johnsons identified these attributes by observing teachers structuring groups. They then connected their observations with social theory, and in doing so, merged theory and practice.

The five attributes are all interdependent and critical for success in this area. They are applied both to design effective group work, and to determine how to fix group work that is considered "broken" or less effective. It is perilous to ignore them. When teachers do not pay attention to all five of these elements, they find themselves believing that cooperative learning does not work.

1. **Individual Accountability:** From my experience, individual accountability is the most important of the five attributes. The larger the group, the less likely you are able to invoke individual accountability. Groups of two to four tend to work effectively; once you go to groups of five or above you usually find less effective learning situations. The larger the group, the easier it is to hide or "hitch-hike" off the efforts of others. Also, the larger the group, the less time there is for each group member to talk/share their ideas. This attribute of effective group work is easy to understand and much more complex to implement.

   One of the mistakes teachers make, for example, is assigning the role of "reporter". As soon as one person in the group is assigned this role, the others in the group realize that reporting is not their problem, and this lets them off the hook for participating more rigorously in the task. The person assigned this role, however, is not off the hook, and often ends up being the person who does most of the work. Wisdom would tell us that informing the students that randomly calling on one of them to share the group's finding is a better way to increase the chances that they are all involved.

   From a parent's perspective, if individual accountability is not present, they often see their child as the one who does all of the work. It is frustrating for the student and their parent. As a teacher, it is important to explain to parents that you are structuring groups in such a way that everyone is responsible.

   Using *Numbered Heads (Person 1, 2, 3)* and *Lettered Tables (A, B, C)*—the work of Spencer Kagan—also work effectively. When students know you are going to ask, *"Table C, person 2, what was your group thinking?"*,

Jackie Eldridge and Denise McLafferty

they are more likely to feel accountable and to participate. When students understand they are accountable, it increases their social responsibility and interpersonal relationships (see Classroom Resources).

2. **Promoting Face-to-Face Interaction:** This attribute refers to how students are sitting, how many are in the group, and the skills they have to interact in a face-to-face situation. Students in pairs maximize face-to-face when it comes to how they are sitting. As the group size goes up, the face-to-face interaction goes down. With groups of two to four, if they are sitting looking at each other, you still promote face-to-face interaction. Once you go to five it really drops off; students can also start to "hide" in the group. Of course, social skills like "equal voice" and "attentive listening" are key regardless of group size. Again, it gives us an opportunity to help our students develop their interpersonal relationships and emotional intelligence.

3. **Teaching the appropriate collaborative skills**: Note that collaborative skills divide into three types: (1) social skills (e.g., taking turns, using quiet voices, equal voice); (2) communication skills (e.g., attentive listening, paraphrasing, suspending judgment); and (3) critical thinking skills (e.g., examining both sides of an argument, considering all factors, making inferences and predictions).

The collaborative skills component is the most infrequently and unintentionally applied during group work. These skills are exceedingly important in developing emotional intelligence. We can never assume that students have fully acquired these skills. Additionally, when teachers help children explore and practise collaborative skills, the classroom is more likely to be a safe place for learning. Safety only increases when the teacher holds the students accountable.

Below is a chart that illustrates examples of the range of collaborative skills. The key point to remember is that social skills, such as "equal voice", are required to implement the communication skill of "attentive listening", and those two skills are required to implement the more complex critical thinking skill of "examining both sides of an argument" (see Classroom Resources).

Social Skills	Communication Skills	Critical Thinking Skills
Using quiet voices	Disagreeing agreeably	Looking for sweeping generalizations
Equal participation	Accepting and extending the idea of others	Fallacy of either/or thinking
Being polite	Paraphrasing	Examining both sides of an issue
Using people's names	Probing for clarification	Looking for the unknowable statistic
Being on time	Personalizing a response	Examining the aims, goals, objectives of others
Sharing resources	Responding to an incorrect response	Looking for false analogies

4. **Processing the Academic and Collaborative Learning:** This is somewhat like meta-cognition, where students take time to think about what they learned and how well they functioned as a group. This reflection would also fit into assessment as being learning because students are providing feedback to each other—taking responsibility for their learning and group interaction. This component is another one lacking in most group work.

Of course, one cannot reflect on, or process how the group functioned, if nothing was consciously being applied. They can discuss how well they are achieving their goals and maintaining effective working relationships, and they can use this time to set goals for next time. While processing, the students might discuss what went well, what didn't go well and why, and how they can improve for the next time.

When students reflect upon their skills, they are more inclined to take ownership and responsibility for their actions (as discussed in the chapter on the brain). They are also building their emotional intelligence while working cooperatively.

5. **Invoking Positive Interdependence (PI):** Positive Interdependence refers to the extent students care about their learning and the learning of others in their group. Although PI may appear as jargon, keep in mind that jargon refers to the language specific to an area of inquiry such as music, computer, welding, or medical jargon. Positive interdependence connects to social theory, and as a concept, it has been around for over half a century.

In researching teachers using group work, the Johnsons found nine basic ways to invoke Positive Interdependence. They are listed here with a brief explanation. It is important to note that not all of the nine are required to be present all of the time.

It is also helpful to understand the strong connections to social responsibility when students realize they must work together; decision-making, when they are able to support each other; and self-respect, when their actions meet with success.

Nine Types of Positive Interdependence

I. **Goal** refers to making sure the students have a clear academic task and/or social task that they are focusing on as a group. Goal PI is the only one of the nine you must invoke. It is similar to the instructional skill of "sharing the objective and purpose" at the beginning of a lesson. If the task is not worth doing as a group, don't use group work; if the task is not clear, then your chances of experiencing effective group work are almost zero. Put the goal/academic task/social task somewhere clearly visible to all students, and then, explain it and discuss why it is important to focus on this learning.

II. **Resource** refers to the sharing of resources to encourage students to work with one another, i.e., they share the rulers, felt pens, books, etc.

III. **Role** refers to students taking on a job such as timekeeper, recorder, interviewer, etc., to increase the chances they all have to participate. Teachers often assign roles for the moment, "Person, B, come and get a piece of paper." Later, "Person C, you will be the recorder." In this way, students emerge with different roles as the lesson progresses. When doing this, however, just make sure that over time all students have group responsibilities.

IV. **Outside Force** refers to causing students to work together as the result of a force outside the group efforts, for example, time; "You have five minutes to complete your group's rough draft of the Venn diagram. Go!" or, "Any group that has a mean score of seventy or higher on the quiz, has no homework." In this case, seventy percent is the outside force. The situation often forces individuals to work together (e.g., lifting something heavy, climbing a mountain, etc.).

V. **Sequence** is when students have to put together different parts to add to the whole; you can keep them all accountable with their part to complete their task(s). Jigsaw is one way you invoke sequence. Another is an experiment where you also have sequence if each person has a part of the experiment to complete. The issue with sequence is that once a student finishes their part, they may ask, "What do I do when I have completed my section?" You have to make sure you have activities to keep those who finish first, busy. Individual accountability must be invoked here.

VI. **Incentive** refers to something everyone in the group, and in every group can get, if they successfully finish the group task. They may get their homework cut in half, an additional five percent on their test, to hear a joke, or a story, etc. Try to keep the incentive to be one of the "heart" rather than something material like stickers or candy. If only one group can win, it is outside force; you must "beat" the other groups—and those other groups become the outside force. While this experience is invoking a level of competition, when the students already know this classroom is a safe place, they will not feel threatened.

VII. **Simulation** refers to a student's role playing a situation. Perhaps students have to act out how food moves through the digestive system, or how the water cycle works, or role-playing a poem and solving algebraic equations. This is one time when you may have to have larger groups in order to invoke all parts of what is to be learned.

VIII. **Environmental** is a simpler way to enact positive interdependence. It refers to structuring the environment, so students have to sit together, perhaps around a hula hoop, a sink, or a bunsen burner to complete the task.

IX. **Identity** reminds us of the times when we've been parts of groups that have created a name, logo, or handshake, etc. These can be used when the group is going to be together over a period of time. The students come up with a group name or logo, and could also create a physical symbol, e.g., flag, scarf, crest, etc.

The following rubric is provided to help assess your application of the five attributes.

Attribute	Non-User	Mechanical	Routine	Refined
Individual Accountability	Little or no evidence that students are all accountable.	Emerging evidence that some students are accountable.	Clear evidence that most students are accountable.	Clear evidence that all students are accountable.
Promoting Face- to-Face Interaction	Students are not sitting in a way that promotes face-to-face interaction.	Some students are sitting correctly, but group size is too large (one or more groups have 5 or more students).	Most students are sitting appropriately, group size also appropriate (2 to 4 per group).	All students are sitting appropriately and group size is appropriate (2 to 4 per group).
Reviewing or Teaching Appropriate Collaborative Skills	No evidence of a relevant skill being reviewed or taught or mentioned.	Skill mentioned but not taught; skill not always appropriate to the task; at times too many skills mentioned.	Skill taught and, for the most part, relates to the academic task; may mention 1 or 2 other skills but focuses on one.	Skill taught meaningfully and it relates to the academic task; teacher checks to make sure all students understand the skill.
Processing the Academic and Social Objectives	Little or no evidence that students reflected on or processed their academic or social learning. The reason is that the collaborative skill was not presented.	Some evidence, but most processing is done by the teacher. Students don't really reflect as the collaborative skill was not taught that effectively.	Clear evidence that students reflected on or processed their academic and social learning. Collaborative skill was taught or reviewed effectively.	Clear evidence that students and teacher effectively processed the academic and social learning. The collaborative skill was effectively reviewed or taught.
Positive Interdependence (PI)	No evidence of PI; no clear goal stated. The task may not be appropriate for group work.	Some evidence of PI; goal stated but not as clearly or meaningfully as it could be. The goal is not discussed with students.	Clear evidence of PI; goal stated, brief discussion with students. Appropriate types of PI selected and applied.	Clear evidence of PI; goal clearly stated and relevance discussed with students. Appropriate type of PI selected and effectively applied.

Level One: Creating the Safe Classroom/ Building Safety and Inclusion

Level one is the key theme that runs throughout this text; if this piece is not in place, then not much else can be effectively implemented. If someone came to you and asked if your students felt safe in your classroom, if their voices mattered, and if they were respected, what do you think they would say? When reflecting on one's teaching or observing other instructors and discussing key strengths (or missing links), *safety* is most likely one of the most important of all concepts. If students don't feel safe, then not much is going to happen in the classroom, especially when it comes to invoking more complex instructional methods. This is why *Hearts and Minds Matter* focuses on building inclusion as one of the most important concepts for optimizing learning.

Below I provide a few ways to focus on this area. They include instructor actions you most likely do and can observe, which would indicate that an instructor is invoking safety. They vary in complexity: the less complex ways are listed first.

Rubrics are provided to assess your efforts, based on the work of Hall and Hord and their work related to the Concerns-Based Adoption Model (CBAM), and more specifically, their work with Susan Loucks-Horsley on the Levels of Use of an Innovation (LoU).

Note: *Self-assessment* refers to the idea of an instructor's professional efforts at self-regulation. This is no different from what we ask of students. We all need to take responsibility for our thinking and actions about learning.

Less Complex Ways to Invoke Safety

♥ **Knowing and using the students' names**: The way in which instructors say student names communicates degrees of safety. Using a student's name is related to effective classroom management, a piece of the puzzle that correlates strongly to social-emotional learning. The instructor's facial message also communicates safety. For example, an instructor can say a student's name with a smile, or a roll of the eyes that makes students smile or laugh.

Ask yourself, am I sending a kind message or am I using the name to send the message that lets the student know that they are pushing the boundaries of acceptable behaviour (especially if we merge "the look" with saying the student's name). As previously discussed, having those boundaries is part of making a classroom feel safe. (Note that an instructor can use the "glance", the "look", the "stare" and the "glare". All are effective and not threatening when the students know what is expected of them).

Knowing names is also key for school administrators. Marie Whelan is a principal with Edmonton Catholic School. She won an award as one of the top principals in Canada. Whelan was known for placing pictures of all the students in the school behind her desk and working hard to know all the names (about four hundred) within the first two weeks of the school year. To Marie, names were important because it made the students feel seen and appreciated. It also helped her in the management of the school. The students understood that she knew who they were—they were not invisible.

♥ **Facial features** connect to the idea of student's names. Observing instructors for the messages communicated by smiling or giving "the look" are clearly part of the art of teaching. When students trying to achieve power in their classrooms were asked how long it takes a student to "suss out" an instructor at the start of the school year, they told us "about thirty seconds. We just have to look at their face".

Think of the ways we communicate to students that they are safe (or not) in our classrooms. Our eyes, our lips—smiling or not—our words and actions; these all communicate safety. Also note that we produce endorphins when we smile and they are apparently four hundred times more powerful than the strongest opiate (hence the term, the "healing power of humour"). The more we smile the happier the classroom will be.

♥ **Use of humour and being enthusiastic** are two key concepts identified as essential attributes of effective instructors. Both are extensively researched. Humour reduces stress. Instructor enthusiasm increases student "academic engaged time". Mary Collin's research in the late seventies focused on the impact of instructor enthusiasm on student learning. She won a dissertation of the year for her work on assisting instructors to become enthusiastic by focusing on the behaviours listed in the rubric below.

Note: humour does not mean the instructor has to "be" funny (although that could be part of it); rather, it implies that the instructor has a sense of humour, and is able to see and appreciate those classroom situations where humour is present. Likewise, with enthusiasm; the instructor doesn't have to be plugged into 220 volts; rather, it implies the instructor communicates through their attitude and behaviour that they are excited and enthusiastic about being in the classroom, and that they enjoy teaching both the subject and the students.

Instructor's Self-Assessment for Invoking Enthusiasm

Criteria	Mechanical	Routine	Refined
Tone of voice/ voice modulation	A bit too monotone; little variety.	Working at changing voice tone; more varied.	Effectively modulates voice to capture attention.
Hand gestures	Little or no hand movement to engage students.	More frequently employs hands to engage students.	Effectively uses hands to engage students.
Movement around the room	Tends to stay in one part of the room.	More frequently moving around room.	Artfully moves around room to keep students' attention.
Facial Messages re: excitement or interest for learning	Tends to be somewhat bland; little excitement for teaching and learning.	More frequently communicates an excitement or interest for teaching and learning	Frequently communicates an excitement or interest in teaching and learning.

A professor from Memorial University in Newfoundland, Canada recently interviewed secondary students on the attributes of effective secondary instructors. The key concepts that came out of his research were "having a sense of humour, "being enthusiastic" and "caring". These social-emotional qualities are also the ones we want our children to adopt as they increase their emotional intelligence.

♥ **Use an open hand when selecting participants:** Students from elementary school to adult learners tell us they prefer the open hand to share, rather than pointing at the participant and saying his or her name. Using an open hand is more invitational and more respectful. In addition, most learners prefer to talk with a partner first, and then, have the instructor say, *"Deborah, what were you and Enrico thinking?"* Course participants tell us that at least if they are wrong, there is no humiliation because the answer may or may not have been their own. This small act makes students feel more secure.

♥ **Providing wait time when asking questions:** Wait time refers the time allowed for learners to think prior to asking them to share their ideas, again, after they've been selected to respond, and then (when appropriate) again, after they've responded. Wait time is an instructional skill discussed back in the late 1890's, and first researched by Mary Budd-Rowe in 1976. That research was followed by Tobin's research at Deakin University in 1983.

The more complex the question, the more wait time the instructor should provide; the more unpredictable the answer, the more wait time learners should provide. Mary Budd-Rowe's research showed that learners need at least three to five seconds to have an impact on their answer. Interestingly, instructors often say, *"Think to yourself for about a minute"*, and then ten seconds later, pick a student to share.

Wait time provides the opportunity to think privately. In this way, any of the learners' less accurate answers "die" privately, rather than the learner "dying" publicly. Taking the time to think first is often known as *"covert"* or hidden. When students have to share their answer, then it is known as *"overt"*. When instructors are framing questions, they can have the learner shift from "covert" (safe and less accountable) to "overt" (less safe and more accountable). Using wait time is especially important for those children who have trouble processing information because it takes them longer to think about what was asked. Using the strategy, Think, Pair, Share, gives them an opportunity to further process.

Some questions, such as "Where do you live?" don't usually need wait time. Think of wait time as the "science", and how much time you provide as the "art".

♥ **Framing questions and using wait time:** Framing questions provides the information learners require so they know how much time they have to think; whether or not they are being asked to share with someone or in their group first; and how they will be selected to respond. Framing questions using wait time is an instructional skill discussed by Millar back in 1897. Keep in mind that very few instructors frame questions effectively (here I include kindergarten to university instructors). It takes a deeper understanding and practice to master both the art and the science of framing questions well.

For example, *"We've all read the case study. Think to yourself first for about 15 seconds. What were the ethical issues that could emerge? When I say go, share with your elbow partner, making sure you both get a chance to talk. In about 45 seconds, I will randomly call on three of you to share with the class what your partner told you."*

Compare the above to a situation where the instructors ask questions like this, *"Who can tell me? Or "Can anyone explain...?"* or *"Hands up if you have..."*. These questions provide a lot of safety, but most participants will not be involved because the instructor has not invoked the concept of *individual accountability*. There is no depth to the questioning, and as "closed" questions, they elicit a yes or no answer, which shuts the questioning down. Compare these to open-ended questions with increased safety measures, that encourage your students to open up their thinking and to go deeper.

♥ **Using Think Pair Share (TPS):** TPS is a small group instructional tactic developed by Lyman back in the 1980s. By using TPS, the instructor is able to provide time for the learners to think after framing a question, and then, can ask the learners to share with a partner before they share their answers publicly. This tactic is one of the most frequently used with faculty of education students, but few instructors use it well. When applying TPS, you must effectively employ wait time and framing questions, otherwise, Think Pair Share is not that effective. Take the time to practise it before moving on to more complex tactics, strategies, or skills (see Classroom Resources).

♥ **Responding to student responses**: Back in the 1970s, Madeline Hunter explored seven types of student responses: Correct, Incorrect, Partially Correct, No Response, Guess, Silly Response, and Convoluted Response.

Correct response: Be careful not to assume that because students provided the right answer, they actually understood the answer. Check to make sure the learners can explain in their own words or with their own example, and not simply state something they've memorized.

Incorrect response: Students are telling you three things: they have a piece of information; they do not know where that piece of information fits, and they do not have the right answer. Let them know where the piece of information they shared fits; and then, shift to finding the correct answer.

Partially correct response: Acknowledge what was correct; go in search of the rest of the answer. Stay away from comments like, "Who can help Michael?" because it implies that he does not know what is being asked, which will not feel safe for him.

No response: The "scariest" for the student; make sure they feel safe. When students give a *"no response"* it is often because they feel scared. Watch their eyes; if they are looking up—searching—leave them alone. If they look right at you or look furtively back and forth, then they are asking you to "save face for them". For example, you may say something like, *"Sorry Samuel; sorry class, I confused myself with that question. Let me rephrase it"*. So, you rephrase it, do a TPS or Round Table Share, and then re-select a participant to share. It helps if you can down-grade the complexity of the question, and then work your way back to the original question.

Guess: Again, safety is key. Don't judge; say something like, "Okay, interesting, any other ideas?".

Silly Response: In jest there can be truth. If possible, find the piece that connects to the learning.

Convoluted response: This is where a student talks all around the question but does not answer it. The trick is to intervene, "Okay, thanks Edel, that is a lot of information; now I just want to refocus this a bit."

♥ **Bloom's Taxonomy:** Using this taxonomy of thinking provides

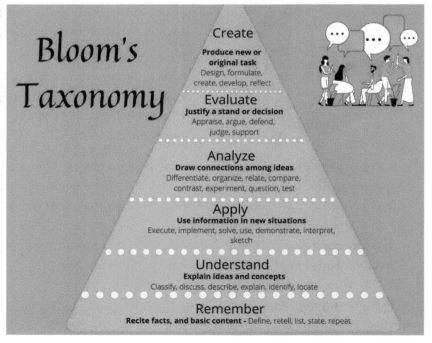

Jackie Eldridge and Denise McLafferty

teachers with a framework for questioning and for moving students from lower levels to more complex, higher-order thinking. It is useful when planning lessons and units and when thinking about differentiating instruction. We can ask students questions based on their achievement levels.

♥ **Teaching learners appropriate social and communication skills:** You might read *Effective Group Work: Beyond Cooperative Learning (Bennett, 2017)*; here, you can see examples of how social skills such as taking turns, appreciation statements, and equal voice; and communication skills such as attentive listening, checking for understanding, and suspending judgment can be taught.

♥ **Inclusion/Belonging (Connects with Safety)**

Clearly, inclusion/belonging and safety overlap. Building *inclusion* or *belonging* is tied with safety as being key concepts that must be invoked in classrooms. The question again is, *"What can effective instructors do and say that creates classroom environments where students feel they are included/belong?"* We could extend the enquiry to ask, *"What administrators can do to make sure the instructors feel they belong?"* What goes around, comes around.

Recent research in Australia reported that around fifty-five percent of employees are looking to work somewhere else. The data showed that two main factors for wanting to leave were organizational culture and not being appreciated/recognized.

In this section, I start by sharing fewer complex ways of invoking belonging, and then, shift to more complex ways of increasing the chances that students feel they belong. I also provide sample rubrics for instructors to self-assess. As stated previously, the rubrics are based on the work of Hall and Hord and their work related to the Concerns Based Adoption Model.

Less Complex Ways to Invoke Inclusion/Belonging

♥ **Have students learn and use their classmate's names:** In addition to classroom management, this is a key area for safety. In terms of belonging, the focus is more on having students learn their classmates' names. Did the instructor take the time for students to learn one another's names? Instructors, for example, who have taken training in this area develop a repertoire of ways to create a more inclusive classroom culture. They acquire several different ways where name games can be applied to learn classmates' names.

You're more likely to see this kind of activity happening in elementary classrooms than secondary classrooms, where we often see primary instructors putting the names of their students on the desks, classroom door or around the room. You also see instructors having students create self-portraits or to trace their body. Students then add things about themselves on that portrait or body tracing, which are discussed and put on the classroom wall.

The 'life map' is a story about oneself, e.g., where they were born, their family, their interests, etc. Some instructors have students do a 'life map' and then share their map with another student. Explaining who they are through a Life Map is a creative way to introduce autobiographies (see Classroom Resources).

When observing other instructors, try to see or find out what the instructor does to make sure students learn each other's names. Some instructors (at the start of the year) have students say their name first before sharing an answer ("Hi, I'm Susan, and I think…….)

♥ **Communicating you care:** For over thirty years we've asked instructors to think back on past teachers, and why they felt those instructors were effective or ineffective. Having a sense of humour and being enthusiastic came up first and second in over ninety percent of the responses; the third was, *"They cared about me"*, (e.g., they understood the student's interests, they did not humiliate students in front of the class, handed out tests/assignments randomly - not low to high). They also cared about students outside of the classroom (e.g., knew birthdays, was aware of special abilities/talents).

As previously mentioned, Madeline Hunter identified "Positive Feeling Tone" as the sense to which students feel safe, included, and respected. Politeness is key here—simply saying *"Please"* and *"Thank you"* makes a difference.

♥ **Learning about and acting on information related to students:** Learning about their home life, their hobbies, sports they play, etc., tells students that they are important and valued. Taking the time to find out that the grandmother of one of the student's is visiting or passed away, or that their parents are having another child or are getting divorced, allows you to communicate care, and gives you an opportunity to find ways to support the student.

In a 1987 book by Ken Macrorie titled *20 Teachers*, the author interviewed twenty great teachers. One of the common attributes of those teachers was the way in which they let students "into their lives". To these teachers, they were not simply students; they cared about them outside the classroom.

♥ **Teach the appropriate social, communication skills:** Social and communication skills drive the more complex critical thinking skills; consequently, you will struggle to implement critical thinking skills if your students do not have the basic communication and social skills.

Less complex processes drive more complex processes. For example, students are not able to critically think about, and examine both sides of an issue, if they cannot suspend judgment, disagree agreeably, probe for clarification, and attentively listen (note that these are emotional intelligence and communication skills). In addition, they cannot suspend judgment, disagree agreeably, probe for clarification, and attentively listen if they are not polite, if they do not take turns, or if they are not able to encourage equal voices. There are ways to teach more complex communication skills. Below is an example of Jerome Bruner's Concept Attainment strategy (Harvey F. Silver, Richard W. Strong and Matthew J. Perini.) More examples can be found under Classroom Resources.

Concept Attainment Lesson: Predator-prey relationships:

The teacher is about to begin a lesson on predator-prey relationships. He wants his students to develop a strong conceptual understanding of what a predator is and how predators are uniquely adapted to the life they lead. As an introduction to the lesson, the teacher tells the students:

"Today I'm going to hold up pictures of different animals. Some of these animals will be *yes* examples of an idea I have in mind. Some will be *no* examples.

All the *yes* animals are examples of an important concept that's going to be at the center of what we study over the next few days. The *no* animals are not examples of this concept, though they may have some things in common with the *yes* examples.

Jackie Eldridge and Denise McLafferty

What I want you to do is to examine each *yes* example and each *no* example to try and figure out what the concept is. The name of the concept will be a start, but what I really want is for you to determine the critical attributes of the concept."

The teacher then holds up pictures of the first three animals—cat (yes), dog (yes), rabbit (no)—and asks students to generate an initial set of attributes.

In surveying the class, Carl finds that some of the initial attributes students have come up with include common pets, runners (instead of hoppers), and meat eaters.

He then presents pictures of four more animals: horse (no), lion (yes), brontosaurus (no), and velociraptor (yes).

"OK," the teacher says, "So what do all the *yes* examples have in common? How are they different from the *no* examples?"

During the student discussion, students explore a number of ideas. One student notices that the brontosaurus is slow, but all the *yes* examples are fast. Another student explains how all the *yes* examples have sharp teeth and that they're all meat eaters. The teacher collects the attributes generated on the board. He then presents two more pictures—an eagle (yes) and a snake (yes).

With these examples, a student points out that the snake isn't fast, but another says, "Yeah, but it strikes fast." Other students focus on the fact that the eagle doesn't have teeth.

One student sums up, "They all have some kind of way to rip into meat. The eagle has the beak and claws; the snake has the teeth. All the other yes examples have claws and sharp teeth. But the *no* examples don't have these kinds of things." At this point, most of the class is reasonably confident that the concept is carnivore and that the critical attributes are eats meat and has a way to tear into meat.

The teacher then holds up one final picture of a vulture, which to many students' surprise is a *no*. With this example, students realize that they have missed something: all the *yes* examples hunt and kill live animals, as opposed to the vulture, which eats dead animals. The class then reviews all the examples and nonexamples and, with the teacher, develops a final set of critical attributes for the concept of a predator:

- ♥ Hunts and kills other animals
- ♥ Has body parts (like claws, sharp teeth, sharp beaks) to kill and eat other animals
- ♥ Is fast or can use stealth to catch live animals

After the class has worked out the critical attributes of predators, the teacher presents them with pictures of various insects, birds, and fish and asks students to determine if each animal is a predator or not based on what they have learned. Later in the unit, as part of their final assessment for their portfolios, he will ask students to design their own predator, one that is ideally suited to an ecosystem of their choosing.

The Concept Attainment strategy is founded on the important work of Jerome Bruner (1973), who conducted extensive research into the psychological process known as *concept formation*. What Bruner concluded is that in order to cope with our diverse environment, humans naturally group information into categories based on common characteristics. For example, a child learns from experience that objects that have four wheels, travel on roads, and transport people belong to a category called cars. The conceptual soundness of the child's emerging concept of a car is then tested by SUVs, minivans, trucks, and motorcycles—and refined.

Concept Attainment draws on this powerful process of concept formation by asking students to analyze both examples (called *yes* examples in a classroom lesson) and nonexamples (called *no* examples in a classroom lesson) of a concept, group the examples into a conceptual category, test their initial categories against further examples and nonexamples and, finally, generate a set of critical attributes that define the concept they are learning.

The effectiveness of Concept Attainment as an instructional strategy is further bolstered by the fact that it engages students deeply in the skills of identifying similarities and differences and generating and testing hypotheses—two of the nine instructional techniques proven to raise students' level of achievement as identified by Marzano, Pickering, and Pollock (2001).

In order to ensure that you get the most out of this tried-and-true strategy, we recommend that you base your Concept Attainment lessons on three simple principles: conceptual clarity, multiple examples, and conceptual competence.

The Principle of Conceptual Clarity. Learning a concept involves more than just learning a label; it involves learning the essential attributes of a concept. To learn the essential attributes of a concept, students must be able to discriminate between examples and nonexamples. Make sure all the essential attributes are clearly present in your examples and that nonexamples embody only some of these attributes. Avoid sending students down misleading and trivial paths.

The Principle of Multiple Examples. When presented with two examples, students can form initial hypotheses about a concept. However, when students see many and varied examples, they can define with increasing certainty the essential attributes of the concept. It is a good idea to lead with more obvious examples and then to introduce more challenging examples as you and your students progress through the lesson.

The Principle of Conceptual Competence. A concept is learned when students can list the essential attributes of the concept and when they can use those attributes to discriminate between examples and nonexamples. Never be afraid to challenge students to apply their new understanding of the concept in a variety of ways. Can they design an imaginary predator? Can they create two imaginary societies—one that fits the concept of a civilization and another that is missing one key attribute? Can they think of 10 different examples of transportation from at least three different sources (e.g., from nature, on the road, at the amusement park)?

How to Use the Strategy

1. Select a concept with clear critical attributes (e.g., tragic hero, civilization, linear equations, alive, mammals, etc.) that you want students to understand deeply.

2. Provide students with *yes* examples, which contain all the critical attributes of the concept, and *no* examples, which contain some but not all of the critical attributes.

Jackie Eldridge and Denise McLafferty

3. Ask students to identify what all the *yes* examples have in common and how the *yes* examples differ from the *no* examples. Students should generate an initial list of critical attributes of the concept.

4. Provide more *yes* and *no* examples that students can use to test and refine their initial list of attributes.

5. As a whole class, review the *yes* and *no* examples and generate a final set of critical attributes.

6. Ask students to apply their understanding of the concept by creating a product or completing a task.

What Does It Look Like in the Classroom?

♥ *ABC's or One to Ten:* This activity is best done in a circle but not necessary. The idea is that everyone feels into the energy of everyone else. When one person feels ready, they will start by saying the letter A. Another person may chime in with B and then C and so on. The idea is that a letter cannot be repeated. If two people say B at the same time you must go back to the beginning and start over. You can use letters or numbers. It may take a few tries, but soon the students will learn that the energy in the room can work for them if they tap into it and concentrate.

♥ *Balloon Bop:* This activity is energetic and fun. You can play it in a small group or the whole class. Have the students start in a circle and then release three or four balloons into the mix. They must work together as a team to keep all balloons in the air at all times. You can increase the level of concern by introducing consequence if a balloon hits the floor. For example, all team members must do five jumping jacks or a one-minute plank!

♥ *Coat of Arms:* Identity builds community and demonstrates the common values of the group. After the group has been together for a while and inclusion has been built, you can have the students brainstorm what is important to them as a community, what symbols represent them and what they identify with. Collectively they will create a coat of arms that will be visible in the classroom. This visual can also be used in terms of classroom management because it is a representation of what their community is about. If something falls outside of that understanding, you can re-visit the coat of arms asking the students if that is what they are really about.

♥ *Mirror, Mirror:* Students will pair off and face each other. They put their palms almost together as they make eye contact. When one person feels called to start, they will do an action and the other person mirrors. Each person takes turns mirroring the other.

♥ *Novel in an Hour* (Jeanne Gibbs, 2014): Choose a novel that is not too complex or deep. Introduce the novel with a strong mental set that really piques their interest. This mental set can also include an inclusion activity. The class will meet in groups of 3 to 5. Each group will be assigned a chapter or chapters of the novel. They will either read the chapter independently or have an assigned reader. For children who have difficulty reading, you might have the resource teacher, or a parent read with them ahead of time. Once the chapter is read, the groups will come up with ways to present the content to the rest of the class. It is a good idea to brainstorm ideas with the class ahead of time so they do not get stuck trying to decide. Some common ideas are a skit, rap, spoken word, story board, newscast, talk show, etc. You will then give each group a certain amount of time to prepare their presentation. When the group preparation is completed, the whole class meets to watch the novel unfold from the first chapter to the last. Following their presentations, have the students reflect on how well they worked as a group and how they might improve next time.

♥ *Our Class Anthem:* As mentioned, identity is important for groups and it is fun to have them compose an anthem that bonds them together. They can write a song or a poem that best describes the group. Once they have rehearsed, it would be fun to make a music video that is shared with parents.

♥ *Placemat:* This graphic organizer helps students to think critically and to prioritize ideas. Have students sit across from each other in a group of four. Letter the students off A, B, C, D. One person will be the recorder where they draw the placemat and place it in the centre for all to reach. Each student has their own colour pen/marker/pencil so that it is easier to see that all are participating. The students all write about the topic at the same time without talking. Once the time is up, they do a round robin sharing of what they wrote. They then have a discussion and come to consensus about the top three ideas that the recorder will write in the centre (see Classroom Resources).

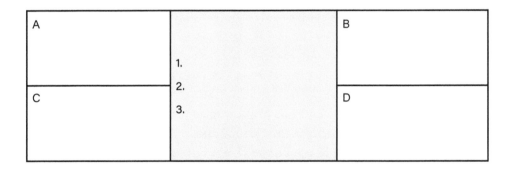

♥ *Rain* Jeanne Gibbs (2014): Everyone sits in a circle with their chairs close to each other. Everyone closes their eyes. The leader will start by making the sound of rain by slowly rubbing their hands together. The person on the right picks up the sound when they hear it, then the next person and the next until the rain goes all around the circle. Start with soft rubbing to represent the rain just beginning and then intensify the sound of the rain by rubbing the hands faster and harder together. When the leader wants to increase the intensity even more, they will add the sound of thunder by stomping their feet. To signal that the storm has passed, stop the foot stomping and reverse the hand rubbing from louder to softer.

♥ *Rock, Paper, Scissors:* This version of an old game is fun and very energetic. The game starts with each person standing with a partner. All pairs will then play the game on the count of 3. They will each play three rounds and the winner scores the best 2 out of 3. Rock will win against scissors but lose against paper. Scissors will win against paper but lose against rock. Paper will win against rock but lose against scissors. When the first round is finished, the partners find another pair and the two winners play each other while the eliminated people are the cheerleaders for their partner. When the winner is established, the group finds another pair to play against and the eliminated become the cheerleaders. The game continues until they are down to only one pair with a whole class full of cheerleaders. Caution: this game can get very loud!

♥ *Six Degrees of Separation:* Have students meet in pairs or small groups. They must begin a dialogue about such topics as where they were born, where they have travelled, what they like to eat, etc., as they try to find at least one thing they have in common.

Literature Resources

Picture Books

A House in the Woods by Inga Moore

Bat's Big Game by Margaret Read MacDonald

Claymates by Dev Petty

Colors vs. Shapes by Josh

Duck and Goose by Tad Hills

Frankie by Mary Sullivan

Frankie Plays the Game by Paulette Bourgeois

Please Please the Bees by Gerald Kelley

Prince and Pirate by Charlotte Gunnufson

Red and Yellow's Noisy Night by Mike Boldt

Swimmy by Leo Lionni

That Fruit Is Mine! by Anuska Allepuz

The Brownstone by Paula Scher

The Little Red Fort by Brenda Maier

The Whispering Town by Jennifer Elvgren

Two Tough Tow Trucks by Corey Rosen Schwartz and Rebecca J. Gomez

Violet and Victor Write the Best-Ever Bookworm Book by Alice Kuipers

What If Everybody Did That? by Ellen Javernick

When Pigs Fly by James Burke

Chapter Books

Appleblossom the Possum by Holly Goldberg Sloan

Beyond Lucky by Sarah Aronson

Mice of the Round Table by Julie Leung

Swim or Sink by Jake Maddox

The Gauntlet by Karuna Riazi

The Last of the really Great Whangdoodles by Julie Andrews Edwards

The Mighty Dynamo by Kieran Crowley

The Wishmakers by Tyler Whitesides

CHAPTER EIGHT

Mindfulness

What Does the Research Say?

According to a recent article in Mindful Schools, "Research shows that stressed teachers impact students' stress levels and student stress impacts learning outcomes. Students learn better in a climate that is more emotionally positive. Studies have demonstrated a link between positive emotional classroom climates and academic achievement." In 2018, The Harvard Gazette released a study that showed "Mindfulness popularity has been bolstered by a growing body of research showing that it reduces stress and anxiety, improves attention and memory, and promotes self-regulation and empathy".

In this chapter, we explore:

✓ *The science of mindfulness*

✓ *The connections between mindfulness and the brain*

✓ *The benefits of mindfulness practice*

✓ *The uses of mindfulness for teachers and children*

In order to begin, it is helpful to understand the science behind stress and the effects of a mindfulness program. There is no question that stress is harmful. Many years of research in the medical and psychological communities have proven that it affects us on many levels: physical and emotional health, relationships, job performance, and the pursuit of happiness. Too much stress is harmful no matter which way we look at it. So how does it work?

As described in Chapter Three on the brain, it is critical to revisit the interconnectedness of the brain and the body, and subsequently, mindfulness. When we receive messages, experiences, or images, they proceed along the neural pathways of our brain and locate themselves in various places. If the conditions for learning are optimal and stress-free, then the received information travels to the cerebral cortex, the area responsible for numerous functions including sensation, language, creativity, motor processing, memory, abstraction, emotion, attention, judgement, problem solving, and the complex processing of auditory information. However, if fear is present, we automatically enter a stress loop. It is our innate way of coping. Fear is a chain reaction in the brain that starts with a stressful stimulus, and ends with the physical release of catecholamines, which include adrenaline and noradrenaline. When these chemicals are released into our bodies:

♥ They cause a racing heart, rapid breathing, muscle tension, difficulty sleeping, and anxiety, among other things. As mentioned earlier, this reaction is also known as the fight, flight or freeze response and is a signal that our sympathetic nervous system (SNS) has been activated.

♥ We experience an emotional high-jacking and our ability to think clearly becomes impaired. The results of the activation of the SNS creates a stress loop that many people find challenging. It can seem impossible to recover from the grip of anxiety.

The SNS is activated by emotional content, especially the more challenging thoughts and emotions of fear, grief, anger, worry, resentment, and aggressiveness. Conversely, the parasympathetic nervous system (PNS) is aroused by feelings of calm, love, peacefulness, contentment, satisfaction, and appreciation.

So, how do we achieve more feelings of calm and fulfillment? We can restore balance by activating our PNS, which promotes healing, regeneration, nourishment of the body and regulation of the immune system. We can easily access our PNS through sleep, meditation, prayer, exercise, and relaxation therapies. The physical results of finding our way back to the PNS are many. We experience decreased blood pressure, slower heart rate, calm breathing, and an ability to reach a deeper sleep. Our minds can see the bigger picture and we are able to turn inward for introspection, receptivity, and creativity.

The following practices can be done by both adults and children. We recommend that you establish your own practice first, so you are comfortable before bringing it to your students. You will ultimately be the model for them. Once you are comfortable, then invite your students to also practise with you. Towards the end of this chapter, there are practices specifically designed for children.

First Baby Steps Towards Your Mindfulness Practice

The research tells us that practising mindfulness for even five minutes per day can re-wire our brains enough to slow us down so that we can become more creative and productive. First determine the amount of time that you would like to meditate. In the beginning, you want to start with a short period of time so that you do not get frustrated. Meditation is a practice and you need to work your way up to a longer period of time instead of trying to do too much at first. One to two minutes at a time is a good starting point.

♥ Find a quiet location with as few distractions as possible. While you might think that the optimal environment is a completely silent room, we do not live in places that are absolutely free of noise. There are sounds everywhere, whether it be the refrigerator, the air conditioner or traffic outside. The practise allows you to work with those noises.

♥ Sit on a chair with your feet flat on the floor. Choosing where you sit is important. Many experienced meditation practitioners prefer to sit on a zafu or meditation cushion, but it is strictly a personal choice; a chair is fine. Finding what is comfortable for you helps you establish your practice.

♥ Whether you choose a chair or a cushion, the next step is vital. Sit with a comfortable yet erect posture. This posture enables the energy to flow through your body in an uninterrupted way. When you are hunched over, you are blocking the energy. Relax your spine and sit up tall.

♥ You also need to concentrate on relaxing your shoulders by slightly rolling them back and down.

♥ Find a way to support your hands by either resting them on a cushion or on your lap, so that your arms are relaxed. It is common to see people sitting in meditation with their index finger and thumb touching. While not required, this gesture or "mudra" is about allowing the energy of the two digits to connect.

♥ Balance your head evenly, with your chin slightly tucked. The back of your neck should be relaxed, long and open.

♥ Relax your eyes, brow, and jaw. It is also a good idea to relax your tongue by lightly touching the back of your teeth.

♥ Get in touch with your breath and start by noticing the inward and outward sensations that go along with natural breathing. Pay attention to breathing in and breathing out. If you are getting distracted, you might repeat the phrase, "I am breathing in, I am breathing out".

♥ Stay with your breath for the amount of time that you have allotted.

♥ While you are focusing on your breath, it is likely that your mind will wander to something that happened in the past or to what you imagine will happen in the future. This mind-wandering is quite common and happens to everyone. Your task is to simply notice that your mind has wandered, and then, go back to your breath without any hesitation. It is our judgement and attachment to thoughts and emotions that gets us into trouble. When we ruminate, we automatically engage the sympathetic nervous system, the centre of our stress loop. Simply notice the thought, watch it fade away, and go back to your breath. By doing so, you are activating your parasympathetic nervous system, that is important when you are attempting to find calm.

♥ This step is perhaps the biggest challenge that beginners face. Instead of recognizing that "monkey mind" is a natural state in the foundational stages of mindful practice, people often say that they knew they would not be able to control their permeating thoughts. However, we all require practice when we are learning a new skill. The more practise, the more skilled we become. Mindful practice is no different. It is mindfulness practise and not mindfulness mastery.

Breath Work

♥ **Stopping and Dropping**: This practice is always with you, no matter where you are or what you are doing. You could be sitting in a peaceful place, but you might also be in a chaotic environment like public transit or a stressful meeting. When you notice the stress loop creeping in, you are going to stop what you are doing or thinking and just drop into your breath. You might close your eyes and take three-to-five breaths. Just that brief reprieve will re-energize you, allowing you to become more present to whatever you are doing.

♥ **4-7-8 Breath:** The *4-7-8 Breath (Relaxing Breath)* is a strategy that is also always with you. It involves breathing in for four seconds, holding the breath for seven seconds, and exhaling for eight seconds. Relaxing Breath takes little time and requires no equipment. It can be done anywhere. It is important to note that if holding for seven and releasing for eight seems too much, you can reduce it to six and seven. Keep your back tall and straight to encourage the breath and energy flow, and your feet flat on the floor.

  ♥ Close your mouth and inhale quietly through your nose for a count of **four**.

  ♥ Hold your breath for a count of **seven**.

  ♥ Exhale completely through your mouth, making a "whoosh" sound for a count of **eight**.

Note that this is one breath. Now inhale again and repeat the cycle **three** more times for a total of **four** breaths. You want to repeat the cycle four times in the beginning in order to avoid getting dizzy from the deep breaths. The more you practise, the less chance you have of experiencing the light-headedness. You can do this exercise twice a day—you'll notice an immediate difference. As you get more used to it, you might increase the practice to eight cycles.

♥ **The Stimulating Breath:** To stimulate the breath, inhale and exhale rapidly through your nose, keeping your mouth closed but relaxed. The in and out breaths should be equal and short. Try breathing for three in-and-out cycles for a second each. Your goal is to have rapid movement of your diaphragm. After each cycle, you will breathe normally. Limit this exercise to fifteen seconds on your first try so you do not feel faint. As you become used to this kind of breathing you can increase your time. Sometimes people find their mind wanders while breathing. If this continually happens, bring your attention back and try repeating the following phrase, "I am breathing in, I am breathing out". You can continue this practice with the goal of eventually removing the phrase. Remember, your breath is your greatest ally on your journey to mindfulness AND it is free!

Daily Opportunities for Mindfulness

Every day activities are filled with opportunities for mindfulness if we simply give ourselves permission to slow down and connect. Find everyday activities in your life that lend themselves to focus and attention. The truth is, we can bring mindful awareness to everything we do:

♥ **In the shower** is a marvelous time to be mindful. The next time you enter the shower, close your eyes and feel the water on your skin, the shampoo on your head, and the soap on your body. Feel every sensation, focussing your awareness on the act of showering and not on past or future events. Now is the time to enjoy every aspect of that shower so that you are not in the stress loop. Instead you are in the present.

♥ **While Cooking** is also an amazing time to enhance your mindfulness practice. As you are cutting vegetables, notice the colour and texture of each one. As the meat is cooking in the oven, take in all of the scrumptious smells. Baking is a perfect way to become mindful since the aromas and textures are very sensual. They draw you in and allow you to connect with the moment. If negative thoughts come into your mind, acknowledge them, and then go back to the present sights, sounds and smells.

♥ **When Cleaning** you can also be very mindful. As you are cleaning the windows or mirrors, be aware of every stroke of the squeegee. Notice as the streaks disappear and the glass becomes clearer. When you are sweeping, mindfully sweep away any negative thoughts or experiences. This mindful activity is not the time to begin ruminating; you are simply sweeping to release the emotion and let the thoughts go.

♥ **With Exercising** people often use runs, treadmill walking, boxing, and other physical activities to vent challenging emotions and stress. Releasing stress mindfully is healthy; staying stuck in the past or future is not. Mindful exercise means you need to let go of judgment during your practise. It is not about thinking that you dislike exercise; you are simply focusing on each movement. When exercising, bring present moment awareness to each activity. For example, when lifting weights, bring awareness to the weight, the feeling in your body, and the strength that you are gaining. You can also bring awareness to your breath as you move through your exercise routine. Not surprisingly, yoga, with its ancient roots in meditation, is one of the best mindful exercises you can do.

♥ **Having mindful conversations** are important on so many levels. Mindful conversations are powerful and they improve your relationships. When we bring mindfulness to our conversations, we connect deeply to the person with whom we are interacting. Being mindful enables us to actually hear what the person is saying, and it validates them. With this validation, the speaker now wants to continue the conversation and potentially go deeper. In order to be mindful in conversation, we want to bring the following attentive listening skills to each experience.

> **Attending** (eye contact, presence, undivided attention—no cell phones)
>
> **Non-verbal encouragement** (nodding, face-to-face, saying "hmmm hmmm," leaning-in)
>
> **Paraphrasing** ("What I heard you say was...," "So, the problem for you is...")"
>
> **Reflecting feelings** ("It sounds like you are feeling...," "I am sensing you are feeling...")

♥ **Email and phone calls** plague our lives and often cause us extraordinary stress. Sometimes the sheer number can be overwhelming. It is all too easy to become a "flitter bug" going back and forth and never really accomplishing much. Bringing mindfulness to emails and phone calls means that we set an intention to spend a period of time doing only emails. At the end of that time, we intentionally move to phone calls for a period of time, and then move on to the next task. Of course, there will be times when we get interrupted. When this happens, we attend to the interruption if necessary, then "stop and drop" into our breath to ground ourselves before we consciously go back to our plan.

Imagery and Objects

Have you ever sat in front of a fireplace or campfire and been mesmerized by the dancing flames and the crackling of the wood? Or have you ever sat by a lake or an ocean and been fascinated by the ripples or the soothing sounds of the waves? These are only two of the many examples of how we bring present moment awareness to imagery and objects.

♥ Find an item or a place that is particularly beautiful to you (e.g., lake, river, flowers, a touchstone, a lava lamp).

♥ Set your intention for the length of time you want to bring your awareness to the imagery or object (e.g., five or ten minutes).

♥ After taking a few deep breaths, bring your attention to the object. Keep your focus on it and if you notice your mind wandering, simply bring it back to the object.

- There are many phone apps that help with this meditation. You can download them and set the timer for the length of time you want. Some favourite ones are: The Mindfulness App, Headspace, Calm, Mind Body, The Insight Timer.

- The object does not actually have to be real. It can be an actual place you remember, or it may be a beautiful place that you imagine. You might have visited a beautiful lake, river, or waterfall. In this case, you are closing your eyes and bringing that place to your mind's eye. Bring all of your senses to the experience as you remember what the object looked like, sounded like and felt like. You are paying attention to the details you remember.

- It is important to understand that you are not going to get attached to any memories that might be associated with the place or the object; you are simply noticing. Take in the colours, the smells and possibly the feel of your memory. During this time, take note of how you are feeling in your mind-body-spirit.

- When we get attached, even if the memory is beautiful, we are taking ourselves away from the present moment.

The Power of Touch

Touch is very grounding. It gives us the ability to ground ourselves anytime and anywhere. The sensation of touch automatically brings us into the present, freeing us from rumination. To understand the power of touch, all you have to do is think about a time when you were given a hug at the very time you needed it most. The hug brings you right here, right now.

- Hug as often as you can. We love the idea of hugging heart-to-heart—your left side touching the left side of the other person.

- Pat and/or cuddle with your pets as often as possible.

- Hold a touchstone in your hand. Jackie has an angel medallion that she holds in her hand when she needs some additional strength. There are many stones and crystals that have healing properties.

- While sitting in meditation, close your eyes and ground yourself by holding your thumb and index or middle finger together. You will feel the energy flowing through you.

- If you are sitting at your desk or in a meeting, you can simply close your eyes and run your fingers over your lips. This act alone will bring you back into the moment and reduce any anxiety that is arising in the moment.

- When you are anywhere in nature, take the time to touch the trees, the flowers or feel the sand on your feet. Nature is very grounding and connecting to it through touch is powerful.

- Add your other senses to touch. Using and integrating our senses helps to deepen the experience of all senses.

- Bring gentleness and your present-moment awareness to all touch.

All of the other suggestions for touch are easily brought into the classroom. Sadly, as teachers, we must avoid hugging children as there is so much fear around improper touch. However, a teacher can easily bring a variety of stuffed animals and sensory objects into the classroom. These help the students understand the importance of touch and gives them something with which to ground themselves.

Mindful Walking

We do not generally bring awareness to our walking. We always seem to be on the run; rushing for the bus, hurrying to meetings, mindlessly going from point A to point B. It means that as we walk through our lives, we often miss interesting parts and experiences. For example, you could live in a neighbourhood for twenty years and never notice the beautiful gardens that are planted at the end of the street, or the unusual colour of the door on your neighbour's house. Instead we get caught up in our thoughts. We fail to "stop and smell the roses" and see the beauty that is right in front of us.

At meditation retreats, mindful walking is slow and deliberate. It is a meditation practice that is powerful and often provides a space for thoughts and emotions to arise that have been buried. When that happens, it is important to avoid attachment to thinking and feeling. Instead, you simply notice that they are there and then let them go. This kind of walking meditation does not appeal to everyone, but like all of the other practices, experiment with ones that work for you.

You can bring mindfulness to your everyday walking. The same principles apply:

- ♥ Set your intention for the amount of time that you plan to engage in mindful walking.

- ♥ Select your path. It can be short, where you walk back and forth or bring mindfulness to your neighbourhood walk.

- ♥ Engage in good posture to ensure that your energy is flowing freely through your body.

- ♥ Hold your hands in a comfortable way so that you are not fidgeting with them.

- ♥ Start with a few deep cleansing breaths, and then begin to breathe naturally.

- ♥ Start with your left foot, feeling it swing forward, feeling the heel hit the ground, then the ball of the foot, and then the toes.

- ♥ Notice and feel the same thing with your right foot.

- ♥ Continue this pattern of walking with awareness.

- ♥ Continue to walk at a steady pace, one that is comfortable for you. When your attention wanders, bring it back to the sensations of your feet touching the ground.

- ♥ When you have finished your walk, pause by taking deep cleansing breaths and then get on with your day.

  With students, this practice can be done in the hallway, gym, schoolyard, or park. It could be the routine for transitions (moving from one class to another). Mindful walking brings all kinds of surprises to children when they are outside in nature. You can let them watch the amazing world of insects that live in the grass or encourage them to count their steps as they are walking.

Connecting to Nature

No matter where we live, we can always find an element of nature somewhere in our surroundings. There are parks, lakes, rivers, and many beautiful flowers everywhere. Of course, escaping the chaos of big city life and actually finding a peaceful place away from the clamour of traffic and populous noise is the ideal. When you find that special place,

you want to simply focus your attention on the sights and sounds of nature by bringing your awareness to all aspects of the object of your choice. For example, when observing a flower, you are noticing the many shades of colour, the intricate patterns on the petals and leaves, the beautiful fragrance and the way it blows in the breeze. When sitting by water, you are taking in all of the many sounds: the splashing against the shore or dock, the waves, the birds hovering. You might also take in the smell of the water or the air all around you. Water has many healing properties. It is worth spending some time both in and beside the water.

♥ Set your intention to be mindful in nature.

♥ Set a time frame for your intended mindfulness practice.

♥ Take some deep breaths to help you become grounded in the present moment.

♥ Cast your gaze upon a particular object or take in the whole picture with all of your senses.

♥ Simply notice the beauty of nature; this is not the time for thinking or planning.

♥ Access all of your senses.

♥ Connecting to nature can happen while you are walking or sitting; it is your choice.

♥ Notice all aspects of your being as you connect to nature, your mind, body and spirit.

♥ Access nature as often as you can.

♥ If you are unable to get out in nature then bring nature to you by having plants, flowers, rocks, or other natural elements as part of your home décor.

♥ Open your windows to let in the fresh air and be mindful of the breeze.

♥ Appreciate the weather instead of fighting it. When it snows, find something beautiful about the snow instead of focusing on how cold it is or how much you have to shovel. When it rains, focus on the positive aspects of the rain—nurturing the flowers, cooling us down instead of how the rain makes you feel gloomy.

♥ Feel gratitude for the beauty of nature and all that it does for us.

Taking your students outside as often as possible really connects them in ways that the confines of a classroom cannot. You might also consider bringing nature into your classroom by using a terrarium, having a class pet, or using murals that are made with natural artefacts. All of this can encourage your students to "stop and smell the roses" as often as possible.

Body Scan

The body scan is perhaps one of the most useful tools in your mindfulness tool kit. In fact, it is one of the best ways to access your parasympathetic nervous system, and achieve that wonderful source of calm, balance, and well-being. The body scan also emphasizes the mind/body connection. This connection is particularly important if you experience stress-related pain. There is an old saying, "What you resist, persists". This phrase resonated with Jackie the first time she participated in the body scan. Because of fibromyalgia, Jackie was in pain twenty-four

hours a day. When she laid down to sleep, the throbbing and aching would take over her mind and she was unable to fall asleep. She would say she was "suffering over the suffering". Upon learning the body scan, Jackie began to acknowledge that the pain was there, but she no longer became attached to it, thinking about the effect on her body.

In order to begin, find a quiet space to lie down. You can also do the body scan seated in a comfortable chair if you are prone to falling asleep. It is best to do this practice away from any distraction. The time of day does not matter, although doing the scan at a time when you are least likely to fall asleep is helpful (otherwise you won't optimize your attention to the mind/body connection). Having said that, the body scan can be helpful if you wake in the middle of the night and have trouble falling back to sleep.

Once you are lying down:

♥ Make yourself comfortable. Think about keeping a blanket close by in case you feel cold.

♥ Close your eyes and begin to focus on your breath. You might start with several deeper breaths or the 4-7-8 breathing.

♥ Relax your body as best you can, taking note of where you are holding tension without becoming overly focused on it.

♥ Spend a few moments taking note of the air around you, the clothes on your body, your body touching the bed, floor, or chair.

♥ Begin by drawing your awareness to the big toe on your left foot. With this awareness, you notice all of the sensations that are present in your toe, tingling, itching, pain, feelings against your sock. Just notice whatever is there.

♥ Note all sensations including those that may not seem pleasant.

♥ Also take note of the life-giving nature of your body parts (your breath, blood flow, energy, etc.).

♥ After acknowledging these sensations, you will let them bring your awareness to the top of your left foot, the ball of your left foot, the heel, etc.

♥ Now bring your awareness slowly and intentionally to all body parts, going up your left side, and then bringing your awareness to the right side, now reversing the order of focus down the right side, and finishing with your right toe. As you do, continue being aware of the sensations mentioned above.

♥ The body scan is a slow process because you are exploring every nook and cranny of your body. You need to set your intention for at least forty-five minutes to an hour for this practice.

- ♥ It is not uncommon for emotions to arise during the body scan, as they are often associated with parts of our bodies. When emotions arise, simply get curious without becoming attached to them. You are not analyzing the emotions, you are simply noticing, becoming curious, and then getting back to the body scan.

- ♥ At the end of the body scan, you can gently wiggle your toes and fingers as you slowly begin to move. Think about taking time for a nice long stretch before actually getting up to resume your activities.

Some further notes about the body scan:

- ♥ Some people prefer to be guided in the body scan. If that is the case, you can find many recorded body scans on You Tube as well as podcasts and cd's devoted to this practice.

- ♥ While it is beneficial to do a full body scan, it is also helpful to do a mini scan for the purpose of calming yourself down. This practice is especially helpful if you find yourself holding a lot of stress in your body.

- ♥ There is no need to change the body scan in any way for children except to say that you will to do it in less time as children's attention spans are not as developed as those of an adult. You could consider breaking the time up and doing different parts of the body on different days.

Loving Kindness Meditation and Forgiveness

Loving Kindness (Metta) is an ancient Buddhist meditation leading to the development of unconditional loving-kindness and friendliness. "Metta" is something you feel in your heart, a positive emotional state towards others as well as each of us. As a result of practicing Metta, we become more empathetic, more considerate, more kind, more forgiving, and in general, more loving, friendly people. Loving Kindness meditation may be one of the most valuable tools when working with children. It helps them to appreciate others and learn the skills of self-love. Practising loving kindness is one of the practices that children can learn and practise on their own.

Metta practice helps us:

- ♥ Develop our emotional intelligence.

- ♥ Develop resilience.

- ♥ Bring harmony into our lives and in our relationships.

- ♥ Rid ourselves of internal and external conflicts.

- ♥ Overcome lacerating guilt.

- ♥ Be open to loving acceptance of ourselves and others.

- ♥ Deepen our connections with all beings.

- ♥ Cope with stresses that are present in the world, especially as we are often inundated with traumatic news events, which we are powerless to change.

- ♥ Move towards forgiveness: When others have hurt you, you have a choice. You can carry that hurt/anger with you, letting it eat away at you or you can send loving kindness to that person and work towards forgiveness. Forgiveness is generally not about the person you are forgiving; it is about freedom for yourself.

To practise Metta:

♥ Bring your awareness to your heart centre by noticing the beating of your heart and realizing the life-giving force that it provides.

♥ Bring someone or something (a pet) who has given you unconditional love into your awareness. Notice all feelings associated with that unconditional love. This is a good time to make the mind-body-spirit connection.

♥ Now take those feelings and bring them to the following one at a time: family and friends, co-workers, people in your: neighbourhood, city, province/state, country, and people around the world. Each time you move to a different person or group of people, take the time to really feel that loving kindness throughout every aspect of your being. It is important to really *feel* it.

♥ Now bring your loving kindness awareness back to yourself, feeling the love you have shared and surrounding yourself in that love. Breathe it in, feel it in your mind-body-spirit.

♥ Take the time to soak in that loving kindness towards yourself and know that you are worthy of being loved.

While the meditation described above is longer, you can bring it to your classroom every day by simply beginning or ending the day with a phrase such as, "May all beings be happy, may all beings be healthy, may all beings find peace".

Practise daily loving kindness, especially towards yourself. You might find it helpful to remember the "oxygen mask" example that comes from the flight attendant just prior to take off. In an emergency situation when the oxygen masks release, the clear safety instruction is for *you* to put on your oxygen mask first before you attempt to help anyone else! You *must* look after yourself first in order to be able to look after others.

Meditation on Thought and Emotion

When we do mindfulness workshops, we show a cartoon where a person has multiple think bubbles above their head with numerous thoughts floating around. The person is saying, "Hi, my name is…and I am a think-aholic". When we ask how many people can relate to this cartoon, most hands go up. We are all guilty of over-thinking from time to time. We all get caught in thoughts of the past or planning for the future.

Emotion is a powerful force within us. Some people are more comfortable expressing all emotion, whereas others have a difficult time revealing and sharing them. Emotion is a natural part of who we are as human beings. If we openly express our emotions, it helps to raise our emotional intelligence. Conversely, if we bury them, they will emerge in one form or another.

Unexpressed emotion is most commonly associated with physical and mental illness. Think about a time when you have felt an emotion and then noticed that you have tension in your shoulders or a pain in your side. Or think about a time when someone has "lost it" over the smallest detail. Both of these examples are associated with unexpressed emotion.

The key to mindfulness practice is to limit the amount of thinking we do, especially when we get attached to the thoughts. Another benefit is how this practice enhances our ability to deal with emotions in healthy and productive ways. When we purposefully meditate on thought and emotion, we begin to see how much time we engage in thinking. It makes us better equipped to make the mind-body-spirit connection because we begin to see that our thoughts and emotions are having a physical effect that could be dangerous to our health.

It does not mean that we are never going to plan or be reminded of the past; of course, we will, and sometimes, this is appropriate and necessary. When we intentionally bring our awareness to thought and emotion, we are simply noticing and then letting them go.

♥ Set your intention to sit in awareness of thoughts and emotions.

♥ As always, start with your breath, grounding yourself there, and opening yourself up to accept whatever comes up for you.

♥ Notice any thought or emotion as it arises. You are not forcing something to come up; it is a natural process.

♥ Allow yourself to feel curious and then watch as each thought and/or emotion fades away.

♥ Understand that bringing awareness here will take the sting out of the challenging thoughts and emotions, especially when you realize that they are just thoughts and emotions, not reality. Be courageous and tell yourself, "This too shall pass".

♥ You may have to consciously push past any fear that arises. That fear is our ego emerging; it tries to shut us down from dealing with thought and emotion.

♥ If you find yourself overcome with emotions and you don't seem able to sit with them and move on, it is probably wise to seek the help of a therapist who can help you process them. There is nothing wrong with asking for help. Potentially, you could combine mindfulness practice with the therapy you may need.

♥ If you are experiencing challenging thoughts that are also filled with emotion, you might explore the Mindfulness-Based Cognitive Therapy program. MBCT combines the ideas of cognitive therapy with meditative practices and attitudes that are meant to help with the cultivation of mindfulness.

♥ It is important to remember your role with your students. If powerful emotions arise for them, you will need to comfort them, alert their parents, and perhaps recommend counselling so that they can get the help needed.

Non-attachment and Non-judgement

As human beings, it is easy for us to get attached to thoughts and feelings, and all of the judgment that goes along with this attachment. It is also common for human beings to live in a total state of judgement. We judge ourselves and others on a regular basis. We also judge experiences, thoughts, and emotions. Attachment and judgement are dangerous to us and to our relationships with others.

Mindfulness is about practising non-attachment and non-judgement. These practices do not mean that we become detached and cold. It does not mean that we do not experience feelings; in fact, just the opposite is true. We are simply becoming aware of our emotions, embracing each one, knowing they exist but not getting sucked into the vortex that keeps us stuck and unable to live fulfilled lives. When we practise non-attachment and non-judgement, we begin to clear our minds from expectation, and we are able to accept things as they are and not as we think they should be.

- ♥ Set your intention to sit in awareness of your attachment and judgment.

- ♥ As always start with your breath, grounding yourself there, and opening yourself up to accept whatever comes up for you.

- ♥ Whenever thoughts or emotions begin to arise, notice them, be curious about them, and then watch them fade away.

- ♥ Take notice of the attachment and judgement that arises for you and breathe into them.

- ♥ Intentionally, let them fade away.

- ♥ Understand that attachment and judgement are part of the human condition; avoid judging yourself for having attachment and judgement.

- ♥ Understand the difference between judgement and discernment; judgement is harmful; discernment is protective; judgement is harsh; discernment is loving and kind. Discernment promotes an open mind to options and choice.

Deepening Your Practice and Future Steps.

You can build your own program particularly suited to your needs. The following tips are ones that we suggest to get you started, and to keep you on the mindfulness path.

- ♥ Do some research into the vast amount of literature that demonstrates the power of mindfulness. Doing this research helps you see how widespread the practices are, and to understand their value in your life.

- ♥ Find mindfulness authors that speak to you and read them periodically to deepen your understanding of mindfulness. Some suggestions include Jon Kabat-Zinn, Jack Kornfield, Tara Brach, Pema Chodron, Thich Nhat Hanh.

- ♥ Start small and work your way up to longer and longer intervals until you reach a place that works for you.

- ♥ Continue your learning in whatever way speaks to you. Follow your intuition about the learning that is calling you.

- ♥ Practise daily, even if it is only for five minutes. As already mentioned, the research shows that just a five-minute daily practice can re-wire your brain to access the para-sympathetic nervous system more easily.

- ♥ Always come back to your breath whenever you are feeling anxious or stressed.

- ♥ Attend yoga classes to increase your mindfulness practice.

- ♥ Take baby steps if you need more time to fully commit.

- ♥ Pick some mindfulness practices to get you started. Once you are comfortable with them, move on to a new one. You can keep adding to your mindfulness repertoire.

- ♥ Join a meditation "sangha". A sangha is a community of like-minded people who "sit" together. There is power in being with people who are also sitting in meditation.

- ♥ Attend day-long or weekend meditation retreats. These will really help you integrate your practice.

♥ Find the courage to start and then stay with your practice.

♥ Have faith in yourself; knowing that you are already creative, resourceful, and whole!

What Does it Look Like for Children?

All the same principles for meditation discussed here apply to children, except that you want to speak to children in language they understand. Even the youngest of children can learn mindfulness practices, but the amount of time you devote each day will be limited. It is important to ensure that you do not put any pressure on the students. They can also learn to meditate anywhere and anytime. You can demonstrate and rehearse with your students and then encourage them to practise outside of the classroom. A helpful start could be reading a picture book like *Peaceful Piggy Meditation* or *Sitting Like a Frog* so that they can more easily grasp the concept.

The most important aspect of beginning a meditation practice with your students is to make the classroom safe and inviting so they do not feel threatened. If they cannot participate in the beginning, let them find their own way. Perhaps there is a quiet area where those who are distracted can sit away from the rest of the group, engage in an art activity or move to a listening centre where they can put on noise-cancelling headphones.

All children can participate in breath work. One helpful strategy is to encourage them to breathe through a straw so they are able to understand the concept in their own way. It is also helpful to have them place their hand on their diaphragm so they can actually feel the breath. It is important that teachers model breath work for their students so they can see it in action. Teachers can use the breath in their daily interactions with students. For example, when you feel stressed because of an event that is happening in the classroom, you can alert the children that you are feeling stressed and you can show them how you are using your breath to calm yourself.

Remember, there are many ways to bring mindfulness to your work with students, but the first step is always to begin with you. Mindfulness is not going to be helpful to your students if you do not know and appreciate the practice.

What Does it Look Like in the Classroom?

♥ ***Practice Focus:*** Many teachers incorporate mind jars or lava lamps into their classroom spaces so that children can focus on an object to still their minds. You could also make a game out of focusing on images and objects by setting a timer to see how long the children can focus. If you choose to make it a game, it is a good idea to make it a competition with self and not others. Remember, the practice is about focus and not about winning! For children who are easily distracted and find themselves lacking the skills to finish tasks, set a timer so they spend a certain amount of time on a task before leaving it and moving to something different.

♥ *Incorporate Mindfulness into Activities*: There are many examples of activities that you can do with your students in a mindful way. For example, you could cook with them; a perfect time to have them engage with all of their senses. In addition, tidying up following the cooking, can be another mindful opportunity. When children are tidying up, try having them do it in silence as they take their time putting things away. Think about including mindful movement into your physical and health education curriculum or during your daily physical activity. Transition times are often challenging for students and moving silently may help with classroom/behaviour management. You might also insist that walking to and from other areas of the school are mindful times, for example, walking silently on their way to the gym or the library.

♥ *Encourage Emotional Self-Regulation*: Children need to learn emotional self-regulation if they are to become emotionally intelligent, resilient adults. Unfortunately, many children do not learn this skill early in life. Instead of being taught how to self-regulate, children are often told not to: cry, get angry, or be sad. These messages are challenging because they are taught to children by adults who have not learned the importance and need to express emotion. These adults may be well-meaning but in reality, they are simply avoiding having to deal with an emotional outbreak, and potentially a child out of control. However, we know from research, the importance of expressing emotions. While having children purposefully bring thoughts and emotion to the fore may be diffi- cult, a teacher can help by encouraging them to inquire into the thought and emotion when they are thinking or feeling. For example, you can ask them to name the emotion, and then you can have them sit with it, feel it, and then let it go. It is important to teach your students about all of the various emotions and to allow them the space to express their emotions. It is also a good idea for them to notice emotion in others and have them help each other through certain challenges. They can learn to use language like, "It sounds like you are feeling sad" or "It seems like you are feeling angry" when they are interacting with their classmates. This kind of work requires your guidance as a teacher. You can model that process for them. You might tell them how you are feeling in certain situations, and then demonstrate deep breathing as you work to let it go. Showing students your human side goes a long way in teaching them. While understanding these concepts and working through them mindfully may be difficult for children, there can be a lot of teaching around the idea of judgement. We can hold children account- able for their judgement of others and we can dissuade them from judging themselves. Judgement is pervasive in our lives. We can use media literacy to discuss judgement and how it plays a role in our everyday lives. We can certainly point it out in literature, technology, and media.

♥ *Create a Peaceful Area in your Classroom*: Create a space where there are nice cushions, a mind jar or lava lamp. You can fill the area with colouring sheets and crayons, listening centre, stuffed animals, etc. You might also consider lowering the lights in your classroom or bring in fairy lights or lamps that bring a peaceful glow to your room. Read through the many resources that are provided in this book and talk to other teachers who have brought mindfulness to their students. Some teachers like to play soft classical or spa-like music while the students are working.

♥ *How to Make a Mind Jar*: Use a clear jar, or plastic water bottle, something you can see through. Fill the jar with water, and then add glitter that sinks rather than floats. Add some glycerin to the water to slow down the fall of the glitter (you can find glycerin at most drug stores). Other alternatives include small beads or a mix of food colouring and oil. Seal the jar with duct tape so that there are no leaks.

Mindfulness Practices for Children

♥ **Blowing Bubbles:** Children love to blow bubbles. Have bubbles and a bubble blower available so that when students are feeling anxious, they can find a quiet space in the room and watch the bubbles and their many shapes, sizes, and colours.

♥ **Heartbeats:** This activity can be done by individual children or in a group. The students sit or lie down and bring their awareness to their breath. Once everyone is calm, they place their hand over their hearts or on their necks or wrists to begin to count their heart beats.

♥ **I Spy:** This old game brings out children's focused awareness as they search their environment for something special. They will begin by saying, "I spy with my little eye, something that is….". The other players will also inspect their surroundings to see if they know what the object is. The person who guesses will then become the spy.

♥ **Mindful Poses:** A little like Follow the Leader, the teacher will do a mindful pose and the children will follow. You can have the children take turns being the leader.

♥ **Mystery Bag:** Place several objects with different shapes, sizes, and textures in a bag/sack. The children will reach into the bag and, using only their touch, try to identify the object.

♥ **Safari:** Connecting to nature is a very mindful experience. Take the students to the schoolyard or a park and tell them they are going on Safari. They must mindfully explore the landscape to find things like, ants, butterflies, birds, etc. They can either take photographs or notes about their excursion.

♥ **Singing Bowls:** Listening to sound vibration is very soothing. Have the students lie down and close their eyes as you walk about and play the sound of a singing bowl, a musical instrument, or a song. The idea is to stay with the sound and to feel it in your body.

♥ **Spidey-Senses:** Using each of their senses, children will examine objects and try to see anything they may have missed when they first looked at the object. You can use the same object for all five senses or you can switch the object.

♥ **Taste Testing:** This activity is a precursor to mindful eating. Instead of rushing through our meals it is a healthier option to eat mindfully. Have the students experience it through taste-testing a raisin or a textured candy. They start by looking at it and telling you what they see, then smelling it. After this initial experience, they will start by placing the food on their lips and then on their tongue and finally swishing it around in their mouths, having them pay attention to all sensations they experience. They should only swallow when they have been mindful about every aspect of the tasting.

Literature Resources

Picture Books

A Handful of Quiet: Happiness in Four Pebbles by Thich Nhat Hanh

Alphabreaths: The ABS's of Mindful Breathing by Christopher Willard

Breathe Like a Bear: 30 Mindful Moments for Kids to Feel Calm and Focused Anytime, Anywhere by Kira Willey

Crab and Whale by Christiane Kerr and Mark Pallis

I Yoga You by Genevieve Santos

Meditation is an Open Sky by Whitney Stewart

Mindful Millie by Louise Tribble

Moody Cow Meditates by Kerry Lee MacLean

Oliver's Tree by Kit Chase

Peaceful Piggy Meditation by Kerry Lee MacLean

Puppy Mind by Andrew Jordan Nance

Quiet by Tomie dePaola

The Present is a Gift by Elchanan Ogorek

Visiting Feelings by Lauren Rubenstein

What Does it Mean to be Present? By Rana DiOrio

Yawning Yoga by Laurie Jordan

Chapter Books

A Quiet Place by Jacqueline Woodson

Brown Girl Dreaming by Jacqueline Woodson

Rain Reign by Ann M. Martin

Sitting Still Like a Frog by Eline Snel

The Secret Garden by Frances Hodgson Burnett

Where the Mountain Meets the Moon by Grace Lin

FINAL THOUGHTS

The act of teaching is both an art and a science, and the impact of these two in tandem is immense. When teachers are able to remember their own learning experiences as a student and incorporate those memories and feelings into their teaching, they are on the right path to developing empathy for their students and creating a relatedness to them. Teachers create a caregiving consciousness that goes beyond curriculum in their daily interactions with their students. They love what they do and they love their students. This strong combination helps teachers understand the art and the science. The great Maya Angelou once said:

> *I've learned that people will forget what you said, people will forget what you did, but people will never forget how you made them feel.*

Through this book, the authors goal was to share the pertinent theory and practice that they feel are most relevant and impactful in the classrooms of today. This resource will prepare all teachers to create learning environments that will develop academic skills and social-emotional attributes in all of their students. We know the difference that teachers can make and how the work they do is one of the most important in society. Who else has the opportunity to "mold" human development and future generations the way that teachers do? What a gift they all give to the world!

Considering all the content areas shared, i.e., Maslow's hierarchy of needs, culturally relevant and responsive pedagogy, the brain research, emotional intelligence, resiliency, trauma-informed practice, cooperative learning and mindfulness, it is important to note that these are not hierarchical or necessary to accomplish one before moving on to the next. Rather, we see them as a whole, each influencing the other in powerful ways. We recognize that there is a lot of theory, but our objective is to balance it with the application as much as possible. We want teachers to have accessible resources and strategies to help them implement the effective instructional tools in a seamless way.

We recommend that you start slowly, build your instructional skill level and strategies repertoire gradually as you gather confidence. Taking on too much, too soon will become overwhelming and frustrating. Dr. Barrie Bennett used to tell his teacher candidates that, "You come to the faculty of education thirsty for knowledge and we stick your heads under Niagara Falls for a drink". So given that thought, start with a few tactics and strategies that you feel comfortable with and can master over time, e.g., Building the classroom alliance/expectations, Inclusion, Wait time, Think-Pair-Share, Numbered Heads, Community Circle, simple graphic organizers (e.g., placemat, Venn diagram) and then incorporate additional ones as you build your skill level. With a grade partner, plan the use of a wide range of tactics, strategies, etc., together and support each other as you "play" with the different approaches and build your repertoire.

There is no doubt that teaching is challenging and there are many demands made on teachers that are not readily apparent when first entering the profession. If teachers lose their *"why"*, i.e., the reason they joined the teaching profession, they are less likely to be able to create the safe classrooms that are so needed. They are also more inclined towards burn-out because they begin to see all of the challenges that go into teaching as insurmountable. However, when teachers are able to hone and develop the skills described in this book, they are more able to stay focused on why they became teachers in the first place. By providing the research, examples, tools and strategies in *Hearts and Minds Matter*, we hope we have helped you find ways to make your classrooms safe and inclusive, and rich with instructional approaches that engage students and impact significantly on their learning. Given this perspective though, remember to look after yourself. The care and attention you will give to your students is only possible if you give care and attention to yourself first.

We hope that this book has provided you with the underlying theory and the relevant practices that will "arm" you with the necessary resources to achieve the goal of building a learning environment that is safe, welcoming, challenging and stimulating.

Teaching is a profession that comes with many rewards. Yes, there are stressors, but the positives far outweigh the negatives when you are able to build an inclusive community where you have engaged learners who *want* to be in your classroom. Keep in mind that when you invest in creating an inclusive culture, where you know your students' needs and wants and their unique learning styles, your commitment will develop their emotional intelligence and resilience and prepare them to be successful in their world of tomorrow. It is also important to fully understand that while curriculum is important, the nurturance of caring, confident human beings who know they belong is at the root of our children being able to learn. We must work with them to create a strong community where they are learning from us and we are learning from them.

In the words of Margaret Mead:

> *Never doubt that a small group of thoughtful, committed citizens can change the world; indeed, it's the only thing that ever has.*

CLASSROOM RESOURCES

Attentive Listening

One of the critical components when creating a productive and success-ful learning environment is to have students who can focus and listen attentively. In today's world of fast-paced technology and stimulation, it is challenging for students to slow down their brains so that they can focus on the verbal messages coming at them and absorb the information. It is essential that in order to clearly establish the expectation of attentive lis-tening, the teacher needs to explicitly teach what attentive listening looks like and once established as a classroom norm, they must consistently focus on building the strength of this skill in all the students.

The Chinese characters that make up the verb 'to listen' tell us something significant about this skill.

EAR
EYES
UNDIVIDED ATTENTION
HEART

As part of the teaching process, it is important to clarify for the students that listening is a multi-faceted skill. Use a 'double t chart' to identify the essential components within attentive listening, i.e., what it "looks like", "sounds like" and "feels like". The graphic represents a Chinese symbol that identifies all the components that are involved when someone is attentively listening. This visual is an extremely useful tool to use with your students when teaching this skill. The next step would be to have them practise in triads all the components as outlined in the graphic. One strategy that is highly effective in teaching attentive listening is Paraphrase Passport described in Chapter Four on Emotional Intelligence. It is in the section on What Does it Look Like in the Classroom.

In order to make an impact on attentive listening over time, it is critical to consistently reinforce the essential elements with the students. Put the completed double t chart up in the classroom outlining the expectations and positively recognize students who exhibit these behaviours on a consistent basis. Attentive listening is a critical life skill and one that could positively impact success in life.

Checklists

Used extensively in assessment and evaluation, a checklist will give your students an opportunity to review what must be done and then a chance to acknowledge they have completed each task.

ACTIVITY	COMPLETE	INCOMPLETE	NEEDS REVIEW
I have designed my story using the story web			
My story has a beginning, middle and end			
I have used adjectives and adverbs			
My message is clear			
I have added appropriate graphics			
I have used appropriate punctuation			
I have had a peer edit			
I am proud of my writing			

Community Circle

The very nature of the seating arrangement builds openness and connection. It builds inclusion and community as you create the atmosphere and the opportunity to share deeply. Students will sit in a community circle for the purpose of sharing ideas, reflecting, creating a space for attentive listening, sharing cares, concerns and compliments, or any activity where you would like the students to be able to interact more intimately.

Ensure that the students are heeding the alliance that you have created as a class. You can begin the community circle with a question or a statement. As the teacher, you will always go first to model what the student contributions should look like. Some teachers will use the community circle daily and others may limit to once or twice per week.

Jackie Eldridge and Denise McLafferty

Concept Attainment (See example in Chapter Seven)

This is an Inductive Thinking Strategy adapted from David Perkins' work on Knowledge as Design (also Jerome Bruner's work):

- ♥ What are the critical attributes of the concept?
- ♥ What are the purposes of the concept?
- ♥ What are the model cases of the concept?
- ♥ What are the arguments for learning the concept?

Phase 1: Present the focus statement and the data set.

- ♥ What is your focus statement?
- ♥ How will you present the data set, all at once or one at a time?
- ♥ Students compare the attributes of the YES examples and contrast them with the NO examples.
- ♥ What medium will you use to present the data set - picture, overhead, objects, role-play, chart, etc.?
- ♥ Students generate and test their hypothesis.
- ♥ When will you decide to present the tester to check for understanding?
- ♥ When will you decide to stop presenting the data and move into phase two?

Phase 2: Sharing the hypothesis and their thinking

- ♥ How will you have the students share their hypotheses and thinking - individually, randomly, pairs, teacher selected, individual from group, etc.?
- ♥ How will you deal with incorrect or partially correct hypotheses? Remember that students may see things you did not realize were in the data set or simply err in their analysis.
- ♥ When students have determined the essence or the critical attributes of the concept, how will you start to move to Phase 3? This is an essential element.

Phase 3: Application or extension of the concept

- ♥ Students describe their thoughts about how their thinking progressed during the analysis of the data.
- ♥ How will you make this concept come alive so that students understand the purpose of the concept and its value?
- ♥ What questions could you ask?
- ♥ What level of Bloom's Taxonomy are your questions?
- ♥ Could you insert any other strategies or critical thinking skills at this point to extend their thinking?

♥ Hasty or Sweeping Generalizations: this refers to the making of a judgement or broad statement based on limited information

♥ The Either – Or – Fallacy: this refers to polarizing an issue when in fact other positions or both positions are possible

♥ The Unknowable Statistic: this refers to the making of a statement based on a statistic that is impossible or unrealistic to calculate

♥ Inconsistencies and Contradictions: this refers to arguing a point while going against or acting in a way that negates your argument

♥ The Loaded Question: this question does not allow for any answer but the one the person who asked it wants; a dead-end question

♥ False Causation: this involves invoking a cause/effect relationship when it is at best a correlation or a coincidence

♥ The False Analogy: this occurs when a comparison is made which is not accurate

♥ The Slippery Slope (Domino Effect): this implies that if one thing happens, then all these other things will happen as a consequence

Designing an Alliance

This image is an example of a Classroom Alliance/Classroom Expectations created by the teacher with the students and then posted in the classroom. This alliance represents the roadmap by which the students and teaching staff will conduct themselves in the classroom. It helps guide them in choices that are made and how they interact with each other. It is an organic tool and can be changed, modified, updated as the year progresses.

Double T Chart

This is an extremely useful tool in creating clear expectations for students and building the classroom expectations and/or the Classroom Alliance. Use this strategy to break down all behaviours in an explicit way for students. To maximize the impact, ensure that students are involved in the process of clearly delineating the expectations within each identified behaviour. As a check for understanding, make sure that all behaviours are observable and measurable.

MUTUAL RESPECT		
Looks Like	Sounds Like	Feels Like
Cooperation Nodding heads in agreement Eye contact	Statements of appreciation Please, Thank you Indoor voices	Safe Welcoming Warm

Examine Both Sides

EBS is a thinking organizer connected to critical thinking and the search for truth. It is a pre-skill for debating or for Academic Controversy. It encourages students to look at both sides of an issue.

Process:

What is the point of the lesson?

- ♥ To understand both sides

- ♥ To apply their newfound understanding to another form such as an essay

- ♥ To evaluate a piece of writing on the subject. In other words, this can be a lesson, or form a foundation for further objectives

How can you generate a statement/question that allows for equal exploration of both sides of an issue?

Read your statement/question carefully.

- ♥ Is it bias free or equally biased for both sides?

- ♥ Does it set reasonable parameters on the dimensions of the exploration (i.e., not too wide, not too narrow)?

You will ask yourself

- ♥ Which organizer, i.e., PMI, Venn Diagram or other, is most appropriate for the type of content being explored?

- ♥ How can the class best be organized? Quiet seat work? Pairs? Groups?

- ♥ What is the most helpful way of reporting their findings?

- ♥ How will I know that they really do understand both sides of the issue?

- ♥ What criteria will you use to evaluate the understanding?

Four Corners (Cooperative learning tactic)

- ♥ Begin with a statement, issue, or question

- ♥ Label your corners: Strongly Agree, Agree, Disagree, Strongly Disagree

- ♥ Students are given a specified period of quiet time in which to make up their minds. At this stage, dialogue is not allowed

- ♥ Students move into the corner which best represents their view of the issue

- ♥ In small groups, students discuss why they moved to the corner they did and record their combined reasons

- ♥ Students then report on their reasons from each corner

Gallery Walk

A Gallery Walk allows the opportunity for students to learn from each other and to celebrate their work. Students can stand with their work and explain it to others or the students can simply go around and visit. There is an excellent opportunity here to have students give each other feedback and appreciations.

Graphic Organizers

The following strategies were adapted from *Beyond Monet, The Artful Science of Instructional Intelligence*, Barrie Bennett/Carol Rolheiser. These include various kinds of graphs and diagrams that organize ideas visually. They help readers classify ideas and communicate effectively. With vivid shapes, symbols and connectors, graphic organizers visualize the relationship between different parts. They are a powerful option for students who process information and make connections in a visual way.

♥ **Concept Mapping** helps the learner to connect existing knowledge with new knowledge; this makes knowledge dynamic rather than passive. As a framework tool, it assists in the formation of connections, in organizing concepts and the relationships between facts, concepts and ideas. It is an analytical process that can be used: to take notes, to study for an exam, to brainstorm, or to make connections between ideas. It enhances memory.

Directions:

♥ Start with a major term or idea from which the next term or idea extends either in a hierarchical or radiating format – Concept Maps usually start at the top of the page

♥ Shift is from more complex to less complex idea or major to minor

♥ Connecting lines are drawn between concepts

♥ Linking words are placed on the lines stating the relationship between concepts

♥ Cross links can be made between one part of the concept hierarchy or classification and another

♥ Optional: Colour can be used to follow relationships

♥ Examples of concepts can be added

Materials:

♥ A sheet of paper for each student or group

♥ Post it notes or index cards

♥ Coloured pens or crayons, even scissors and glue if pictures will be used

Process:

♥ Brainstorm, individually or in a group, the key ideas

♥ Students put their ideas onto cards or post-it notes

♥ Sort/classify the cards, looking for relationships between ideas

♥ Paste or transfer the ideas onto the large piece of paper

♥ Draw lines between concepts and place words on the lines that illustrate their relationships

♥ Look for cross links between different concepts

♥ **Fishbone** (sometimes called herringbone map) is a type of graphic organizer that is used to explore the many aspects or effects of a complex topic, helping the students to problem solve and to identify and organize their thoughts in a simple, visual way. It is a more sophisticated way of Brainstorming or CAF (Considering All Factors). A fishbone diagram is a visual way to look at cause and effect. It is a more structured approach than some other tools available for brainstorming causes of a problem. A fishbone diagram can be helpful in identifying possible causes for a problem that might not otherwise be considered by directing the team to look at the categories and think of alternative causes.

   ♥ The head (circle) of the bone provides the issue or idea that acts as the focus for the thinking. Framing the question/statement is essential in providing the direction for the exercise

   ♥ Possible contributing causes are listed on the smaller "bones" under various cause categories

   ♥ The squares are the classifiers, or main ideas

   ♥ When you are brainstorming causes, consider having team members write each cause on sticky notes, going around the group asking each person for one cause

   ♥ Continue going through the rounds, getting more causes, until all ideas are exhausted

   ♥ Encourage each person to participate in this activity and to voice their own opinions

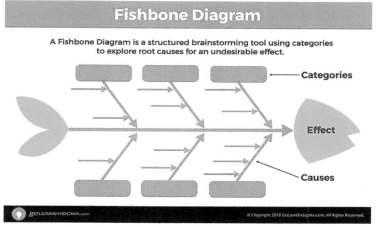

   ♥ To help identify the root causes from all the ideas generated, consider a multi-voting technique such as having each team member identify the top three root causes

   ♥ Ask each team member to place three tally marks or colored sticky dots on the fishbone next to what they believe are the root causes that could potentially be addressed

   ♥ Use the fishbone diagram tool to keep the team focused on the causes of the problem, rather than the symptoms

   ♥ Consider drawing your fish on a flip chart or large dry erase board

   ♥ Make sure to leave enough space between major categories on the diagram so that you can add minor detailed causes later

♥ Graffiti (Cooperative learning tactic)

Graffiti is a creative brainstorming process that involves collecting the wisdom of all or most of the students in the class.

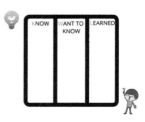

Method:

- ♥ Begin by introducing the concept of Graffiti. It helps make the process more meaningful for students

- ♥ Place students into groups of three or four

- ♥ Provide a large sheet of paper (station) for each group

- ♥ Each piece of paper has a topic/question in the middle (can be same or different for each group)

- ♥ Students get a reasonable amount of Wait Time to think

- ♥ Student are given a specified amount of Record Time to write down their answers/ideas on the sheet

- ♥ Then the group stands up and goes to another station and adds their thoughts to the information already there

- ♥ They should NOT read info already there. Duplication is irrelevant, and often can simply indicate that info is important

- ♥ The process continues until all groups have visited all stations

- ♥ When they return, they now have the collective wisdom of the class

Considerations:

- ♥ Consider giving each group different coloured pens. When inappropriate comments happen, and they do, it is easier to trace

- ♥ Know how you will deal with inappropriate comments before you begin

♥ KWL Chart: (What I Know, What I Wonder/Want to Know, and What I Learned)

KWL charts are graphic organizers that help students organize information before, during, and after a unit or a lesson. They can be used to engage students in a new topic, activate prior knowledge, share unit objectives, and monitor students' learning.

♥ Mind Mapping

This graphic organizer helps the learner to connect existing knowledge with new knowledge; this makes knowledge dynamic rather than passive. As a framework tool, it assists in the formation of connections, in organizing concepts and the relationships between concepts. It is an analytical process that can be used: to take notes, to study for an exam, to brainstorm, or to make connections between ideas. In addition, it enhances memory.

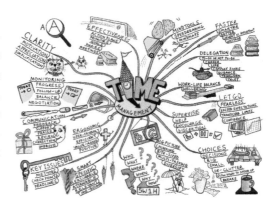

Essentials of Mind Mapping:

- ♥ The central image represents the subject being mapped
- ♥ The main themes radiate like branches from that central image
- ♥ Those branches have a key image or key word printed on an associated line
- ♥ The branches have a connected structure
- ♥ Optional: Use of colour and codes

Materials:

- ♥ A sheet of paper for each student or group
- ♥ Coloured pens or crayons, even scissors and glue if pictures will be used

Process:

- ♥ Select a topic. It helps to think of a visual that captures the essence of that topic and use it in the centre
- ♥ Brainstorm the key ideas related to that topic
- ♥ Record all ideas
- ♥ Group into common categories
- ♥ Draw a picture or symbol that represents each of the key ideas brainstormed
- ♥ Position those visuals around the outside of the visual in the centre of the map
- ♥ Put in the key word then connect the key words to the centre
- ♥ Flow with ideas radiating out from each of the key ideas and continue the above process
- ♥ Reflect alone, with a partner, with a small group or with the class. Talk through the journey you took to conceptualize the key ideas related to the topic. Explore the relationships between different aspects of the map

♥ Placemat

Placemat is a form of collaborative learning that combines writing and dialogue to ensure accountability and participation of all students. It involves groups of students working, both alone and together, around a single piece of paper to simultaneously involve all members.

- ♥ Chart paper is preferable (but not necessary), different colour pens or pencils
- ♥ The paper is divided into sections based on the number of members in the group with a central square or circle (samples below)
- ♥ Students work alone at first responding to the teacher's prompt in their own section, e.g., brainstorm around a curriculum concept and their understanding, generate new ideas around an upcoming topic, or decision making on a class celebration
- ♥ Ensure that each student has their own colour to establish accountability

- Students share information with their group. Results are recorded in the centre of the page. Eliminate any repetition. The expectation may be that each group presents a specified number of ideas, e.g., top 3

- Sharing then takes place with the rest of the class. This can be done with Walkabout, Round Robin, reporting to the whole class or other techniques depending on purpose or time

- **Venn Diagram**

  Venn diagram is an illustration that uses circles to show the relationships among things or finite groups of things. Part of the circles that overlaps have a commonality while the part of the circles that do not overlap, do not share those traits. Venn diagrams help to visually represent the similarities and differences between two concepts.

  - Students are placed in small groups (maximum 4), and on a piece of chart paper they draw two overlapping circles (see example)

  - In this example, students are comparing the differences and similarities between Canada and The United States

  - Students discuss the topic and decide what is the same and what is different between the two countries

  - In each circle, the two items are identified at the top, e.g., Canada and The United States

  - Students discuss and list things that are distinct about Canada and place in that portion of the circle. Similarly, they list the things distinct about The United States and place in that circle

  - In the overlapping portion in the centre, they discuss and list the things that both countries have in common

  - Venn diagrams operate at the analysis level of Bloom's Taxonomy

  - There is more than one type of Venn diagram

  - They are particularly powerful when used in combination with tactics such as: Numbered heads, Walk About, Place Mat

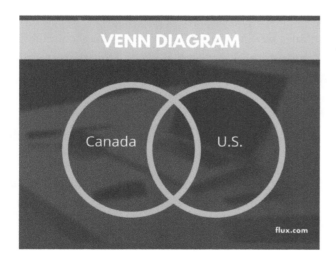

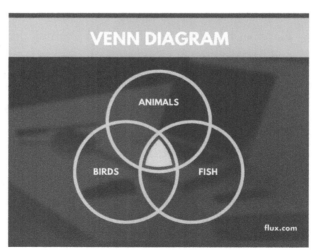

Jackie Eldridge and Denise McLafferty

Inside Outside Circles

Inside outside circles provide a mechanism for students to share with each other, and then by shifting positions in their circle, the opportunity to meet with a new partner to continue or begin a new conversation.

Method:

- ♥ Assign half of the class to be A and the other half B
- ♥ It can be used with groups of 6 or more – one half are inside and the other half outside
- ♥ Students face each other between circles
- ♥ Put a question/problem on the board
- ♥ Give the students wait time to process the question and answer
- ♥ The person on the inside of the circle will share how they would answer the question or solve the problem. Outside circle is attentively listening and when the inside person finishes, they paraphrase what they heard
- ♥ Now the outside circle will share while the inside circle attentively listens
- ♥ When both have shared and the signal is given, people on the inside move one person to the right to be ready for the next question/problem

Interest Inventories

As we work daily to develop the skills of young readers, writers, speakers, listeners, and thinkers, we constantly consider this: What will engage them? How will we help them relate the school content to their lives?

As teachers strive to be culturally relevant, we do our best to include relatable materials into our curricula: articles, media, song lyrics, speeches, websites, and film and documentary clips. For many teachers, this is exciting stuff, but for others, particularly new teachers who already feel overwhelmed by planning, grading, and management, it is worrisome. Finding relevant, engaging material to use with students takes time and effort.

What is the easiest way to know what students are interested in? What are the issues most on their minds? Ask them. Ask them often, and in multiple ways. Find out what they are into—the latest music, fad, or Netflix series they are all watching. It is our job to know the culture of our students. and culture goes beyond ethnicity and includes age group, trends, concerns, and interests.

Jigsaw

This cooperative learning strategy allows a student to become an 'expert' in some aspect of a topic, then return to a 'home' group to share what he or she has learned. Expertise is developed, acknowledged, and shared among the members of each group as they encourage each other in the learning process. *Note:* Previous work in pairs and small groups will help students be successful with this sophisticated strategy.

Steps

♥ Decide how to divide students into Home groups of no more than four

♥ Ask the students in the groups to each assign themselves a letter (A–D)

♥ Have students form new groups (of all A's, B's, etc.) to become expert groups

♥ Ask one member of each group to pick up sheets providing information and questions about their topic

♥ Allot enough time for students to become familiar with their topic, jot down notes, and check their understanding

♥ Have students thank their expert group and return to their home group. The A's present their expert information to their home groups first, the B's next, until everyone has presented and shared the research on their topic, and checked that the information has been understood

Hints and Management Ideas

♥ Pre-assign groups. You can incorporate letter heads (a-d) and divide the class

♥ Give ample time for expert and home groups to gather, discuss, and share their research (15 minutes is a reasonable time)

♥ Make sure that your instructions are clear and that they are visible for students

♥ Monitor the discussions for common confusions and to be sure students are staying on track

Benefits of Jigsaw

♥ When students have appropriate 'think time', the quality of their responses improves

♥ Students are actively engaged in the thinking and in becoming 'mini' experts on the topic assigned to them

♥ The activity facilitates interaction among students and gives them time to communicate and check for understanding prior to presenting to the Home group

♥ Many students find it safer or easier to enter into a discussion with a classmate, rather than with a large group; in this activity, everyone gets a chance to share

Jackie Eldridge and Denise McLafferty

Journals and Learning Logs

The value and positive impact of reflection is well documented. When we encourage reflection, we know through the research that it can help boost students' critical thinking skills; can enhance student ability to remember information and turn it into knowledge; can encourage students to think about their own thinking (meta-cognition) and can help students prepare for assignments and examinations.

- ♥ Be clear about the journal's purpose: voice personal feelings and responses, develop and apply critical thinking skills, or some combination of both
- ♥ Offer personal examples to help students understand what is expected of them
- ♥ Evaluate only journal content, not form, spelling, or grammar
- ♥ Types of Reflection Journals: Observations, Questions, Speculations, Self-awareness, Integration of theory and ideas, and Critique
- ♥ The Reflection Cycle: Reflect (think); Analyze (explain & gain insight); Record (what)

Multiple Intelligences

This was a theory first posited by Harvard developmental psychologist Howard Gardner in 1983 suggesting human intelligence can be differentiated into nine modalities: visual-spatial, verbal-linguistic, musical-rhythmic, logical-mathematical, interpersonal, intrapersonal, naturalistic, bodily-kinesthetic and existential. Behind the theory of Multiple Intelligences is that people learn in a variety of different ways.

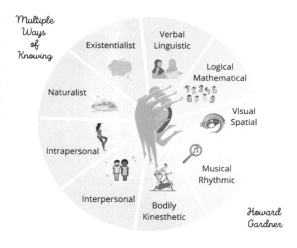

These Multiple Intelligences range from the use of words, numbers, pictures, and music, to the importance of social interactions, introspection, physical movement and being in tune with nature. Accordingly, an understanding of which type(s) of intelligence a student may possess can help teachers adjust learning styles, teaching styles, student groupings, student tasks, and potentially suggest certain career paths for learners. There are assessment tools available for teachers to use with their students to determine their intelligences.

Numbered or Lettered Heads

Increases student accountability without increasing stress when used in combination with other tactics such as Think-Pair-Share, Placemat, PMI, EBS, Three-Step Interview, Inside/Outside Circles

- ♥ Is one of simplest and useful group tactics
- ♥ Randomly groups students

- ♥ Simply means to have groups number off (1,2,3...) or letters (A, B, C...)
- ♥ Assists in initiating a transition or handing out, collecting materials

PMI: Positive, Minus, Interesting

PMI is a thinking organizer. It assists in making wise decisions, critical thinking (analysis) and evaluation. It invites exploration of an issue from the point of view of what will or will not work.

- ♥ *'Positive'* refers to reasons why something is a good idea or decision
- ♥ *'Minus'* refers to why something will not work or is unwise
- ♥ *'Interesting'* refers to the position or action one takes having balanced out the positives and minuses
- ♥ This strategy involves brainstorming around a topic/issue and collecting the ideas on a PMI chart

Reading and Analyzing Non-fiction (RAN)

A RAN (Reading and Analysing Non-fiction) Chart is a graphic organizer that students can use to organize their thoughts and learning as they work through an inquiry. To start, students record their prior knowledge and wonderings they have about the topic or inquiry question. As they progress through the gathering and analysing information phase, students confirm what they knew, record any misconceptions that were part of their prior knowledge, and add new knowledge they gained.

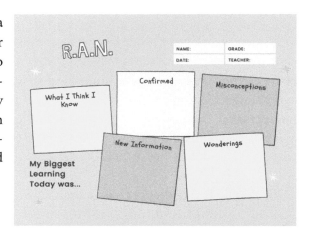

Resilience

Below are two charts. The first identifies the characteristics of resilience, the factors that influence its development and the personal strengths most often identified when one is resilient. The second makes the connections between resiliency and the development of emotional intelligence.

Resiliency Framework
Characteristics that Elicit and Foster Natural Resiliency in Children

Family   School   Community

Protective Factors

Caring Relationships   High Expectations   Opportunities for Meaningful
& Positive Messages   Participation & Contribution

Characteristics Most Often Associated with Resilience

Social Competence	Sense of Autonomy & Identity	Sense of Purpose & Belief in a Bright Future	Problem-Solving & Metacognition
• Empathy • Communication Skills • Cross-cultural competence • Sense of Humour	• Self-efficacy • Internal locus of control • Mastery • Self-awareness • Detachment from negative influences • Stress tolerance	• Special Interests • Imagination • Goal Direction • Achievement • Motivation • Educational Aspiration • Persistence	• Planning • Goal-setting • Critical Thinking • Resourcefulness

What are you consciously doing to foster resilience with your students?

Resiliency Framework
Characteristics that Elicit and Foster Natural Resiliency in Children

Family   School   Community

Protective Factors

Caring Relationships   High Expectations   Opportunities for Meaningful
& Positive Messages   Participation & Contribution

Characteristics Most Often Associated with Resilience

Social Competence	Sense of Autonomy & Identity	Sense of Purpose & Belief in a Bright Future	Problem-Solving & Metacognition
• Empathy • Communication Skills • Cross-cultural competence • Sense of Humour	• Self-efficacy • Internal locus of control • Mastery • Self-awareness • Detachment from negative Influences • Stress tolerance	• Special Interests • Imagination • Goal Direction • Achievement • Motivation • Educational Aspiration • Persistence	• Planning • Goal-setting • Critical Thinking • Resourcefulness

Making Connections: Emotional Intelligence and Resilience

Self-Perception	Self-Expression	Interpersonal	Decision-Making	Stress Management
• Self-respect • Self-actualization • Emotional self-awareness	• Emotional expression • Assertiveness • Independence	• Relationships • Empathy • Social responsibility	• Problem-solving • Reality-testing • Impulse control	• Flexibility • Stress tolerance • Optimism

Snowball

The objective of snowball is to provide students with an opportunity to make suggestions, answer questions, give opinions, etc., anonymously. Have students sit in a community circle and give each an 8 x 10 piece of paper. The students fold the paper in four, creating four clear sections. When prompted by the teacher, for example, "How do we want to celebrate the end of the school year?" each student will write their suggestion in a pre-designated spot, e.g., top left quadrant. When the teacher observes that all students are finished, they call out: "Snowball" and all students crumple up their piece of paper and throw into the centre of the circle (place a hula hoop or an empty container in the centre to give the students a target).

The teacher then instructs each student to take one of the snowballs, being careful not to take their own, and read the suggestion to the community. The activity continues until all four sections are completed. The teacher then gathers all snowballs so that there is a written record of all student responses. This strategy can be used to answer anonymous questions, review work, write a story or a poem.

Student Groups

To build Inclusion, all students need the opportunity to get to know every other student in the classroom. To achieve this, teachers need to ensure that students are grouped in a variety of ways, e.g., pairs, triads, and quads, on a daily basis. And as part of these groups, an inclusion starter is always included, e.g., What is your favourite food? Through this process of "Getting to Know Each Other", we build inclusion and community throughout the school year. Additionally, inclusive classrooms, where students know each other, are aware and understand each other, results in learning environments where there is tolerance and acceptance.

Student Portfolios

This way of documenting learning is widespread among schools. It is a meaningful and safe way for students to provide evidence of their academic and social growth, set their own intentions and goals and provide reflections and exemplars of their work. Students gain a sense of control when using portfolios, unlike what can happen when assessment is continually forced on them. Portfolios are often used in student-led conferences and are a way for children to present their learning to their parents and teachers.

Advocates of student portfolios argue that compiling, reviewing, and evaluating student work over time can provide a richer, deeper, and more accurate picture of what students have learned when compared to more traditional measures, such as, quizzes, or final exams that only measure what students know at a specific point in time.

Teaching using the Performing Arts

Singing, drama, storytelling, role-play, music and/or movement, are all ways to engage the learner and to stimulate the brain for more significant learning and retention. Performing arts are an essential method of communication and learning and are strongly linked to language. We perceive the world through the senses, and the arts allows us to understand (observe), explore, experiment, and express ourselves. The performing arts provide another outlet for children to interact with others. When combined with dance, music and drama, children can use language to understand and express more complex ideas.

- ♥ **Music**, according to the Ministry of Education, Ontario Curriculum, will help students find a source of enjoyment and personal satisfaction and will gain creative problem solving skills, individual and cooperative work habits, knowledge of themselves and others, a sense of personal responsibility, and connections to their communities. Music experiences include (but are not limited to): singing, playing instruments, creating or composing music, listening to and reciting rhymes (with or without music), creating rhymes or raps, listening to and viewing live performances, interpreting and discussing music, performing to an audience, combining music with movement/dance, and reflecting on and appreciating music. Some musical concepts that can be explored include rhythm, pitch, volume, duration, tone/quality, and patterns.

  - ♥ Embed language in music. Experiment with different instruments and encourage children to find the words that describe what kind of sounds they are making (e.g., loud, soft, sharp, twangy, strong, scratchy)

  - ♥ Use songs and rhymes to help children learn new words and concepts, e.g., "Head, Shoulders, Knees and Toes" for body parts, or "Going on a Bear Hunt" for prepositions (over, under, around, through)

  - ♥ Play mystery sound games where children hear an unknown sound or instrument and are asked to describe what they hear

  - ♥ Use repetitive songs to give children multiple opportunities to practise words and phrases (e.g., "B-I-N-G-O", "Ten Green Bottles Standing on the Wall")

  - ♥ Change the lyrics to well-known songs to introduce new concepts (e.g. change "Old Macdonald Had a Farm" to "Old Macdonald Had a Ship" where he has a sail, anchor, wheel, lifeboat, and map)

- ♥ **Dance and Movement**, according to the Ministry of Education, Ontario Curriculum, introduces students to the notions that movement is a medium of expression and that the human body is an instrument. Dance transforms images, ideas, and feelings into movement sequences. Learning in dance requires a balance of knowledge, skills, and attitudes, and embraces movement, creation, and performance. Appreciation of dance expands students' awareness of the richness of various cultures around the world. In an educational context, dance offers children an opportunity to learn by involving the whole body in kinaesthetic exploration, cognitive processing, aesthetic experimentation, and social engagement. (Deans, Meiners, Young and Rank (2017, p.95)

- ♥ As a teaching practice and learning mode, dance and movement offer further opportunities for language learning

- ♥ Children can use the universal "language of dance" to express their ideas and make meaning. Some types of dance experiences include developing a dance/movement vocabulary; improvisation using language, sound and music; creating dances; learning traditional or cultural dances; performing dances; linking dance to other art forms; appreciating the history and culture of dance

♥ **Drama,** according to the Ministry of Education, Ontario Curriculum, drama provides students with an opportunity to take on roles and to create and enter imagined worlds. They learn about themselves in a unique way, the art of drama, and the world around them. Students engage in social interaction and collaboration as they create, perform, and analyse drama. Through informal presentations and more formal performances, students use drama to communicate their aesthetic and personal values. Students develop their awareness and use of the elements of drama (role/character, relationship, time, and place, focus and emphasis, and tension) to create drama works that are related to their personal interests and experience.

- ♥ Drama enables students to imagine and participate in exploration of their worlds, individually and collaboratively. Students actively use body, gesture, movement, voice, and language, taking on roles to explore and depict real and imagined worlds

- ♥ Drama is powerful because of its multiple purposes as a tool for teaching (pedagogy), an artform, and as a socio-cultural experience (sociodramatic play). (Bird, Donelan, & Sinclair, 2017)

- ♥ Some key dramatic elements that can be explored and learned through drama experiences include: *role*: different parts that performers take, such as parents, children, doctors, teachers, construction workers, sailors, scientists, kings, and queens; *character*: the identity of the parts that are played, including their characteristics, motivations, desires, histories, and cultures; *focus*: the ability of the performer to concentrate and channel their energy into the performance; *tension*: how conflict or suspense is communicated through the performance; *climax*: the highest peak of tension/conflict; *transformation of spaces and objects*: how spaces and objects can be transformed from one thing to another through the actors' use of voice and body language; and, *symbolic use of spaces and objects*: how the actors pretend that spaces and objects are representative of something else.

Think-Pair-Share

This is an instructional tactic where students are asked to think for a moment first, then pair with a classmate to compare their experiences/thoughts, then share them with a larger group.

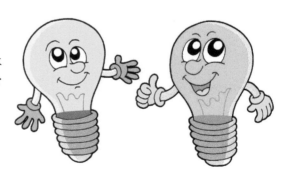

Pre-skills:

- ♥ Can students listen effectively and actively to one another?

- ♥ Can they paraphrase what another person says?

- ♥ Can they suspend judgement?

Jackie Eldridge and Denise McLafferty

Factors to consider beforehand:

- ♥ Do students perceive the classroom as a safe environment for sharing?

- ♥ How long should each part of the process take?

- ♥ Are there an odd or even number of students?

- ♥ Who will work with the ESL student or those who, for example are 'loners'?

- ♥ How will you pair up people? Number them off? Let them choose? Alphabetical order?

- ♥ How accountable will you make each student? How will you do so and still keep the environment an emotionally safe one?

Think

What background information do students need to be able to think effectively about the question?

Pair

How can you frame the question to indicate the level of thinking you expect: recall, comprehension, application, analysis, evaluation, or synthesis (Bloom's Taxonomy)? How directed do you wish this to be? Discussion or listen, repeat, record or something between?

Share

Who will report? Make it random so all are equally accountable (e.g., the person wearing a red shirt) or a more directed process. What will you do with correct, incorrect, partially correct responses; a silly response; a convoluted response; a guess, a 'no' response, and still maintain an emotionally safe place?

Three Step Interview (Cooperative Learning Tactic)

- ♥ Three Step Interview (Cooperative Learning tactic)

- ♥ Encourages students to share their thinking, ask questions and take notes

- ♥ Works best with 3 per group, but can be modified for groups of 4

- ♥ Assumes a knowledge base is in place about which the interviewee can talk. This may be from prior research, a report, homework

Pre-skills:

- ♥ Asking questions: types, levels of difficulty, sequence, open and closed questions

- ♥ Note taking skills

- ♥ Interview skills: are there questions that you should not answer? What if you do not understand the question?

Method:

- ♥ Assign a letter to each student: Interviewer; Interviewee; Reporter
- ♥ The roles rotate after each interview
- ♥ Gauge time needed for each interview
- ♥ When they are done, they do a Round Robin and share the key information they recorded when they were Person C: The Reporter

Value Lines

These are thinking and emotion organizers. They are:

- ♥ A simpler version of Four Corners. They use a continuum between opposites to place a student's thoughts/emotions
- ♥ Used in combination with other tactics and strategies
- ♥ Opposite ends can consist of: Agree --------------Disagree; Is an example of ------------------Is not an example of... Should ------------Shouldn't

For example: use value lines at the beginning and end of a lesson to see how students' positions have shifted; in combination with Think, Pair, Share to examine why students have chosen their particular spot on a continuum; Mental Set creation at the beginning of a lesson; or a form of closure

REFERENCES

Aronson, E. & Patnoe, S. (1997). *The Jigsaw Classroom*. New York: Addison-Wesley Longman.

Beattie, M. (1995). *Constructing Professional Knowledge in Teaching: A Narrative of Change and Development*. New York: Teachers College Press.

Benard, B. (2003). *Resiliency: What we Have Learned*. San Francisco, California: WestEd Publisher.

Bennett, B. & Smilanich, P. (1994). *Classroom Management: A thinking and Caring Approach*. Ajax, Ontario: Bookation.

Bennett, B. & Rolheiser, C. (2001). *Beyond Monet: The Artful Science of Instructional Integration*. Toronto, Ontario: Bookation.

Bruner, J., Goodnow, J. J., & Austin, G.A. (1986). *A Study of Thinking*. New Brunswick, NJ: Transaction.

Burgess, A. W. & Holmstrom, L. L. (2015). *Rape Trauma Syndrome*. American Journal of Psychiatry. American Psychiatric Association.

Cohen, E. (1994). *Designing Group Work: Strategies for the Heterogeneous Classroom*. New York: Teachers College Press.

Collins, M. L. (1978). *The Effects of Training for Enthusiasm on the Enthusiasm Displayed by Preservice Elementary Teachers*. Unpublished Doctoral Dissertation, Syracuse University.

DeVries, D. L., Mescon, I. T., & Shackman, S. L. (1975). *Teams Games Tournament in the Elementary Classroom: A Replication*. (Tech. Rep. No. 190). Baltimore: John Hopkins University.

Dweck, C. S. (2012). *Mindset: How you can fulfill your potential*. Constable & Robinson Limited.

Edutopia. (2001). *Reflection and the Enhancement of Brain Retention*. San Rafael, California: George Lucas Educational Foundation.

Edutopia. (2018). *Research Tested – Benefits of Breaks*. San Rafael, California: George Lucas Educational Foundation.

Gardner, H. (1999). *Intelligence reframed: Multiple Intelligences for the 21st Century.* New York: Basic Books.

Gibbs, J. (2006). *Reaching all by Creating Tribes Learning Communities.* Windsor, California: Center Source Systems.

Goleman, D. (2006). *Emotional Intelligence: Why it Can Matter More Than IQ.* New York: Bantam Books.

Goleman, D. & Boyatzis, R. (2017). *Emotional Intelligence has 12 Elements. Which do you Need to Work on?* Brighton, Boston: Harvard Business Review.

Grant, A. & Sandberg, S. (2016). *Originals: How Non-Conformists Move the World.* New York: Penguin Random House.

Hall, G. E. & Hord, S. M. (1996). *The Concerns-Based Adoption Model (CBAM): A Model for Change in Individuals.* Reprinted with permission from the chapter entitled " Professional Development for Science Education: A Critical and Immediate Challenge." National Standards & the Science Curriculum. Dubuque, Iowa: Kendall/ Hunt Publishing Company.

Havens, L. (1989). *A Safe Place: Laying the Groundwork of Psychotherapy.* Washington, D.C.: APA.

Henry, F. & Tator, C. (2006). *Racial Profiling in Canada: Challenging the Myth of 'a Few Bad Apples'.* University of Toronto Press

Hunter, M. (1994). *Enhancing Teaching.* New York: MacMillan College.

Jensen, E. (2004). *Teaching with the Brain in Mind.* Alexandria, Virginia: ASCD.

Johnson, D. W. & Johnson, R. T. (1994). *Learning Together and Alone: Cooperative, Competitive, Individualistic Learning.* Boston MA: Allyn & Bacon.

Jones, E. D., Greenberg, M. & Crowley, M. (2015). *Early Social-Emotional Functioning and Public Health: The Relationship Between Kindergarten Social Competence and Future Wellness.* American Journal of Public Heath, November issue.

Kagan, S. (1994). *Cooperative Learning.* San Juan Capistrano: Kagan Cooperative Learning.

Knost, L. R. (2013). *Two Thousand Kisses a Day: Gentle Parenting Through the Ages and Stages.* Little Hearts Books.

Kohn, A. (1993). *Punished by Rewards: The Trouble with Gold Stars, Incentive Plans, A's, Praise, and Other Bribes.* Boston: Houghton Mifflin.

Kugler, J. & West-Burns, Nicole (2010). *The CUS Framework for Culturally Responsive and Relevant Pedagogy.* Centre for Urban Schooling, OISE, University of Toronto.

Lopez, A. & Messina, R. (2011). *Inquiry into Practice: Reaching Every Student Through Inclusive Curriculum.* OISE, U. of Toronto.

Loucks-Horsley, S. & Stiles, K. E. (1998). *Professional Development Strategies. The Science Teacher.* Volume 65, Issue 6. Washington.

Lyman A. Glenny (1980) *Demographic and Related Issues for Higher Education in the 1980s.* The Journal of Higher Education, 51:4, 363-380, DOI.

Macrorie, K. (1984). *20 Teachers.* New York: Oxford University Press.

Marzano, R., Pickering, D. & Pollock, J (2001). *Classroom Instruction that Works.* Alexandria, VA: ASCD.

Masten, A. (2011). *Resilience in Children Threatened by Extreme Adversity: Frameworks for Research, Practice, and Translational Synergy.* Cambridge, United Kingdom: Cambridge University Press.

Mate, G. (2019). *In the Realm of Hungry Ghosts: Close Encounters with Addiction.* Post Hypnotic Press.

Mayer, J.D., Caruso, D.R., & Salovey, P. (2000). *Models of Emotional Intelligence.* Port Chester, New York: Dude Publishing.

McLaughlin, M.W., & Talbert, J.E. (1993). *Contexts That Matter for Teaching and Learning: Strategic Opportunities for Meeting the Nation's Educational Goals.* Washington, D.C.: Institute of Education Sciences.

Millar, J. (1897). *School Management.* Toronto, ON: William Briggs.

Murray, Karen &West-Burns PhD. (2020) *Equity Continuum: Action for Critical Transformation in Schools and Classrooms.* Toronto, ON. A Different Publisher.

Muskat, L. (1995). *Education as empowerment: A revolutionary concept? Issues of assessment and diagnosis revisited.* International Association of Special Education Monograph.

Narayan, K. (1989). *Storytellers, Saints and Scoundrels: Folk Narrative in Hindu Religious Teaching.* Philadelphia: University of Pennsylvania Press.

Noddings, N. (1988). *Schools Face 'Crisis in Caring'.* Bethesda, Maryland: Education Week.

Olson, A. (2013). *The Theory of Self-Actualization Mental illness, Creativity, and Art.* Psychology Today.

Rowe, M.B. (1974). *Wait time and Rewards as Instructional Variables, Their Influence on Language, Logic and Fate Control: Part 1. Wait-time.* Journal of Research in Science Teaching, 11, 81-94.

Salovey, P. (2004) *Emotional intelligence: Key readings on the Mayer and Salovey model.* New York: Dude Press.

Salzberg, S. (2011). *Meditation: The Key to Resilience in Caregiving.* HuffPost Contributor Platform.

Scuderi, R. (2018). *Cultivating Human Potential for happiness, Health and Fulfillment*: Lifehack.

Silver, H. F., Strong, R. W. & Perini, M.J. (2007). *The Strategic Teacher: Selecting the Right Research-Based Strategy for Every Lesson* (Chapter 7: Concept Attainment). ASCD

Smykowski, J. (2020). *Getting to Know Yourself: True Happiness Comes from Within*. BetterHelp.

Thelen, H. A. (1972). *Education and the human quest: Four designs for education.* University of Chicago Press.

Tobin, K. (1980). *The effect of an Extended Teacher Wait Time on Science Achievement.* Journal of Research in Science Teaching, 17, 469-475.

Tomlinson, C.A. (2001). *How to Differentiate Instruction in Mixed Ability Classes.* Alexandria, Virginia: ASCD.

Wenk, L. (2017). *The Importance of Engaging Prior Knowledge.* Hampshire College: Center for Teaching and Learning.

Wolfe, P. (2010). *Brain Matters: Translating Research into Classroom Practice.* Alexandria, Virginia: ASCD.

http://www.edu.gov.on.ca/eng/policyfunding/growSuccess.pdf

https://www.youtube.com/watch?v=57hPu0foQ3Q

www.youtube.com/watch?v=SFnMTHhKdkw https://www.youtube.com/watch?v=57hPu0foQ3Q www.youtube.com/watch?v=SFnMTHhKdkw

(2013). *Optimizing Attachment and Learning in the Classroom.* The Social Neuroscience of Education.

www.publicsafety.gc.ca/cnt/ntnl-scrt/cbr-scrt/cbrbllng/prnts/cbrbllng-en.aspx

https://www.mindfulschools.org/about-mindfulness/research-on-mindfulness/

United Nations Office www.unodc.org

ABOUT THE AUTHORS

Dr. Jackie Eldridge

With many years as an elementary school teacher, a teacher educator, university administrator, keynote speaker and coach, Jackie is passionate about inspiring teachers, parents and leaders to be the best they can be so they will be agents of change. Her work at Hearts and Minds Matter is grounded in her belief that living, learning, and working environments must be safe, nurturing communities where people have what they need to thrive and grow. Jackie believes that all people can make a difference in the world when they are able to tap into their own understanding of self and others. Jackie's doctoral research on the ethics of care, demonstrates her core value of the importance of caring connections in all of life's relationships.

Currently Jackie teaches in The Master of Teaching Program at the Ontario Institute for Studies in Education at the University of Toronto where she teaches The Fundamentals of Teaching and Learning.

Jackie is also the author of Mindfulness: 15 Tips to Get You Started and the creator of Intentional Emotional Intelligence cards. Jackie is currently writing a new educational text entitled: *Trauma-Informed Classrooms: Hearts and Minds Really Matter.*

Denise McLafferty

As an educator for 35 years, Denise has worked in many different capacities, including consultant, teacher, Vice-Principal and Principal. In each of these roles, she has consistently focused on enhancing the culture and climate within her school communities.

As a school Principal, and after opening two new schools in the York Region District School Board in Ontario, Denise realized the challenges of sustainability with the myriad of school-based initiatives and innovations. As a result, she worked hard with students, staff, parents, community members and other school administrators to create learning and working environments that moved impactful initiatives forward in the spirit of inclusion, collegiality, positivity, and mutual respect.

Dr. Barrie Bennett (Guest Author)

Dr. Bennett is professor emeritus at the Ontario Institute for Studies in Education: University of Toronto. His research interests relate to teacher thinking, learning, and action focused on instructional practices. He seeks an understanding of how teachers acquire an instructional repertoire, how they extend and integrate it, and what effect this has on student learning (kindergarten to adult).

Dr. Bennett's work has focused on long-term systemic/sustainable change in twelve districts in three countries, working to establish graduate work, graduate programs, and courses for classroom teachers. One of Dr. Bennett's goals is to make research a normal part of what a teacher does; to create research agendas that are part of building the internal capacity to enact change rather than relying on external researchers and external research grants.

He has written three books related to instruction, is completing another related to integrating instructional methodology, and has written for a number of referred conferences.